Strategic Conflict Management

To our children
Jan Niklas, Simon Lukas, Paul Jonas,
Tabo, Miro, and Liam

Strategic Conflict Management

A Game-Theoretical Introduction

Peter-J. Jost

WHU – Otto Beisheim School of Management, Vallendar, Germany

Utz Weitzel

Utrecht School of Economics, Utrecht University, the Netherlands

Edward Elgar
Cheltenham, UK • Northampton, MA, USA

Published by
Edward Elgar Publishing Limited
Glensanda House
Montpellier Parade
Cheltenham
Glos GL50 1UA
UK

Edward Elgar Publishing, Inc.
William Pratt House
9 Dewey Court
Northampton
Massachusetts 01060
USA

A catalogue record for this book is available from the British Library

Library of Congress Cataloguing in Publication Data

Jost, Peter-J.
  Strategic conflict management : a game-theoretical introduction / Peter-J. Jost, Utz Weitzel.
    p. cm.
  Includes bibliographical references and index.
  1. Conflict management. 2. Game theory. I. Weitzel, Utz. II. Title.
  HD42.J67 2008
  658.4'053–dc22

                                                                    2007039422

ISBN 978 1 84064 837 9 (cased)

Printed and bound in Great Britain by MPG Books Ltd, Bodmin, Cornwall

Contents

Preface

Conflicts in organizations are a fact of everyday life: in families, in child education, in sports clubs, in companies, etc. They accompany virtually all areas of life in which humans interact and constitute an integral part of organizations. Whenever a group of individuals come together and interact in order to reach a common goal, differing individual preferences of these group members can lead to a clash of interests. This creates a situation of conflict. If every group member tries to implement her individual preferences within this situation, the clash of interests becomes manifest in a conflict. A conflict can arise in the organization 'married couple', when there is disagreement about how to spend the holiday together. She might want to go hiking, while he is more interested in sunbathing on a long white beach. Both members of this organization have different interests. If they both try to get their way, the clash of interests becomes manifest in a conflict and the couple may find themselves in a marital argument.

Next to such internal conflicts within an organization, there also exist external conflicts between the organization and its environment. These conflicts can arise when there is a clash of interests between the organization as an entity and other actors in its environment. External conflicts of the organization 'married couple', for instance, could be due to disagreements with the neighbors or the tax authorities.

This book lies in the realm of business economics and focuses on internal conflicts, more specifically, on internal conflicts within business organizations. External conflicts between such organizations and, for example, public bodies, suppliers, or competitors, are mentioned for explanatory purposes, but without more detailed elaboration. Although internal and external conflicts share many common features, there also exists one fundamental difference. Conflicts within business organizations can always be managed by a superior authority, while this is often not the case in external conflicts. This is the main reason why internal conflicts in business organizations allow for a much richer spectrum of instruments and measures in their management, which again influences the course of the underlying conflict itself.

In discussing and analyzing internal conflicts we choose a scientific approach that focuses on the strategic aspects of the situation. We study how parties with individual preferences strategically interact in situations of conflict and formulate simple principles of strategic behavior that can explain their behavior. For the deduction of these principles we use examples out of the domain of business organizations. On this basis we then also develop specific measures and instruments with which a conflict manager can influence the strategic actions of the parties in conflict.

The scientific approach we employ to study the strategic behavior between parties is commonly referred to as game theory. As the original objective of game theory was conflict analysis, this book can also be used as an introduction to game theory. In contrast to many other introductory books we do not focus on pure game theory with formal definitions and mathematical proofs, but rather concentrate on the application of game theory on strategic conflict management. By means of examples of internal conflicts in organizations we will introduce and explain basic concepts and definitions of game theory. Most of these examples are wellknown to practitioners and are also discussed from different perspectives in the pertinent business and management literature. We explicitly use such examples to re-examine our intuition on wellknown conflicts in a new light. We hope that readers who are interested in conflict management, but have never come into contact with game theory before, can use this book to approach and assess organizational conflicts from a more strategic perspective.

This book is not intended to be a guide for all kinds of conflicts in organizations, as each situation is characterized by specific framework parameters with regard to the parties' interests and goals, the cause of their conflict and their organizational relation to each other. However, this book shows how organizational conflicts can be analyzed strategically and how parties that are involved in such conflicts can act strategically. Strategic behavior assumes rational parties. As irrational behavior is unsystematic we include it in the systematic analysis of conflict management.

The structure of the book is as follows. In the introductory chapter, we present two case studies that show how game theory can be used as a theoretical approach for organizational conflicts. After this, the book is divided into two parts: conflict analysis and conflict management.

Part I covers the analysis of conflicts. Here, we will discuss some basic principles of strategic behavior and successively introduce the most important concepts of game theory. In doing this, we distinguish between two types of conflict. First, we study conflicts with independent decisions, in which one party can not condition her action on the action of the other party. In game theory, these situations are called static games. Second, we look at dynamic conflicts, where one party can react on the behavior of the other party and where parties can try to influence the behavior of the other. In game theory these situations of conflict are referred to as sequential games.

Part II focuses primarily on the management of conflicts. A manager can anticipate how the parties in conflict will behave and what influence framework parameters of the conflict will have on its outcome. We will use the concepts and findings of Part I to show how the strategic behavior of conflicting parties can be influenced by direct governance or by changing the organizational framework parameters. We distinguish two forms of conflict management. Vertical conflict management deals with the question how a supervisor can ensure that an employee completes her task adequately. Lateral conflict management focuses on the appropriate organizational design of a situation of conflict, such that the parties involved work cooperatively towards a common corporate goal.

Without the invaluable help of a number of people this book would not have been published. First and foremost, we want to thank our spouses, who are both professionally interested in business economics, not only for their understanding of our sometimes very odd and long writing hours, but also for the many constructive discussions and suggestions for improvements. Further, we sincerely thank Petra Helming, Tobias Hoereth, Jürgen Kumbartzki, Elke Renner and Dirk Simon for further suggestions, editing work and valuable help with the exercises. We are also especially indebted to Karin Senftleben for her coordinative efforts, the production of the figures, numerous modifications and final editing. Of course, all remaining errors are ours.

1. Introduction

> In defense of the assumption that actual behavior is the same
> as rational behavior, it could be argued that, while this is likely
> to lead to mistakes, the alternative of assuming any particular
> type of irrationality is likely to lead to even more mistakes.
> (Sen, 1987)

According to Schelling (1960, p.3) the numerous theories of conflict can
be divided into two major groups. One group of theories treats conflict as
a pathological state and studies its causes and treatments. To this group
belongs, for example, the psychoanalytical theory of Freud, which tries to
understand conflicts within a party by the dominance of stronger motives
against weaker motives. A second group of theories takes the conflict as
granted and studies the behavior that is associated with it. The theory of
Marx, for example, discusses the conflict between capital and labor and the
consequences of this antagonism.

Within this framework, game theory belongs to those theories of conflict
which analyze the behavior of the participants in a given conflict situation.
Building on the theory of normative decisions, game theory is a science
that analyzes strategic behavior in situations where several parties interact
with each other.[1] In other words, a party does not act in a vacuum but its
decisions also depend on the decision of other parties who are involved in
the situation.

In game theory a 'game' is any kind of interaction, irrespective of whether
it has an economic, political, military, or social background. When the
opposition in parliament proposes a motion of no-confidence, when the
supermarket around the corner increases its prices for milk, when a general
decides to attack today instead of tomorrow, when parents want to get
their son to tidy up his room, ... all these situations can be subject to
game theoretic analysis. A prominent feature of these situations is the
interdependence of the parties involved. This means that the result of an
action by one party does not solely depend on her own behavior, but also
on the actions of another party, or on the behavior of several other parties
that are also involved in the same situation. Whether the manager of the
supermarket really makes more profit by increasing milk prices depends
on the reaction of the customers, and maybe also on the reaction of a
competitor across the street. Whether the parents get their son to tidy up
his room may depend on corresponding rewards or punishments, and also
on the son's aptitude. Who knows, tidying up might be his favorite activity
at home.

As game theory assumes that interacting parties pursue their own interests, it can also be interpreted as a theory of social conflicts. Our definition
of a *situation of conflict* corresponds to a game as understood in game

1

theory: several parties interact with each other, while pursuing their own interests, which are, at least partially, conflicting against each other. We can interpret every situation of conflict as a game, although in game theory we do not talk of parties in conflict, but of players. In game theory, conflicts in organizations are an important object of investigation. The players that are involved in such conflicts are the various stakeholders of the organization.

In a game-theoretical analysis the parties in conflict are not considered in their entire complexity. Game-theoretic approaches rather focus on the strategic actions of the parties. For this, the assumption of rational behavior of the parties is essential. This means that the parties are considered to weigh the advantages of a certain action against the disadvantages and then decide for the alternative that promises the greatest individual utility. Game theory provides us with a number of analytical tools to study the behavior of parties in situations of conflicts. Such an analysis always starts with a given conflict, which is characterized by (a) interdependency and (b) a conflict of interests between the parties involved. By focusing on these two causes for a conflict we can study and understand the whole situation more easily. This is important, because once we understand the causes for a conflict, we are able to anticipate the behavior of the parties and manage the situation of conflict more appropriately from the beginning or even avoid the manifestation of the conflict at all.

Conflict management is dealing with the strategic design of situations of conflict. For this, we have to analyze the strategic behavior of the parties in conflict. And in order to do this, we first need to understand the structure of the situation of conflict. Without appropriate knowledge about the framework parameters that affect the situation of conflict, we can neither analyze the parties' strategic behavior, nor manage the conflict in question. Thus, for the quality of the analysis of the parties' strategic behavior it is very important to build a sound model of the situation of conflict.

As with all game-theoretical models we always take the situation of conflict as a given. Hence, we do not question the relationship between the parties, their goals, or the subject matter of the conflict. In game-theoretical modeling the focus rather lies on the identification of the parties' collaborative or conflicting interests with regard to the matter of the conflict, which in turn determine their behavior. According to our definition of a conflict, this involves the following framework parameters.

1. Parties in conflict

   First we have to determine who is involved in the conflict and which interest she pursues. Are the parties directly involved right from the beginning or can they intervene at a later point in time? Do they act individually or as a group? The last question is important, because the other party's interests in the conflict may depend on whether she represents an individual or a group. The individual interests of, for example,

an employee are determined by personal and structural factors. To identify the interests of a group we have to additionally analyze the social
structure within this organizational unit. Who is responsible for the actions of the group? Who determines the group's interests? In such a case
the identification of key persons in the group and their relationship with
other group members may be required. Which cohesion has the organizational unit? This might indicate to which extent the group's actions
are based on homogeneous interests.

2. Matter of conflict

   The matter of a conflict represents an aspect where the parties in conflict
   have a conflict of interests. The matter of conflict can be subjective or
   objective. An example for an objective matter is an unclear division of
   responsibilities in a matrix organization, where a regional manager and
   a product manager pursue partially different goals. A subjective matter
   may be the misinterpretation of an instruction.

   We also have to analyze the interests that the parties have with regard
   to the matter of conflict. This includes finding out how important the
   matter is to the different parties. Further we have to clarify to which
   extent the interests of the parties are actually competing with each other,
   as opposed to pursuing a (partially) cooperative goal.

   Further, it is important to find out to which extent the parties can
   appraise each other's interests. In general a party only knows about her
   own interests, but has incomplete information about the other party's
   interests. Hence, the parties will form expectations about each other's
   interests and behavior.

3. Course of interaction

   The sequence of actions in the conflict also determines the parties' strategic behavior. We therefore have to specify individual decision points
   at which one of the parties or all of them can act. The chronological
   sequence of these actions and reactions determines the course and the
   outcome of the conflict. We can differentiate between simultaneous and
   sequential interdependencies in conflicts. The type of interdependence
   between the parties not only determines the extent of their uncertainty
   about each other's actions, but also the sequence of actions in the conflict. In case of sequential interdependencies one party is able to make her
   decision with the knowledge of and subject to the other party's previous
   action(s). With simultaneous interdependencies, both parties have to
   form expectations about the actions of the other. In many companies,
   the course of interaction is largely predetermined by its organizational
   structure, with a predominance of simultaneous interdependencies in
   horizontally differentiated structures, and more sequential interdependencies in vertically diversified structures.

4. Strategies of the parties

   At each of the decision points in the course of the interaction, we have to identify the potential actions that a party can choose. The availability of different actions is mostly also predetermined by a company's organization, because the responsibility of a certain position and the access to certain resources largely defines the number and quality of options that are available to a party in conflict. A strategy of a party is then defined as a plan for her actions at each of the decision points in the situation of conflict.

5. Consequences of the interaction
Finally, we have to determine all possible benefits and drawbacks for each of the parties and each of the possible courses of interaction. This includes the individual utility that the parties gain by pursuing their interests and possible sanctions that may be used to influence the other's behavior.

These aspects show which parameters are of general importance for the modeling of a situation of conflict. The analysis can be conducted at several levels of detail. The highest level is not always the most appropriate for the modeling of the situation of conflict. In order to analyze the strategic behavior of the parties, only those aspects which have a significant influence on their actions are relevant. Ideally, a game-theoretic model chooses a level of abstraction that extracts only those aspects of a situation of conflict that are relevant for the understanding of the conflict or cooperation.[2]

Up to this point we have presented the framework parameters of a situation of conflict, and have also shown that it essential to carefully identify these parameters prior to modeling and analysis. For instance, we should bear in mind that the interaction is most probably not isolated. A situation of conflict between two parties is often part of another, larger conflict. In such a case we can not expect that an isolated analysis of the behavior in the sub-conflict corresponds with the actual behavior in the larger conflict. Also, we should take account of the fact that many conflicts organizations also have a dynamic dimension. The individual parties or organizational units interact over a long time period. To model such a conflict as a static one-shot situation, or possibly even as a game with a finite number of repetitions, would fall short of an appropriate analysis for conflict management implications.

With the help of the following two case studies we want to exemplify our introductory explanations with the application of a simple game-theoretic analysis to real economic situations. Both case studies consider market conflicts, that is conflicts that are external to the companies' internal organization. The focus in the case study on General Motors vs. Ford lies on illustrating the strategic analysis of a given situation of conflict. The second case study on regulation of the US cigarette industry exemplifies the application of game-theoretical considerations in conflict management.

In both case studies we proceed as follows. First, we briefly present the historical situation as a starting point or our case. In a second step, we discuss the possibilities and the implications of a strategic analysis in each case. Finally, we present the actual development of the situation of conflict.

1.1 CONFLICT ANALYSIS: GENERAL MOTORS VERSUS FORD, 1921-1927

1.1.1 Historical Starting Point

In 1921 two large automobile companies ruled the US-American auto market: the Ford Company and the General Motors Corporation (GM). Jointly, both companies had a market share of over 65 percent of the US automobile production. With a market share of 57 percent, Ford had by far the highest production. The Ford Company, solely owned by Henry Ford since 1920, produced the famous Model T. This car was built in only one version with very few extras and was priced low accordingly. Although GM had a far lower production of only 10 percent of the US market, its revenue was barely lower than Ford's. From Chevrolet to Cadillac GM produced seven different models ranging from medium-sized to luxury cars.

Up to 1921 neither of the two firms directly competed with each other. Ford produced for the lower-price segment and GM for the middle and upper segment. However, in 1920, this began to change when Pierre du Pont became CEO and chairman of the board. He decided to attack Ford's monopoly position in the lower-price segment. The plan was to launch a new version of GM's cheapest model, the Chevrolet, for the upper end of the lower price segment. This car was supposed to be a bit more expensive than the Model T, but also qualitatively superior. GM hoped that this would not only convince former Ford customers to buy the Chevrolet, but also attract new buyers from the medium-price segment.

1.1.2 Conflict Analysis

First, we have to clarify which interest the two parties pursue. The intention of GM is obvious: to attack Ford's monopoly position by successfully introducing a product that directly competes with the Model T. Ford's interest is to prevent such a market entry by GM. Hence, we face a situation of competing interests (as opposed to cooperative interests).

Let us now examine the situation of conflict in more detail. If we take GM's entry into the low-price segment as a given, we can formulate five possible counter-reactions of Ford:

1. Ford behaves passively and observes how the launch of the new Chevrolet is developing. At a later point in time they can then choose the right countermeasure to fend off this attack more effectively.
2. Ford lowers the price for the Model T and thereby puts a greater distance between the competing models.
3. Ford also introduces a new model into the upper lower-price segment, which has similar extras and also a similar price to the new Chevrolet.
4. Ford lowers the price for the Model T and concurrently launches a new version of it that directly competes with the new Chevrolet.
5. Ford strikes an agreement with GM to split the market.

What would be the consequences of Ford's potential actions on the further course of conflict? The answer to this question depends on, first, the counter-reaction of GM, and, second, on the development of relevant external factors that neither of the two companies can influence. Part of such exogenous uncertainty is, for instance, the general development of the US economy. In the middle of 1921, the USA was in a recession. However, it was generally expected that the economic situation would slowly but surely improve. A few expected more extreme developments, like an economic boom or a further deterioration. Virtually nobody expected that the economy would not change at all over the medium term.

If we assume that these were the expectations of the two parties with regard to the economic development, then we can assess Ford's potential actions and the potential counter-reactions of GM as follows (also see Figure 1.1).

Suppose Ford observed GM's market entry passively, then the success of the new Chevrolet would at first solely be determined by the development of the US economy. In case of a sharpening recession, GM would not have enough demand for a sufficient mass production and for corresponding economies of scale. The market launch would most probably fail. However, this scenario is unlikely. Much more likely is the case that the positive economic development enables GM to reach its sales targets. The new Chevrolet would then be successfully established in the market, such that later price discounts of the Model T would not be able to seriously affect GM's newly gained position in the lower-price segment.

A second option for Ford could be to immediately reduce the price of the Model T in response to the launch of new Chevrolet. Here, we have to consider the possible counter-reactions of GM, which could either leave the introductory price unchanged, or sweeten the initial offer in proportion to Ford's discount. In the first case, GM could only expect a successful launch in the rather unlikely situation of a booming US economy. In any other economic scenario, the high price premium in relation to the Model T would generate sufficient demand for mass production above a critical scale. However, a reduction of GM's introductory price would have a higher

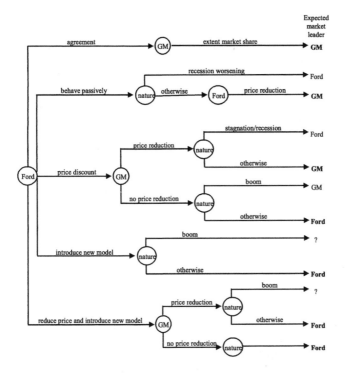

Figure 1.1. Discussion of Ford's alternatives and possible outcomes of the conflict

probability of success. Due to lower prices, GM would have to produce with higher economies of scale and sell more cars, but in an improving economy, GM can expect that the price discount generates a higher than planned demand, effectively increasing the production numbers to a profitable level. Only for the much less likely case of a deepening recession would this price reduction strategy lead to a failed market launch.

A third option that, in 1921, would have been available to Ford, was to introduce a new version of the Model T that would directly compete with the new Chevrolet. Although such a new version would cannibalize the sales of the old Model T, it would also attract more buyers from the medium-priced segment, which would probably lead to a market failure of the new Chevrolet. Only in the unlikely case of an economic boom would GM face enough demand out of both segments to establish the new Chevrolet.

The fourth option for Ford is to combine the strategy of a price reduction of the Model T with the introduction of a new version. The answer of GM could be a price reduction for the new Chevrolet or a passive response. As explained above, none of these alternatives is promising for GM. Only in the unlikely event of a booming US economy could the launch of the new Chevrolet still be a success.

The last option for Ford to strike a deal with GM in which they split the market would not prevent a sustained market entry by GM. In fact, splitting the market ex ante guarantees a successful market penetration by GM. Even worse for Ford, it could allow GM to strengthen and expand its position in the long run, as GM has a more differentiated product portfolio. As contracts are always incomplete, Ford would not be able to contractually prevent GM's expansion in the long run.

In conclusion we can determine that the best strategic response of Ford to the market entry of GM would be an immediate price reduction on the old Model T, in combination with the launch of a new version as a direct competitor for the new Chevrolet.

1.1.3 Historical Development

In September 1921, GM introduced the new Chevrolet for a price of $525 into the lower market segment. Ford reacted with an immediate price reduction of $60, resulting in a price of $355 for the old Model T. When considering all the extras of the new Chevrolet the effective price difference was $90. In combination with the positive economic development in the fall of 1921 this price difference was too small to directly fend off the market entry of GM. One year later, in September 1922, Ford cut the price of the Model T to $300, but this reduction came too late. The new Chevrolet was already so established in the market that GM did not even react to Ford's price reduction. Despite the higher price, GM was able to increase the sales of the new Chevrolet, supported by the setting in of an economic boom. As a result, GM not only successfully entered the market, but also succeeded in building up a significant and sustainable market position.

1.2 CONFLICT MANAGEMENT: PUBLIC REGULATION IN THE US CIGARETTE INDUSTRY, 1970

1.2.1 Historical Starting Point

Since the beginning of the 1960s the US-American cigarette industry was challenged with massive problems. Following a study of the Royal College of Physicians in London, which provided comprehensive evidence on the health risks of smoking, President Kennedy founded an Advisory Committee on Smoking and Health in the very same year. In January 1964, this committee published a report that created a large public awareness of the issue. The report came to two important conclusions. First, the risks of smoking are so serious that anti-smoking measures have to be taken immediately. Second, there is a direct causality between smoking and lung cancer.

In the same year cigarette consumption dropped by 2 percent. Further, the Federal Trade Commission and the Federal Communications Commission led a large anti-smoking campaign. An important goal of the two public authorities was to prohibit unfair and misleading practices in the advertising and labeling of cigarettes. This resulted in three new regulations:

1. The Cigarette Labeling and Advertising Act of 1965 stipulated that the health risk warning had to be printed on every cigarette pack.
2. From 1967 onwards, the Fairness Doctrine guaranteed that non-smoking advertisements were broadcast without any charge. Each radio and television station was obliged to act in the public's interest and to offer enough air time for public discussions on topics of general importance. Non-smoking advertisements warned against the danger of smoking.
3. The Public Health Cigarette Smoking Act of 1970 prohibited any radio or TV advertisements for cigarettes, effective January 1, 1971.

1.2.2 Conflict Analysis

In the 1960s, the US-American cigarette market was dominated essentially by six companies: R.J. Reynolds, Philip Morris, American Tobacco, Brown and Williamson, P. Lorillard, and Liggett and Myers. These companies controlled 99 percent of the market. The cigarette market was a supply oligopoly.

An important peculiarity of this cigarette oligopoly was the absence of price competition. The production costs of cigarettes were largely determined exogenously by cigarette taxes, the quantity of tobacco used per cigarette, and the tobacco price. All firms have fully exploited any economies of scale in the cigarette production. Hence, the cigarette price was inflexible and could only be reduced, by all firms together, if one of the three exogenous factors was reduced.

However, nevertheless there was tough competition in the cigarette market, namely a crowding out of competitors by means of advertising. The goal of cigarette advertising was not to increase cigarette demand at large, but rather to gain market shares from the competitors: 'TV advertising was never designed to create new smokers; its main purpose is to switch people from one brand to another'.[3]

What impact do the regulations have on the behavior of the US-American cigarette companies? To answer this question we first analyze the behavior of two firms that compete for market shares in an unregulated environment. On the basis of this behavior we then discuss the firms' strategic best responses to the government's conflict management.

9

Suppose we have a market that is controlled by two firms, A and B. In this duopoly competition only takes place via advertising and not via prices. This does not lead to an increase in the total market. For simplicity we assume that both firms only have two competition strategies: S_1 denotes a strategy where a firm chooses a small advertising budget; with S_2 a firm chooses a large advertising budget.

If both firms choose S_1, there will be no change in market shares. Both firms keep their market share and spend little on advertising. The same happens if both choose S_2, only that both advertising budgets are large now. However, if one firm invests a lot in advertising, while the other does not, then the more intensive advertising will lead to a larger market share to the costs of the competitor.

Figure 1.2 shows how the market shares depend on the strategy combinations of the two firms.

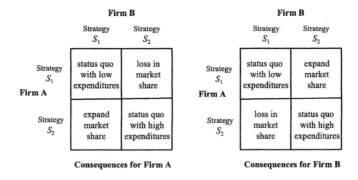

Figure 1.2. The 'competition dilemma'

This situation represents a 'competition dilemma'. If Firm A chooses S_1, then Firm B would benefit from high advertising expenditures (S_2). She would then be able to expand her market share. Firm B would also choose a high budget if she expects Firm A to have chosen a high budget. In this case Firm B can prevent a loss in market share. Hence, Firm B will always choose high advertising expenditures (S_2), irrespective of Firm A's budget decision. As this applies analogously to Firm A, both parties will heavily advertise for their brands.

We can now infer which consequences a public ban on radio and TV advertising will have. In our duopoly situation, government regulation would restrict the firms' options to only one: both firms would be forced to choose S_1 and reduce their advertising expenditure accordingly. This would be in the interest of both firms, as they can agree on the status quo without spending as much on advertising as in the unregulated scenario.

1.2.3   Historical Development

The regulation of the US cigarette industry first led to a substantial increase in advertising expenditure from 1964 to 1970 (see Figure 1.3). Thanks to the required educational advertising the cigarette consumption decreased by 1.6 percent per annum. From 1967 onwards, probably due to the Fairness Doctrine, the market even shrank by 2.6 percent per annum. In order to hold onto their share in this shrinking market, the cigarette firms intensified competition. On average, their annual total advertising expenditure in the period from 1964 to 1971 was 50 percent higher than in the period from 1956 to1963. However, in the 1970s, the advertising ban reduced these expenditures significantly. The cigarette industry was able to increase profits and despite a sharp increase in print advertising the whole industry spent $80 million less in 1971 than in 1970. In the following five years the average annual advertising expenditure of the industry was still significantly lower than before the introduction of the advertising ban.

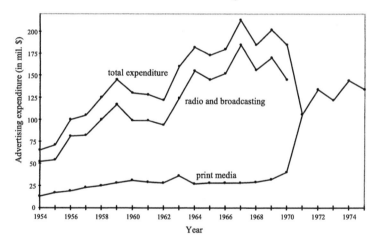

Figure 1.3. Advertising expenditure of the US-American cigarette industry, 1955-1975

But the regulation also had other positive effects on the cigarette industry:

First, the US-American cigarette market expanded again, because with the ban, advertising for non-smoking had to be stopped as well. As non-smoking advertising has effectively reduced the market, the cigarette consumption increased again, despite less advertising expenditure by the cigarette manufacturers. In fact, from 1971 to 1976, the cigarette market grew by 2.5 percent per annum.

Second, the advertising ban represented a substantial barrier to entry for the US-American cigarette market. Without the possibility to advertise nationwide on radio or TV, the chances for a potential entrant to successfully launch a new brand were close to zero.

Third, the cigarette manufacturers were able to lower their production costs. Due to the increased public health awareness, consumers preferred lighter cigarettes with less nicotine and tar. The market share of light cigarettes increased from 1 percent at the end of the 1960s to 16 percent in 1976. Despite lower production costs, the cigarette manufacturers managed to keep prices at the level of the heavier cigarettes. Thus, by pushing the lighter version of their brands the cigarette industry enjoyed additional profits.

1.3 NOTES

1. Several authors also tried to analyze psychological conflicts game-theoretically. See for example. Aumann et al. (1996), or Güth and Kliemt (1996).
2. Certainly. it is virtually impossible to include all these aspects of a real situation into a game-theoretical model. These are typical boundaries for any form of theory building and modeling.
3. Frank Saunders, top manager at Philip Morris. 1971, in News and Observer.

PART I
Conflict Analysis

2. Conflicts with Independent Decisions

'All that I have to say has already crossed your mind,' said he.
'Then possibly my answer has crossed yours,' I replied.
(Holmes to Watson in Doyle, 1990)

We begin our analysis of the strategic behavior of the parties involved in a conflict with the consideration of situations in which the interactions between the parties are simultaneously interdependent. The parties decide independently of each other which alternative to choose. This is the case either when the parties decide at the same time or when the parties decide sequentially, but neither party can observe the decisions of the other parties.

To describe the situation of conflict we have to identify the interests of the different parties as well as the form of interaction between the parties. Since the individual decisions are independent of each other, we can simplify the course of the interactions. The modeling of a conflict situation in a strategic form then is covered by the following three parameters:

1. The parties involved in the conflict situation
2. The alternatives or strategies, which are available for each party
3. The payoffs or consequences for each party for every outcome of the conflict situation, that is, for every possible strategy combination of the parties.

The strategic form of a conflict situation visibly shows how each party is aware of the conflict: The issue of the conflict is indirectly considered by the set of alternatives. Moreover the strategic form comprises the assessment of the individual interests of each party, which can be derived from the payoffs or the consequences of each strategy combination. The consequences of the interactions specify the benefits and costs of each party connected with each strategy combination. From a strategic perspective only the individual assessment of a conflict is important, independent of whether this assessment is objectively correct or not.

In the following chapter we consider the modeling of these conflict situations. In the first section we first model the simplest strategic situation that is possible: Two parties interact with each other and each party has exactly two alternatives. We will see that with these simple interactive decision situations we can describe a variety of different conflict situations.

How parties interact strategically in these situations will be analyzed in the following section. Here we derive the different principles of strategic behavior.

For the behavior of a party in conflict situations it is important whether it has complete knowledge about the strategic form of the conflict situation or whether there are informational asymmetries concerning specific factors.

15

In the last section, we consider conflict situations in which one party has incomplete information about the conflict situation.

2.1 A CLASSIFICATION OF CONFLICTS I

In this subsection we focus on the simplest form of conflict with independent decisions: two parties are involved in a situation of conflict and each of them has to choose between two actions. In this situation of conflict all strategic elements are given, except for the consequences of these choices. Despite its simplicity, this basic form can be used to depict a multitude of situations of conflict. In the following classification Schelling (1960) uses the possible consequences of interactions to define various situations of conflicts.[1] In Figure ?? the payoff for player 1 is shown on the x-axis, while player 2's payoff can be found on the y-axis.

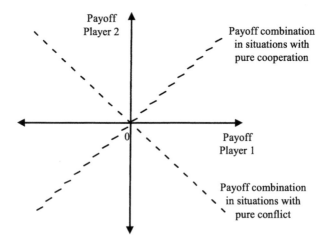

Figure 2.1. A classification of situations of conflict

As can be seen, various payoff combinations determine different situations of conflict. Two extremes are possible: one class of situations characterizes directly competing interests of the parties. Here, the gain of one party inevitably leads to a loss for the other party. A second class of situations delineates purely cooperative interests where payoffs are positively related to each other. Thus, a gain for one party is always associated with a gain for the other party as well. Between these two extremes, competing and cooperative interests may coexist in the same situation of conflict.

The intensity of a conflict in a certain situation is then determined by the relative importance of competing vs. cooperative interests.

In the following we will discuss several idealized situations of conflict by means of an example. Although idealized situations can not depict the richness of reality, they do help to analyze the fundamental structure of real conflicts by extracting constituting behavioral elements. The cooperative and competing interests are disentangled, which facilitates the investigation of the resulting behavior of the parties involved.

Collaboration between the marketing and the production department in an innovation project

---

A company wants to introduce a new product to the market. This new product can be either customer oriented or production oriented. In the first case, a number of production changes would be necessary and the product would have to be produced in small lot sizes. In the second case, the product could be produced in a more standardized way, allowing for greater lots and economies of scale, but this comes with the disadvantage of less customer orientation. For this the collaboration of the marketing and production department is needed. Consequently, a project team is formed in which the departments can work together and contribute their expertise. Since competitors are working on similar products, time-to-market is important. The company's board fears that without some concrete product designs to choose from, the representatives of the two departments in the project team will engage in endless discussions. Therefore the board decides that each department should first come up with an own product idea and design. Subsequently the interdisciplinary project team can evaluate the product designs in a kick-off meeting and then decide on one of the two for further development and market introduction.

From the conflict in this example we can infer the following strategic form: The nature of the innovation project determines the parties involved, in this case the marketing and the production department. Both parties have to work on a product idea where they can choose between two alternative actions. Their efforts can be either oriented towards the customer and product differentiation, or focused on larger lot sizes and lower production costs. Due to their specializations the departments have competing interests. These are expressed in differing preferences with regard to the focus of the product innovation. While the marketing department prefers the customer-oriented design to the lot-size-maximizing design, the production department has exactly the opposite preferences.

The competing interests of the departments coexist with the cooperative interest to complete the joint project successfully. The payoffs that are assigned to the choices of actions have to reflect such a mix of competing and cooperative interests. This mix depends on the relative importance of cooperative and competing interests, effectively determining the intensity of conflict. On this basis we can characterize different types of conflicts, which will be discussed in the following subsections.

2.1.1 Situations with Pure Cooperation

Assume that the company in our example is young and needs an expeditious market launch of a new product to survive. The success of the new product is vital for the firm and, of course, also for the two departments. Since the key for success is the speed with which the product is launched, an effective and efficient coordination between the marketing and the production department is of utmost importance. An inefficient coordination, where both departments pursue differing product designs, would endanger the success of the whole project, irrespective of the final product design.

Both departments know that their survival depends on the fact that they plan their next steps on the basis of the same product orientation. Consequently, we observe a situation of pure cooperation, where joint interests will determine the behavior of the departments, while conflicts of interest are of little or even no importance in this project.

The strategic interaction of the two departments can be described in the form of a matrix. Since the number of columns and rows is defined by the number of choices that each party has, we use a bi-matrix as depicted in Figure 2.2. Each cell in this bi-matrix shows the payoffs for both parties (separated by commas) with respect to the specific combination of choices that are represented by the cell. By convention, the payoff before the comma relates to choices of the party depicted in rows (here, marketing), while the payoff behind the comma is associated with choices of the party depicted in columns (production). Figure 2.2 shows the payoffs for the above example of pure cooperation.

If both departments work on the same product orientation their plans and efforts can be easily integrated. This would lead to a quick launch of a new product, which may either generate higher margins because of superior customer orientation, or sell in greater numbers due to production efficiencies and a lower price. In both cases we assume that a payoff of three is realized for the marketing and for the production department. In contrast, if both departments simultaneously work on two different product designs, the introduction of the new product will be delayed to such an extent that it trails behind competing market launches and fails to break through. In this case the payoff is assumed to be zero.

Although this situation of pure cooperation does not pose a conflict of interests, there nevertheless exists a coordination problem between the two departments. Let us take the view of the head of production. If she assumes

**Production
department**

		customer-oriented product innovation	production-oriented product innovation
Marketing department	customer-oriented product innovation	3,3	0,0
	production-oriented product innovation	0,0	3,3

Figure 2.2. A situation with pure cooperation

that the marketing department is choosing the customer friendly design, then it would be advantageous to also make this choice. Similarly, if she assumes that the marketing department chooses the design that maximizes lot sizes, she should also pick this alternative. The considerations of the marketing department are analogous. However, since we assume that there is no direct coordination, it is a priori not clear how the two departments can agree on a joint proceeding.

2.1.2 Situations with Pure Conflict

In contrast to above, now assume that the company in our example is established and has a lot of different products in the market. The launch of a new product is thus a project, which both departments have done several times. The management of the company knows that the marketing department prefers a customer-orientated design while the production unit would like to introduce a more cost-effective version. The prestige and future organizational importance of each department depends on its ability to implement its preferences into the new product. The final product design will therefore determine a winning and a losing department. Cooperative (corporate) interests do not exist. The situation of conflict is purely competitive: the interests of the two parties are diametrically opposed such that the gain of one party represents a respective loss for the other party. In game theory this situation is also called a zero-sum game. The matrix in Figure 2.3 shows the payoffs of such a game.

If both departments support a customer-orientated design, the marketing department will enhance its future prestige and position by three units, while the production department loses three units. Analogously, the marketing department loses three units and the production department wins three units if both departments support the lot-size-orientated design. If

19

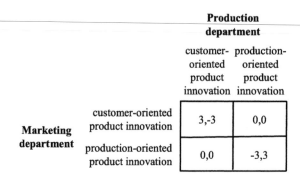

Figure 2.3. A situation with pure competition

both departments simultaneously work on separate product designs, irrespective of whether these meet their individual preferences or not, their organizational status will not be influenced.

Let's look at the position of the marketing department: if she assumes that the production department will work on their own preferred design, that is the lot-size-orientated version of the new product, then marketing is better off in also pursuing its own favorite design. Although this would be inefficient for the whole company, since the launch of the new product will be delayed, the marketing department can nevertheless save its original status and prevent that the production department gains organizational importance. Analogously, if production assumes that marketing will work on the customer-orientated product version, it has no incentive to abandon its lot-size-orientated design.

2.1.3   The Cooperation Dilemma

Assume that both departments prepared their preferred design prior to the first meeting: the marketing department focused on the design of a customer-orientated product version while the production department has worked out a lot-size-orientated product version. Before the meeting the two departments have to determine a negotiation (bargaining) strategy. Two alternatives are possible: either the department accepts a compromise about its design or it is unaccommodating and insists on its own design proposal.

If both departments make a compromise they can use the meeting to agree on a joint procedure for the launch of the new product. This is equally beneficial for the organizational status of both since both can refer to their contribution in a successful project. Furthermore, a joint development that takes both customer orientation as well as production costs into account, promises maximum revenues and profit. Although such a design would be superior since it could combine the advantages of the two proposals, both departments also have an interest to insist on their individual concept. If a proposed design is implemented without compromise the respective department gains organizational status while the other department loses some of its internal importance. The payoff matrix in Figure 2.4 shows this situation of conflict.

		Production department	
		accept a compromise	insist on own proposal
Marketing department	accept a compromise	3,3	0,4
	insist on own proposal	4,0	1,1

Figure 2.4. The cooperation dilemma

In this case both parties pursue cooperating as well as competitive interests: if both parties insist on their product design and behave uncompromisingly, in the meeting they will nevertheless come to an agreement about how to proceed with the project. However, due to insufficient integration the project is less successful such that each department only gains one unit. In a situation where one party is willing to accept a compromise while the other is not we assume that the uncompromising party can implement its design proposal without any changes and gains four units of organizational status. The other party does not win anything. If both departments are willing to accept a compromise and agree upon a joint design, they receive three units each since their project has the highest probability of success.

This situation of conflict is characterized by a cooperation dilemma: both departments have the cooperative interest to come up with a joint design. However, if the marketing department assumes that the production department will be willing to accept a compromise, then it would be better off insisting on its own proposal. This would allow marketing to maximize its future organizational status at the expense of the production unit, which would gain nothing. The dilemma arises if now both departments decide to insist on their proposals, since this uncompromising behavior leads to lower status payoffs for each of them than if both would have cooperated.

In game theory this cooperation dilemma is commonly referred to as *Prisoners' Dilemma*. The name originates from the following exemplary story: after a robbery two suspects are arrested and imprisoned on remand. The police do not have any evidence except illegal possession of a firearm, which would allow the suspects to get off lightly if they were responsible for the robbery. The two suspects are therefore separated and interrogated in two different rooms. A police officer makes each of them the following offer: if the suspect confesses to the crime, she will be used as a principal witness to prosecute the other suspect, provided the latter remained silent or lied to the police. The principal witness will then be free to go without any punishment. The penalty for the one who did not confess is likely to be severe since there are no extenuating circumstances. If both confess, each of the suspects will be prosecuted, but their confession will mitigate the sentence. Their punishment will then be lower than the maximum penalty, but more severe than the punishment for illegal possession of a firearm.

2.1.4 Conflict with Two Leaders

In our initial example, assume that the coordination process between the two departments leads to significant delays in the project. Seen individually, both product proposals are sound and have a high probability of success, but the coordination of a joint product design requires a significant amount of extra time and resources, which endangers the success of the whole project. Hence, if both departments accept a compromise in their project meeting, they can not expect to gain as much status and internal approval as they would with a more successful project.

In this situation of conflict we assume that the launch of the new product would be fastest if one department takes the leadership of the project. The chances for success are best if the leader insists on her original product proposal, while the other department accepts changes to its product design. Since an uncompromising attitude leads to the implementation of the own design proposal the leading department gains additional organizational importance. However, this only applies if the other party goes along. If both departments strive for leadership they will delay the project even more than they would with a mutual compromise.

Again, this describes a situation of conflict in which both parties have competitive as well as cooperative interests. Figure 2.5 depicts the payoffs of this situation.

If one department is willing to agree to a compromise and the other is not, both parties gain three units. The leading department, whose initial design proposal is implemented, obtains an additional one unit of organizational importance since it can claim a greater contribution to the successful project. If both departments agree to integrate their product proposals into a new third design, the delayed launch will reduce their payoff to two units each. The payoff is even lower, just one unit each, if the two parties can not agree on any design, because they both strive towards project leadership.

**Production
department**

		accept a compromise	insist on own proposal
Marketing department	accept a compromise	2,2	3,4
	insist on own proposal	4,3	1,1

Figure 2.5. Conflict with two leaders

This specification is called a conflict with two leaders since both parties want to adhere to their preferences for a specific product design. Accepting a compromise leads to a minimum payoff of two units and a maximum of three. An uncompromising attitude, however, allows a potential gain of four units, but can also lead to the lowest possible payoff if the other department insists on its own product design. This is the risk inherent to the otherwise attractive strategy to leadership.

In game theory this situation of conflict is often referred to as the *Battle of Sexes*, where a newly wed couple visits a bigger city. In the evening he wants to go to a boxing event while she prefers to see a ballet. Being on their honeymoon they certainly do not want to spend the evening separately, but before they can decide where to go together they accidentally lose each other in some turmoil downtown. Unfortunately the boxing arena and the ballet theatre are at opposite ends of the city so that they only can get to one of the two venues for the evening. Now each of them has to decide independently of where to go to in the hope of meeting each other.

2.1.5 Conflict with Two Heroes

This situation of conflict is comparable to the one above with one qualitative difference: if a department insists on its product design then this is considered to have a detrimental effect on the department's reputation or status. Thus, as shown in the payoff matrix in Figure 2.6, uncooperative behavior leads to a lower payoff than the cooperative behavior.

As in the previous example, identical strategies of the two departments generate a payoff of two units each in the case of mutual cooperation, and of only one unit each if both departments insist on their original design proposals without any compromise. If one department cooperates while the other insists on its design, a quick product launch will generate three units each. The department that accepted the other party's design as a

**Production
department**

		accept a compromise	insist on own proposal
Marketing department	accept a compromise	2,2	4,3
	insist on own proposal	3,4	1,1

Figure 2.6. Conflict with two heroes

basis for the project increases its reputation as a constructive team player and gains an extra unit.

By cooperating, a department not only secures a minimum payoff of two units, but also has the chance to get the highest possible payoff of four units. For both departments, accepting a compromise is the strategy with the highest minimal payoff. Such a strategy is also called a *maximin strategy*, since it maximizes the minimum payoff. However, if both departments cooperate, this would lead to a suboptimal outcome. Both parties would be better off if one of the two does not cooperate, although it is less attractive to be uncooperative. One department therefore has to act as a hero by suppressing its individual interest for maximal reputation in order to increase joint (corporate) payoff. To make things worse, such a heroic decision runs the risk of the lowest possible payoff if the other party also decides to be heroic, which effectively delays the product launch.

2.1.6 Conflict with Two Cowards

This situation of conflict is similar to the cooperation dilemma, but with a significant difference. Suppose both departments make differing choices prior to the meeting. One department decides to accept a compromise, while the other is determined not to cooperate. In this case, the non-cooperative department will be able to implement its product design without any changes. However, in contrast to the cooperation dilemma above, in this situation of conflict the willingness to accept a compromise is considered to be positive and therefore does not lead to a loss of organizational importance. The bi-matrix in Figure 2.7 depicts this conflict in its strategic form.

According to Figure 2.7, a department can reach the highest payoff of four units if it chooses non-cooperative behavior while the other department accepts a compromise. Due to its cooperative behavior the latter increases

**Production
department**

		accept a compromise	insist on own proposal
Marketing department	accept a compromise	3,3	2,4
	insist on own proposal	4,2	1,1

Figure 2.7. Conflict with two cowards

its organizational importance by two units. If both departments decide to insist on their product design, they end up with the lowest possible payoff of one unit each. Thus, non-cooperative behavior may on the one hand promise a maximum gain, but it can on the other hand also lead to maximum losses. In contrast, the willingness to compromise maximizes the minimum payoff (maximin strategy), effectively securing the smallest disadvantage.

Interpreting the willingness to compromise as the strategy of a coward, and the alternative strategy as a bold one, we find the following conflict of interests between the two departments. If the marketing department thinks that the production department will act cowardly and accept a compromise, then it is advantageous for marketing to act boldly and insist on its design. However, if the marketing department thinks that the other department is bold in its choice, then it will opt for the strategy of a coward.

The game-theoretical literature commonly refers to such a situation of conflict as a *Chicken Game*. The following story is told to illustrate the situation: as a test of courage, two teenagers drive towards each other. The one who leaves the collision course first and swerves off is chicken-hearted and loses the test. If both swerve off, nobody has won, but at least they get off lightly. In contrast, if both are determined not to give in, they provoke the worst possible outcome.

2.1.7 Conflict with Two Conformists

In this setting, analogously to the situation with two cowards, both departments' willingness to compromise leads to a joint design, which ensures the most successful market launch for the corporation and the highest payoff for both departments. Again, a non-compromising attitude by the departments reduces the probability of corporate success, consequently leading to a lower payoff for both departments. In contrast to the situation of conflict with two cowards we here assume that a non-compromising attitude by one department already endangers the success of the project. In such a case, both departments receive a very low payoff. Moreover, a department's compromising attitude leads to a lower payoff since the implemented design, albeit not very successful, originates from the other department (see Figure 2.8).

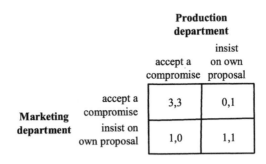

		Production department	
		accept a compromise	insist on own proposal
Marketing department	accept a compromise	3,3	0,1
	insist on own proposal	1,0	1,1

Figure 2.8. Conflict with two conformists

If both parties are willing to compromise, both their payoffs are three units. If both insist on their own design the reduced probability of success generates a payoff of only one one unit each. Additionally, if one department compromises on its design, its payoff decreases by another unit since it can not credibly claim any more that it made any observable contribution to the implemented design

In this situation both departments are conformists: whether a specific alternative is advantageous or not critically depends on conforming to the behavior of the other department. If the production department assumes that the marketing department will be willing to compromise, then it makes sense to choose the same strategy since this will maximize payoffs. However, if the production department assumes that the marketing department will not be willing to compromise on its design, then production would be better off to stand its ground and also insist on its own design. Both departments thus try to attune their behavior to the expected choice of the other party. However, in contrast to the situation of pure cooperation the departments have to deal with a conflict of interest: if one department is willing to compromise it is not only worse off than the party that insists on its design, but also worse off than not cooperating in the first place.

In the game-theoretic literature a situation of conflict with two conformists is referred to as a *Stag-hunt Game*. Two hunters go on a hunt. Each of them has to decide whether she wants to shoot a stag or a hare. A stag they can only successfully hunt jointly. A hare both of them can hunt individually. However, one of the two hunters values half a stag more than a single hare.

2.2 STRATEGIC BEHAVIOR IN CONFLICTS WITH INDEPENDENT DECISIONS

The previous section showed that even very simple relations between two parties with two alternatives each can already lead to a multitude of situations of conflict with various constellations of cooperative and competing interests. What is the parties' behavior in these different situations? Which of the two alternatives are they going to choose? Can we deduce general implications for the strategic behavior of parties in a situation of conflict, and if yes, what do they look like?

In this section we will take a closer look at these questions and analyze the strategic behavior of parties in different situations of conflict. We will develop principles of strategic behavior that can be used as guidance for strategic actions in conflicts. We start with simple principles and then systematically refine these into more complex approaches.

When we study the strategic behavior of party in a specific situation of conflict we have to keep in mind that the attainment of individual goals does not only depend on one's own decisions. Due to interdependencies between parties, we also have to consider the interests of the other party and its decision. Typically, as to its own behavior, a party has to make some assumptions about the behavior of the other party. Additionally, the attainment of goals may also be influenced by exogenous factors, which none of the parties can influence.

Both the parties' strategic as well as exogenous uncertainty, make it necessary to also evaluate consequences that are happening with less than absolute certainty. Decisions which are taken under exogenous uncertainty are commonly labeled as decisions under risk. For this, we not only have to specify all advantages and disadvantages for all parties in a specific conflict, but also the preferences of all parties for certain over uncertain payoffs. These preferences are expressed in the parties' acceptance of so-called lotteries.

Here decision theory provides an instrument for the analysis of decisions under risk: if the decision maker possesses certain intuitive axioms, then his behavior under uncertainty can be described with the help of a utility function. This utility function provides a quantitative description of the party's preferences for different lotteries. The behavior of a decision maker is then characterized by the maximization of her expected utility. Consequences out of strategic interaction constitute utility values or payoffs, with which a respective party evaluates various outcomes of a situation of conflict.

2.2.1 Dominant Strategies

Let us take another look at the previously mentioned example of collaborative efforts in a production team. For simplicity we assume that only two employees work in the production team. Each employee can contribute a low or high effort to the team: a high effort, which we assume to cost ten units, generates a productivity increase of 16 units; a low effort, costing five units, makes an increase of ten units possible. Considering the costs and payoffs of these efforts, we can illustrate the situation of conflict between these two team members with the bi-matrix in Figure 2.9.

Employee 2

	high effort	low effort
Employee 1 high effort	6,6	3,8
low effort	8,3	5,5

Figure 2.9. Team production with two employees

The conflict resembles the cooperation dilemma or Prisoners' Dilemma discussed previously. If both team members work with a low effort, their payoff is lower (five units each) than what they could achieve with a joint high effort (six units each). If one employee shirks and thus chooses a low effort, her payoff increases, while the payoff for the one with the high effort decreases. The average increase in productivity is 13 units. The employee with a low effort has lower costs and receives a payoff of eight units (13-5), which is two units higher than she would have gotten with a high effort. In contrast, the employee who contributed the high effort, costing her a total of ten units, experiences a reduction of her payoff, due to the shirking of her team mate, from six to three units (13-10).

How are the two team members going to behave in this situation of conflict? To answer this question we simply have to put ourselves in one of the two employee's place and then assume that the other party once decides for the lower and once for the higher effort:

- If we assume that the other employee contributes a high effort, then we know that we can reach the maximum payoff of eight units by shirking, that is choosing the low effort. In contrast, if we also contribute a high effort, our payoff will only be six units. Thus, we decide for the low effort.
- If we assume that the other employee chooses a low effort, we can still reach five units if we keep costs down and also contribute a low effort. In

contrast, if we should decide to put in a high effort, our payoff decreases to three units. Thus, again, we decide for the low effort.

If one alternative, independently of the behavior of the other party, always leads to a higher payoff, we call this a *dominant strategy*. In our example the choice to contribute a low effort is a dominant strategy: independent of the behavior of the other employee we always prefer shirking, since it guarantees the higher of the two alternative payoffs in a given situation.

If a party identifies a dominant strategy in a situation of conflict, her choice of action is simple. She chooses the dominant strategy since it will always generate the highest possible payoff, independently of the decision of the other. Thus, with a dominant strategy, no consideration of the possible behavior of the other party is needed, which allows us to formulate the first principle of strategic conduct in conflicts of situation:

Principle of Strategic Behavior I:
In a situation of conflict, always choose a dominant strategy, if it is available to you.

This first principle needs only minimal assumptions about the behavior of the other party and is therefore very plausible. A party that opts for the dominant strategy makes a rational choice. For this choice it is irrelevant whether the other parties involved also behave rationally. Even if they acted completely irrationally the dominant strategy would still be better than any other alternative. Furthermore, a party that follows this first principle of strategic conduct does not need to have any information about the other party's consequences of its behavior.

Let us go back to the example of the team production with two employees. We already argued that one employee has the dominant strategy to contribute a low effort. Due to the symmetry of the situation of conflict, the other employee will conversely come to the same conclusion. As a result, she also has the dominant strategy of choosing a low effort, irrespective of the behavior of the other. With this the behavior of both employees in this situation of conflict is fully determined: both team members will only contribute a low effort. Based on this interaction they receive a payoff of five units each.

Thus, both employees are worse off than they would be with a joint high effort, which could generate an individual payoff of six units. The problem therefore is that both would prefer a higher payoff, but each party individually chooses for a worse alternative, because the other alternative carries the risk of a minimal payoff. In other words, individual rationality leads to a worse outcome than collective rationality. This exactly is the strategic dilemma, which the production team faces in the described situation of conflict.

The situation is aggravated by the fact that even communication between the two employees does not solve the cooperation dilemma. To illustrate this, simply assume that both parties would be able to agree on a joint behavior, prior to contributing their effort. Assume that both parties would agree on the higher net utility associated with a high joint effort. What is going to happen after this conversation when the parties have to decide to which effort they now really contribute? Are they going to stick to their agreement? No, because for each of the two it is individually more attractive to break the agreement and shirk: if one party assumes that the other behaves as agreed upon, she will gain the highest possible payoff of eight units. If she assumes that the other party adopts the same reasoning and thus shirks, sticking to the agreement would leave her with the lowest possible payoff.

Situations of conflict, where each party has a dominant strategy are simple to analyze from a strategic perspective: both parties have an alternative at hand, which is always better than any other option, irrespective of the behavior of the other. In these situations the outcome is clear from the very beginning since the behavior of the parties is predetermined.

2.2.2 Elimination of Dominated Strategies

In most situations of conflict the parties involved do not have dominant strategies. It is therefore interesting to expand the concept of dominant strategies so that we can analyze a more general class of conflicts. As an example for discussion let us examine the following situation of conflict:

Election of the workers' council

In the campaign for the election of representatives for the workers' council, the electorate is split. 40 percent of the employees prefer a policy of change. This policy supports the top management, which wants to reorganize the company in order to secure and strengthen its competitive position. 60 percent of the employees are not in favor of this strategy and support a policy of continuity without drastic changes, because they fear for their jobs.

Two new members have to be voted into the workers' council. A long-serving employee of the company (Candidate 1) and a just recently employed worker (Candidate 2) have announced that they would be interested in these positions. As they are the only candidates they will definitely be voted into the workers' council. The two candidates are interested in winning the elections with as many votes as possible, because this strengthens their power basis in the council.[2] Neither of the candidates has strong political ideologies so they are open to support any policy that seems to be best suited for the election campaign.

30

An employee only votes for a candidate who represents her preferred policy. If her preferred policy is not supported by any of the candidates, the employee will abstain from voting. If both candidates support the same policy, 70 percent of the employees would vote for the older and longer-serving Candidate 1, and 30 percent for the younger, recently employed Candidate 2. Due to her network in the company, the older candidate has the additional possibility to support a policy of compromise. This policy finds a middle ground between the two factions and would get 80 percent of the votes for change and 25 percent of the votes for continuity.

In this example the proportion of votes is determined by the policies of the candidates. Figure 2.10 shows which policy combination is supported by which percentage of votes.

Candidate 2

		policy of change	policy of continuity
	policy of change	28,12	40,60
Candidate 1	policy of compromise	58,30	58,12
	policy of continuity	60,40	42,18

Figure 2.10. Percentage of votes in the election of the workers' council

If, for instance, Candidate 1 chooses a policy of compromise and Candidate 2 a policy of change, then the workers' council would be elected with the following voting percentages: 25 percent of the supporters of a policy of change (10 percent of the workforce) and 80 percent of the supporters of a policy of continuity (48 percent of the workforce) vote for Candidate 1. Thus, she receives 58 percent of all votes. Candidate 2 will be voted for by 75 percent of those employees that want a policy of change (30 percent of the workforce), while employees that favor a policy of continuity abstain from voting (20 percent of the workforce). Voter participation is thus at 88 percent.

A strategic examination of this situation of conflict shows that neither of the two candidates has a dominant strategy: Candidate 1 would prefer a policy of continuity, if she assumes that Candidate 2 decides for a policy of change; but if Candidate 2 rather chooses to campaign on continuity herself, Candidate 1 would be better off with a policy of compromise. Thus, the optimal choice of policy of Candidate 1 depends on the decision of her rival candidate. The same applies to Candidate 2: she would prefer a policy of continuity if she assumes that Candidate 1 campaigns on change. However, with any other campaign topic of Candidate 1, Candidate 2 would be better off with a policy of change. As with Candidate 1, the optimal choice of Candidate 2 also depends on the decision of her rival candidate.

In this situation of conflict one alternative of Candidate 1 is characterized by a special property: the policy of change is, irrespective of the choice of her rival candidate, always worse than any of the other two possible choices. Consequently the policy of change for Candidate 1 is referred to as dominated strategy.

Generally we call a party's strategy a *dominated strategy*, if there exists an alternative for this party which, independently of the behavior of the other party, generates at least one higher and never a lower payoff. This strategy is *strictly dominated* when another alternative always leads to a higher payoff.

To predict the behavior of a party with a dominated strategy is equally simple as in the case of a dominant strategy. While a dominant strategy is always better than any other alternative, a dominated strategy is always worse than at least one other alternative of the party in question. Hence, a party should never choose a dominated strategy since she definitely has a better alternative.

This principle is equivalent to our first principle of strategic conduct when a party has only two alternatives. If one of the two alternatives is a dominant strategy, the other must be a dominated one. In this situation, the principle 'always choose a dominant strategy' is identical to the principle 'never choose a dominated strategy'.

Candidate 2

		policy of change	policy of continuity
	policy of compromise	58,30	58,12
Candidate 1			
	policy of continuity	60,40	42,18

Figure 2.11. Percentage of votes in the election of the workers' council, reduced form

If we apply this to the above example of workers' council elections, we find that Candidate 1 will never choose a policy of change. If Candidate 2

32

anticipates this behavior of Candidate 1, then she will analyze the situation of conflict in the reduced form of Figure 2.11.Assume that Candidate 2 expects that Candidate 1 behaves according to the principle 'never choose a dominated strategy'. Then the behavior of Candidate 2 in the reduced strategic form is uniquely defined: for Candidate 2 a policy of continuity is then always worse than a policy of change, irrespective of the decision of Candidate 1. Hence, Candidate 2 will decide to campaign for a policy of change and not for a policy of continuity.

If we further assume that Candidate 1 knows that Candidate 2 does not expect his rival candidate to pursue a dominated strategy, and that Candidate 2 herself would never choose such a strategy either, then Candidate 1 can reduce the situation of conflict to the following strategic form, as shown in Figure 2.12.

In this situation the decision of Candidate 1 is very simple: she will prefer 60 percent of the votes to 58 percent of the votes and thus decide for a policy of continuity. With this the policy combination for the campaigns is set and the expected outcome of the election is clear: both candidates are voted into the workers' council. Candidate 1 decides to campaign on continuity and can expect to receive 60 percent of the votes. Candidate 2 will choose a policy of change, supported by 40 percent of the workforce.

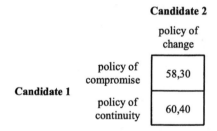

Figure 2.12. Percentage of votes in the election of the workers' council, twofold reduced form

In summary, we can generalize the above procedure in our second principle of strategic conduct for situations of conflict.

Principle of Strategic Behavior II:
In a situation of conflict, iteratively eliminate dominated strategies whenever they are available to one of the parties of conflict.

2.2.3 Strategically Stable Strategies

Although the principle of the iterative elimination of dominated strategies can be used in some situations of conflict to predict the actions of the interacting parties, in many cases the strategic form can not be reduced or simplified any further, neither by identifying a dominant strategy, nor by iteratively eliminating dominated alternatives. Therefore, with these instruments, predictions about a unique behavior of parties are often not possible, even after some complexity reduction of the situation of conflict. This is shown in the above example of conflicts between two leaders, two heroes, or two cowards. In the following, we therefore introduce another concept that does allow us to make predictions about the unique outcome in such situations of conflict. This concept will be the basis for our third principle of strategic conduct, which we will explain with a modified version of the previously introduced example of effort decisions in a production team:

Team production with continuous effort

A production team consists of two employees. In choosing her effort in the team, each employee can not only decide between routine work with low effort-related costs of production and qualified work with high effort-related costs, but also choose any other non-negative effort. The payoff of the joint production is shared equally between the two team members.

We specify the situation of conflict as follows: let $e_1 \geq 0$ and $e_2 \geq 0$ be the effort which the two team members can individually choose. The production of the team is given by the following production function: $e_1 \cdot e_2 + 3 \cdot (e_1 + e_2)$. The costs of production, which are influenced by the effort e_i, are given by $\frac{1}{2}e_i^2$ with $i = 1, 2$. This leads to the following net utility or payoff for Employee 1 with an own effort

$$U_1(e_1, e_2) = \frac{1}{2}[e_1 \cdot e_2 + 3 \cdot (e_1 + e_2)] - \frac{1}{2}e_1^2.$$

The payoff for employee 2 is determined analogously. In analyzing the behavior of the two employees we assume, like before, that both study their best alternative on the basis of the possible behavior of their team mate. This best alternative, which generates the highest payoff for one party, under a given behavior of the other party, is called the *best response*. The *reaction function* represents the best response of a specific party to each possible alternative of the other party in a situation of conflict.

In the framework of the above example, each of the two employees thus considers which effort would maximize its individual net utility when contributed as a best response to every possible effort the other team member could choose. Let us imagine ourselves in the place of one of the employees. Assume we think that our colleague will contribute effort e_2. What would be our best response? Which effort $e_1^*(e_2)$ leads to a maximum net utility, if we believe that the effort of the colleague is e_2? We will get the answer to this question by solving the following maximization problem

$$\max_{e_1} U_1(e_1, e_2)$$

with a given effort level e_2 of our colleague. As a first order condition we can specify $e_2 + 3 - 2e_1^*(e_2) = 0$, hence

$$e_1^*(e_2) = \frac{1}{2}e_2 + \frac{3}{2}.$$

Since the second order condition for a maximum is satisfied, the above equation represents the reaction function of Employee 1. For instance, if she assumes that her colleague is choosing an effort level of $e_1 = 1$, then her best response would be to contribute an effort of two units, $e_1 = 2$. In contrast, an effort of $e_2 = 5$ by the colleague would lead to a best response of $e_1 = 4$ by Employee 1. Figure 2.13 shows the reaction function of Employee 1 and also the respective function of Employee 2, which we can derive analogously since this specific situation of conflict is symmetric.

Based on this situation of conflict, what will be the behavior of Employee 1? In an attempt to answer this question Employee 1 will probably consider the following:[3] if Employee 1 plans to contribute an effort of $e_1 = 1$ and if Employee 2 anticipates this, then Employee 2's reaction function would lead to the contribution of an effort of $\frac{1}{2}e_1 + \frac{3}{2}$ that is $e_2 = 2$ units. But then it would be better for Employee 1 to choose an effort of $\frac{1}{2}e_2 + \frac{3}{2}$ that is $e_1 = 2, 5$ units. However, based on such a change in the level of effort of Employee 1, Employee 2 would prefer to an effort of $\frac{1}{2}e_1 + \frac{3}{2}$ that is $e_2 = 2, 75$ units, and so on.

But where does this seemingly endless chain of best responses end? For an answer we can examine the reaction functions of the two employees in Figure 2.13: the chain of best response converges toward the intersection point of the two reaction functions. This applies irrespective of the starting point of best response considerations:

$$e_1^* = \frac{1}{2}e_2^* + \frac{3}{2} \text{ and } e_2^* = \frac{1}{2}e_1^* + \frac{3}{2}, \text{ that is } e_1^* = e_2^* = 3$$

If Employee 1 contributed an effort of three units, Employee 2 would also prefer an effort of three units. Vice versa, if Employee 2 decided on an effort of three, the same effort would be optimal for Employee 1.[4]

Thus, at the intersection of the reaction function, both, Employee 1 and Employee 2 decide on an optimum effort of three units.

The properties of the efforts e_1^* and e_2^* are such that they are the mutual best responses of both parties: on the one hand, for a given effort e_2^* of

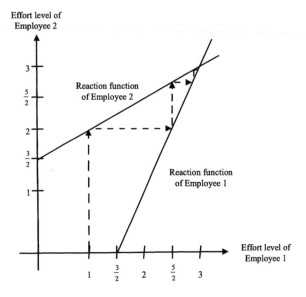

Figure 2.13. Reaction function of two team members

Employee 2, e_1^* is the best response of Employee 1. In fact, by choosing another effort level $e_1 \neq e_1^*$ Employee 1 can only be worse off. On the other hand, for a given effort e_1^* by Employee 1, e_2^* is the best response of Employee 2. Again, also she can not be better off by choosing another $e_2 \neq e_2^*$.

Such a strategy combination, in which none of the parties is better off by choosing another alternative, represents an *equilibrium*. Since Nash (1950a) developed this concept it is commonly referred to as *Nash equilibrium*.

In equilibrium none of the parties has an incentive to choose a different alternative, provided that the other parties orientate themselves towards the equilibrium. If the other parties pursue an equilibrium strategy, then for each party an equilibrium strategy is the best alternative available. Since this applies to all parties that interact in a situation of conflict, such equilibrium is strategically stable in the sense that no party has an incentive to deviate from it. We can thus formulate our third principle of strategic conduct:

Principle of Strategic Behavior III:
In a situation of conflict, always choose a strategy that is stable.

The above explanations of the concept of a Nash equilibrium in a situation of conflict are based on specific assumptions of rationality: each party behaves rationally. But each party must also know that all other interacting parties behave rationally, and all these other parties on their part must also know that all other parties make rational decisions, and so on. These endless steps of knowledge must be *common knowledge*. The concept of equilibrium thus assumes that all parties are rational, and that this fact, together with the strategic form or design of the situation of conflict, is common knowledge.

This very strong assumption as to the rationality of interacting parties inevitably poses some critical questions: how does this concept of equilibrium relate to our previous principles of strategic conduct? Why should it be an appropriate method to predict the outcome of a conflict at all? We will answer these questions, as follows: first, we will explain that the concept of equilibrium allows more precise predictions about the outcome of a situation of conflict than the iterative elimination of dominated strategies. Second, we will then argue that if a unique outcome can be predicted for a certain situation of conflict, this outcome necessarily has to be strategically stable.

To answer the above questions we will study a modified version of our previous example of workers' council elections.

Modified election of the workers' council

Assume the electorate does not support the older Candidate 1 so strongly anymore. The recently employed Candidate 2 succeeded to build up a positive image and enjoys the support of a significant share of the workforce. If both candidates were to represent the same policy, 60 percent of the employees would vote for her and 40 percent for Candidate 1. Furthermore, Candidate 1 is now also able to credibly stand for a policy of compromise. If she chooses to support this policy, she could get 30 percent of the votes for continuity and 20 percent of the votes for change. Due to her improved image she can now reckon with the majority of the votes if both candidates happen to campaign for a policy of compromise. In this case 70 percent of the work force would cast their votes.

Now, both candidates are confronted with the modified situation of conflict in Figure 2.14. In contrast to our previous example of the workers' council elections, neither of the two candidates has a dominant or dominated strategy. Neither choosing a dominant strategy nor iteratively eliminating dominated strategies can help us to determine what decisions the candidates are likely to take.

Candidate 2

		policy of change	policy of compromise	policy of continuity
	policy of change	16,24	32,26	40,60
Candidate 1	policy of compromise	58,30	28,42	58,12
	policy of continuity	60,40	42,26	24,36

Figure 2.14. Percentage of votes in the modified election of the workers' council

Now, let us see whether we are able to make such a prediction with the concept of equilibrium: if, for instance, Candidate 1 chooses a policy of change, the best response of Candidate 2 would be a policy of continuity. This, however, would make Candidate 1 prefer a policy of compromise, which would then prompt Candidate 2 to campaign on the same issue, whereupon the best response of Candidate 1 would be a policy of continuity, such that Candidate 2 would be better off with a policy of change. This last choice of Candidate 2 gives Candidate 1 no incentive to change her policy.

These considerations lead directly to the equilibrium of this situation of conflict – irrespective of their starting point: a policy of continuity is the best response of Candidate 1 to a policy of change by Candidate 2, and, vice versa, a policy of change by Candidate 2 is the best response to a policy of continuity by Candidate 1. The two alternatives, policy of continuity for Candidate 1 and policy of change for Candidate 2, form a combination of strategies that is stable: neither of the candidates has an incentive to change her policy, provided the other candidate chooses an equilibrium strategy. Hence, the concept of equilibrium allows the prediction of a unique behavior in situations of conflict.

In situations where an elimination of dominated strategies is not possible, the concept of equilibrium can still allow us to make statements about the outcome of a situation of conflict. This superiority of the concept of equilibrium over the concept of iterative elimination of dominated strategies can be generalized as follows:[5] if the iterative elimination of dominated strategies leads to the prediction of a unique outcome, then this outcome is strategically stable. Conversely it can be said that an equilibrium always survives an iterative elimination of strictly dominated strategies.

Therefore, the concept of equilibrium is the stronger approach than the iterative elimination of strictly dominated strategies. Moreover, it can be shown that in nearly all situations of conflict at least one equilibrium exists.

Due to these properties the concept of equilibrium is of special importance in the strategic analysis of situations of conflict. It can easily be shown that equilibrium strategies are coercive if the parties involved are rational, if rationality is common knowledge, and if a unique equilibrium exists: assume a conflict manager expects that two parties in a situation of conflict are not going to behave in a strategically stable manner. According to our definition the conflict manager then expects that at least one of the parties, for example Party 1, will choose a strategy that is not a best response on the behavior of the other party. However, this would not be rational for Party 1, since there would then exist a better alternative for Party 1. Therefore, Party 1 would always have an incentive to choose the best response instead, effectively deviating in her behavior from the expectation of the conflict manager. Hence, rational behavior does not allow any deviation from the equilibrium.

2.2.4 Unpredictability of Strategic Behavior

Up to now we assumed that a party in a situation of conflict decides on an alternative either with absolute certainty or not at all. In equilibrium, a party thus chooses exactly one strategically stable strategy of all the alternatives available. In this context, all other parties involved know about the equilibrium strategy and on their part will respond with a strategically stable strategy. All parties a priori thus know the outcome of the conflict. The behavior of each party is calculable such that all systematic thinking can be anticipated. Of course, anticipation of behavior is not always advantageous for parties involved in situations of conflict, as we will explain with the help of the following example.

Effort control of a field worker

A field worker is responsible for servicing the company's equipment and facilities in remote areas. The supervisor of the field worker wants to determine a fair pay. However, the supervisor finds it hard to make the payment depend on any kind of performance measures, as she can not directly observe how well the field worker has serviced the equipment. The supervisor nevertheless wants to offer the field worker some payment-related incentives to ensure due fulfillment of the service tasks. She therefore asks the field worker to write a weekly service report, so that she can monitor the field worker's effort. The supervisor checks the report. The payment of the field worker depends on the result of this check. If the check reveals a low servicing effort, the supervisor is entitles to withhold the payment of the field worker's weekly premium. For the supervisor, the only disadvantage of this system is that she has to spend a substantial amount of time and money on fact-checking the reports.

The described situation of conflict between the supervisor and the field worker depicts a typical situation in which neither party wants that the other can anticipate her behavior with certainty. If the field worker knew with certainty that the supervisor will check next week's service report, then she would work hard next week to make sure that she will receive the promised bonus. Any control of her effort would thus be unnecessary. It would only confirm that the field worker made an exceptional effort. Since the supervisor could have known this in advance, she could forgo checking the report and save the respective control costs. However, if the supervisor does not check the report, the field worker would have received the bonus in any case and thus has no incentive to work hard. In turn, if the supervisor expects that the field worker is not working hard enough, she would definitely check the reports to discover shirking and to cut bonuses. Now it would again be of advantage for the field worker to work hard enough to qualify for a bonus.

In this situation of conflict, each party wants to be unpredictable in her behavior: the supervisor with regard to checking the reports and the field worker with respect to her real effort. Every time that one party (implicitly) decides on an alternative, the other party reacts with her best response, which would give the first party an incentive to switch to another strategy. The first decision is, given the best response of the other party, not optimal anymore. Hence, both strategies are strategically unstable.

In order to make their behavior unpredictable, no party may choose an alternative with certainty. They rather have to decide for alternatives at random. In the literature we refer to the alternatives of a party as *pure strategies*. In our example there is no equilibrium in pure strategies. A party will rather determine probabilities with which she will pursue certain pure strategies. Within these parameters, the actual implementation of one of her alternatives is then left to chance. Such a probability distribution over a party's pure strategies is called a *mixed strategy*. If a party decides to pursue a mixed strategy, she will receive an expected payoff, rather than a certain one. To maximize this expected payoff, a party will choose an optimal probability of playing pure strategies, that is decide on a specific mixed strategy.

Let us look at our example again: the supervisor will choose a strategy where she controls field reports with a positive probability, but not with certainty. The field worker can not be sure whether her effort will be checked. In other words, she knows that some reports will go through unchecked. Hence, the field worker will choose a strategy where she does not work hard all the time, but also shirks with a certain probability. Now the supervisor can not be sure anymore, whether the field worker puts in the required effort or not.

The stability of their strategic behavior critically depends on the probabilities that both parties choose for their alternatives. In the following we will explain this decision making: first, we will further specify the example of the supervisor and the field worker, to carve out the conflict of interest in more detail. After that, we will analyze the probabilities of strategic behavior of both parties.

The field worker has two alternatives: she can either choose a low effort, that is shirk, or she can decide to make a high effort, which we interpret as adequate to qualify for a bonus. The field worker experiences a high effort as costs of ten units, while shirking reduces these costs to five units. The productivity of the field work is assumed to be ten units for a low effort and twenty units for a high effort. The field worker receives a fixed salary of five units, plus a bonus of seven units, which is cut if the supervisor discovers shirking. This can only be done by checking the field reports, which costs the supervisor one unit. Thus, if the supervisor does not check the reports, the field worker gets the benefit of the doubt and receives the bonus, which she claims to deserve. Since the supervisor represents the organization, she is interested in as high as possible productivity, while the field worker wants to maximize her net income. This leads to payoffs in pure strategies as depicted in Figure 2.15.

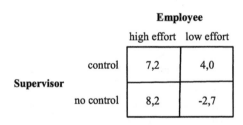

| | | **Employee** | |
		high effort	low effort
	control	7,2	4,0
Supervisor			
	no control	8,2	-2,7

Figure 2.15. Effort control of a field worker

A mixed strategy of the supervisor can be represented by a tuple $(k, 1 - k)$, where the probability $k \in [0, 1]$ determines to which extent the supervisor is controlling the field worker. Similarly, a mixed strategy for the field worker can be represented by $(a, 1 - a)$. Here, $a \in [0, 1]$ specifies the probability with which the field worker shirks. In the extremes, when k or a take on the values 0 or 1, the mixed strategy is equivalent to a pure strategy. The concept of mixed strategies is thus a natural extension of pure strategies.

From a strategic perspective it is however not sufficient to simply choose any mixed strategy at random. This would make the own behavior quite unpredictable, but probably not strategically stable: the best response of the other party would generally give the first party an incentive to deviate from its initial strategy. For example, if the supervisor would check the field reports with a randomly assumed probability of 50 percent, then the expected payoff for a shirking field worker would be $3.5(= 0.5 * 0 + 0.5 * 7)$. With a 50 percent chance the field worker would be checked upon and, according to Figure 2.16, receive a payoff of zero units, and with a 50 percent chance an unjustified bonus is paid, generating a net income of seven units for the worker. If the field worker decides not to shirk, her expected payoff is two units $(= 0.5 * 2 + 0.5 * 2)$. Thus, the field worker would prefer to shirk, which would give the supervisor an inventive to always check the field reports. Rather than unpredictability of behavior per se, it is the optimal degree of unpredictability that is important.

To find a strategically stable behavior we first study how the field worker's payoff depends on the supervisor's probability of control:

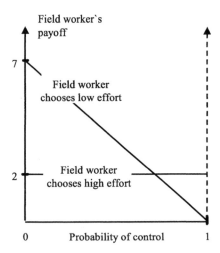

Figure 2.16. Field worker's payoff, subject to the choice of effort and to the probability of control

In the extreme cases, where the supervisor does not check the reports at all, $k = 0$, or always checks them, $k = 1$, the net income of the field worker corresponds to the payoffs in the bi-matrix of Figure 2.15. For example, in the case of shirking, the payoff for the field worker would be either zero or seven units. If the supervisor now randomizes between her alternatives by choosing a probability of control seven or zero, then the field worker receives a payoff of zero units with a probability $k \in [0, 1]$, and a payoff of seven units with a probability k. If the field worker chooses not to shirk, she receives a payoff of two units, which is independent of the probability of control.

Figure 2.17 shows that, up to a critical value k^*, the expected payoff for the field worker is always higher when she shirks. However, if the supervisor chooses to check the field reports with a probability higher than k^*, the field worker is better off without shirking. With this we have determined the reaction function of the field worker, that is the full range of all her best responses on all possible mixed strategies of the supervisor.

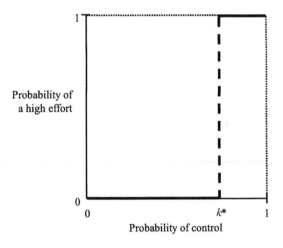

Figure 2.17. Field worker's reaction function

If the probability of control lies below a critical value k^*, then the field worker has an incentive to shirk, above k^*, her expected payoff is higher when she chooses in favor of a high work effort. For the case that the probability of control is exactly at the critical level k^*, the field worker will be indifferent between the two alternatives.

To calculate the critical value k^*, we first determine the expected payoff for the field worker subject to the probability of control $k \in [0,1]$ by the supervisor. If the field worker chooses a high effort with a probability $a \in [0,1]$, then her expected payoff is determined as $a\,[2k + 2\,(1 - k)] + (1 - a)\,[0k + 7\,(1 - k)] = 7 - 7k + a\,(7k - 5)$. Consequently, the field worker will choose a high effort level with the probability $a = 1$ if $k > \frac{5}{7}$. If $k < \frac{5}{7}$

she will shirk with certainty $(a = 0)$ and at the critical value $k^* = \frac{5}{7}$ she is indifferent:

$$a^*(k) = \begin{cases} 0 & \text{if} \quad k < \frac{5}{7} \\ \in [0,1] & \text{if} \quad k = \frac{5}{7} \\ 1 & \text{if} \quad k > \frac{5}{7} \end{cases}$$

Analogously we can examine the behavior of the supervisor. As Figure 2.18 shows, the supervisor's payoff with control exceeds the payoff with no control if the probability of shirking is sufficiently high, with $1 - a > 1 - a^*$, that is $a < a^*$.

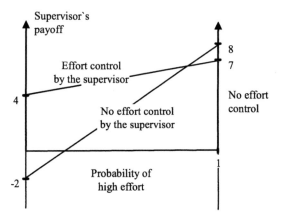

Figure 2.18. Supervisor's payoff, subject to choice of control and to the probability of shirking

Hence, the best response of the supervisor to a given mixed strategy $(a, 1 - a)$ of the field worker is determined as follows: if the probability $a \in [0, 1]$ for a high effort in the field exceeds the critical value a^*, then the supervisor will not check any of the reports. Conversely, if this probability a lies below the critical value a^*, the supervisor will rather bear the costs of control and conduct checks with certainty. If the probability of shirking is equal to the critical value a^* the supervisor is indifferent between checking the reports or not. Together, this leads to the supervisor's reaction function as shown in Figure 2.19.

By maximizing the supervisor's expected payoff we can analytically determine the critical value a^*. If the supervisor assumes that the field worker will choose a mixed strategy $(a, 1 - a)$, then the probability of control

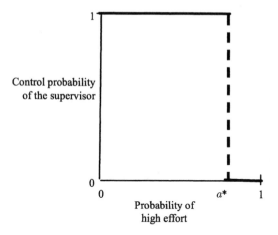

Figure 2.19. Supervisor's reaction function

$k \in [0, 1]$ generates a payoff $k\left[7a + 4\left(1 - a\right)\right] + \left(1 - k\right)\left[8a - 2\left(1 - a\right)\right] = 10a - 2 + k\left(6 - 7a\right)$. Therefore, the critical value is $a^* = \frac{6}{7}$ and it follows:

$$k^*(a) = \begin{cases} 0 & \text{if } a > \frac{6}{7} \\ \in [0, 1] & \text{if } a = \frac{6}{7} \\ 1 & \text{if } a < \frac{6}{7} \end{cases}.$$

After we have analyzed the best responses for both parties we can now directly infer their strategically stable behavior. According to the concept of equilibrium a strategically stable behavior of both parties is achieved, when the mixed strategies are mutual best responses. As shown graphically in Figure 2.20, this is nothing else than the intersection between the supervisor's and the field worker's reaction functions.

Figure 2.20 shows that there exists a unique equilibrium in mixed strategies: the supervisor chooses a probability of control of $k^* = \frac{5}{7}$, while the field worker chooses to adequately fulfill his duties to the extent of $a^* = \frac{6}{7}$. As the following argumentation shows, this is in fact a stable strategic behavior for both parties:

1. Let a be smaller than the critical value a^*. According to her reaction function, the supervisor would then check the field reports with certainty, $k^*(a) = 1$. However, following the reaction function of the field worker, we would then observe no shirking anymore, which is in contradiction to our assumption.

2. Let a be greater than the critical value a^*. Here, it would be advantageous for the supervisor to forgo any control, $k^* = 0$. Since $a^*(0) = 0$,

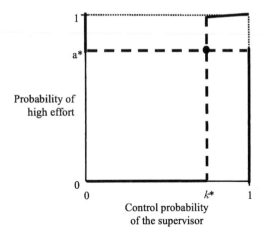

Figure 2.20. Strategically stable behavior of both parties

the field worker would then shirk with certainty, which, again, is in contradiction to our assumption.

3. The last case left is a situation where $a = a^*$. This means that the supervisor is indifferent with regard to her control, $k^*(a^*) \in [0, 1]$. If the probability of control would not be identical to $k^* = \frac{5}{7}$, then the field worker on her part would have an incentive again to either certainly shirk or not. Both of these reactions would contradict $a = a^*$. Hence, the only consistent alternative left is given by $k = k^*$.

2.2.5   Focal Points

Many situations of conflict have multiple equilibria. In such a case we can not make specific predictions about the behavior of the parties and the outcome of the conflict. Thus, to make sure that all parties in a conflict expect the same outcome, we have to extend our principle of strategic behavior III that stipulates only to choose stable strategies. Only if such a mechanism exists do all parties make strategically stable decisions, which satisfy the conditions of equilibrium.

Let us once again look at the conflict between the marketing and the production department. Both departments have to choose whether they are willing to accept a compromise in their product design, or rather insist on their original proposal without any further changes. In the following we refer to the situation of conflict with two leaders (see Figure 2.21).

In this situation there exist two equilibria in pure strategies: the marketing department is willing to compromise, while the production department

Production department

		accept a compromise	insist on own proposal
Marketing department	accept a compromise	2,2	3,4
	insist on own proposal	4,3	1,1

Figure 2.21. Conflict with two leaders

is not; or the production department is willing to compromise and the marketing department is not. Furthermore there exists a mixed equilibrium in mixed strategies: both departments decide independently from each other with a probability $\frac{1}{2}$ either to compromise or not to compromise.

From the definition of equilibrium we can infer the following. If both parties expect a specific equilibrium they will also choose the equivalent equilibrium strategies. The equilibrium would then be a self-fulfilling prophecy. For example, if both departments expect that the marketing department will be willing to compromise and that the production department will insist on its design, then both departments will behave accordingly. No party will have an incentive to choose a different strategy, even though the marketing department would prefer the higher payoff from the other equilibrium.

On the basis of our current modeling we can not answer how the parties could coordinate their expectations in such a way that they reach an equilibrium. After all, the only elements that characterize the strategic form of our situation of conflict are the relevant parties, their alternative actions, and the consequences of their interaction. Of course, with such a parsimonious specification we omit a number of details that might also be relevant to the situation of conflict. For example, we did not consider the gender of the parties, other relationships the parties might have, or the societal environment in which they interact. Of course, such elements can have important effects on the parties' behavior. Specifically, these factors might contribute to the coordination of behavior and thus to the selection of an equilibrium. Anything that focuses the attention on a specific equilibrium leads the parties involved to expect and select this equilibrium. Following Schelling (1960), such strategy combinations are referred to as focal points. Focal points enable parties to reach the most prominent outcome of a conflict.

Principle of Strategic Behavior IV:
Choose the strategically stable strategy that leads to the most prominent outcome of a conflict.

To exemplify which mechanisms may lead to the establishment of a focal point, we refer back to the conflict between the marketing and the production department. Suppose that the marketing department always dominated similar meetings on several earlier occasions. In our example we can then expect that the marketing department will (again) insist on its position, such that compromise is the best response of the production department. Even if the head of production is reluctant to accept the tough position of the marketing department (again), it is still in her interest to stick to this focal point in order to reach an equilibrium. A prominent outcome of this conflict could also be established through, for instance, a corporate strategy that is focused on customer orientation. Both departments would then implicitly agree to the more customer-oriented design of the marketing department.

Next to conventions that often lead to a selection of an equilibrium, communication between the parties can also establish a focal point. Suppose the head of marketing tells the head of production prior to the meeting: 'There is no way around a customer oriented design'. We can then expect that the two departments will decide on a customer-oriented design when they actually meet.

Up to now we only examined exogenous factors that support the selection out of multiple equilibria. Additionally, certain aspects of the conflict itself can possess features of a focal point, for example decision criteria like fairness. In the following we discuss this for the criteria's payoff efficiency and risk dominance.

Research collaboration of two colleagues

Two researchers in a corporation are asked to collaborate in a research project to solve a complex problem. Since the project has a tight deadline, both researchers are briefed to prepare some preliminary solutions before the kick-off meeting. The researchers have the following alternatives: they both either invest in substantial preliminary work and thereby increase the probability that the project will be finished before the deadline. Or they invest minimally and wait and see how the joint work develops. This would drastically reduce the probability of being finished in time. Since the individual commitment of each researcher can not be properly assessed, they receive a joint payoff, which mainly depends on whether they meet the deadline.

We specify this situation of conflict between the research colleagues as follows: both can invest a low or a high initial investment into the joint project. The success of the project depends on this decision. The probability of success for the joint project is specified in Figure 2.22. If both researchers decide to invest low then the project is going to fail with certainty (probability 0). If both invest high then the project's success is certain (probability 1). If one of the two invests high and the other low then the probability of success is 20 percent (probability $\frac{3}{15}$).

Researcher 2

	low investment	high investment
low investment	0	$\frac{3}{15}$
high investment	$\frac{3}{15}$	1

Researcher 1

Figure 2.22. The probabilities for a successful project

The investment decision of the researcher depends on the costs involved and the payoff: a low investment incurs costs of two units; a high investment incurs ten units. The payoff of the researcher largely depends on the project's success: each researcher receives a fixed payoff of ten units, irrespective of the outcome of the project; additionally each researcher gets a bonus of 30 units if the project is successful. If the project is a failure, no bonus is paid at all. This leads to the payoffs in the bi-matrix in Figure 2.23.

Researcher 2

	low investment	high investment
low investment	8,8	14,6
high investment	6,14	30,30

Researcher 1

Figure 2.23. Incentives to invest in a joint project

There exist two equilibria in pure strategies: either both researchers choose a low investment or both choose to invest high. The latter payoff dominates the former, because the payoffs in the latter equilibrium are higher for both researchers. A naïve argumentation could be that both researchers will automatically agree to the payoff dominant equilibrium, that is both colleagues decide to make high initial investments. However, it is also possible that risk dominance is used as an alternative selection device: a low investment generates at least eight units, whereas a high investment may lead to only six units.

Which of the two criteria will now be the focal point? If we assume that the two researchers do not have the opportunity to communicate before they have to decide on their initial investment, then a mutually high investment is not necessarily a focal point. If Researcher 1 assumes that Researcher 2 chooses a low investment with a probability greater than $\frac{8}{9}$, then she should not make a high initial investment into the project. This would at least guarantee her a payoff of eight units. In fact, Researcher 1 knows that Researcher 2 shall invest low if Researcher 2 expects Researcher 1 to choose this alternative with a probability greater than $\frac{8}{9}$ herself. Thus, without communication it is not warranted whether the payoff-dominant equilibrium really coordinates the expectations of the two researchers.

Does this argument change when we assume that the two researchers can communicate about their input before the project starts? To answer this question, let's assume that both researchers agreed on a joint high initial investment in an unofficial meeting before the actual project kick-off. In analyzing this situation from the perspective of Researcher 2, we find that she always has an advantage if Researcher 1 makes a high investment. Researcher 2 has a clear incentive to convince her colleague to invest high, irrespective of the investment strategy she really pursues. Hence, in front of Researcher 1, Researcher 2 will always pretend to invest high herself. However, knowing this, Researcher 1 doubts Researcher 2's commitment to invest high. Despite their efforts to coordinate their strategies, for either researcher it is not clear whether the payoff dominant equilibrium is really reached.

Normally, organizations have a preference for a specific outcome or equilibrium. In our example it would be disadvantageous for an organization if both researchers make low investments. In such situations, in which organizations prefer a specific equilibrium, while there does not exist a prominent equilibrium for the parties involved, conflict management is needed to act as a selection device.

2.3 INCOMPLETE INFORMATION ABOUT THE CONFLICT

Up to now we have always assumed that the parties are fully informed about all decisive characteristics of the situation of conflict. Each party knew exactly which alternatives and payoffs the other party had at hand. Such situations are referred to as conflicts with *complete information*. For most cases this is not a very realistic assumption. Rather there will be some uncertainty about the other's alternatives or about the consequences that follow from different actions.

If a party is not completely informed about all elements of the strategic form of the conflict, then she faces a situation with *incomplete information*. The information deficit of the not so well informed party is countered by the information advantage of the better informed party. The better informed party thus possesses private information, which the other party does not enjoy. This leads to situations of conflicts as in the following example:

Monitoring of a field worker under incomplete information

The field worker, who is responsible for servicing the company's equipment and facilities in rural areas, has to send weekly work reports to her supervisor. The field worker's pay depends on the result of the supervisor's fact-checking of these reports. The worker is uncertain about the supervisor's monitoring costs. As the supervisor is very busy, the field worker assumes that she will hardy be able to check the work reports in detail. Thus, the worker expects that the supervisor's opportunity costs for such monitoring are rather high.

The higher the monitoring costs of the supervisor the lower is her payoff if she really decides to check the work reports. The field worker can only estimate the monitoring costs of the supervisor by assigning probabilities to different levels of monitoring costs. By doing this, she implicitly assigns probabilities to the supervisor's payoffs, too. The uncertainty about the monitoring costs of the supervisor is thus directly reflected in uncertainty about the payoffs of the supervisor.

Payoffs can also be used to model incomplete information about other characteristics of a situation of conflict. Assume that a party is uncertain about the potential alternatives available to the other party. From a strategic perspective it is equivalent, whether the other party does not have a certain alternative, or whether this alternative is associated with a very disadvantageous payoff. Similarly, uncertainty about other aspects of situations of conflict, for example about the level of information of the other party, can be taken into account: if they are relevant for the strategic

51

behavior of the parties, then they also have to be reflected in the consequences of the interaction.

At first sight it seems that we have departed from our general framework when analyzing conflicts with incomplete information. Until now we have assumed that the general framework of the situation is common knowledge to all parties involved. On the basis of this knowledge each party was able to put herself in the position of the other party to deduce the other's behavior. The common knowledge about the general framework of the situation was a necessary condition for the development of the concept of strategically stable strategies.

In situations in which one party possesses private information, this condition is no longer satisfied. Here the question is how far the modeling of incomplete information is compatible with our previous analytical setting. We will answer this question in the following subsections.

2.3.1 The Consideration of Uncertainty in the Strategic Form

The answer to this question can be traced back to Harsanyi (1967, 1968a, 1968b). He argued that the present framework can also describe situations of conflicts with incomplete information. Hence, the consideration of incomplete information does not go beyond the scope of the hitherto existing model. In fact, a situation of conflict with incomplete information can be interpreted as a situation with complete information. In the following we explain this with the example of monitoring a field worker.

Let's assume the uncertainty of the field worker with regard to the real monitoring costs of her supervisor can be described as follows: checking the work report causes either low costs, $c = 1$, or high costs, $c = 2$. Of course, the supervisor knows her monitoring costs. She knows whether the checking of a field report costs one or two units. However, the field worker does not know this. But from the general workload of her supervisor she can deduce a certain expectation of how high the monitoring costs are likely to be. Let $\theta \in [0, 1]$ the probability with which she expects the monitoring costs to be low. With probability $1 - \theta$ she assumes that monitoring costs two units. If we assume the same framework as in our explanation of mixed strategies, this leads to the strategic forms in Figure 2.24.

According to Harsanyi we can describe the situation as follows: before the two parties interact, a random draw determines the monitoring costs of the supervisor. With probability θ the monitoring costs are low, with probability $1 - \theta$ the costs are high. The outcome of the random draw determines the type of supervisor. In our case the supervisor can represent two types: Type 1 has low monitoring costs, a supervisor of Type 2 has high costs.

Field worker

		high effort	low effort
Supervisor with low costs	control	7,2	4,0
	no control	8,2	-2,7

Field worker

		high effort	low effort
Supervisor with high costs	control	6,2	3,0
	no control	8,2	-2,7

Figure 2.24. Monitoring with uncertain costs

We can therefore interpret the uncertainty of the field worker about the monitoring costs as an uncertainty about the type of her supervisor. Thus, instead of saying that the field worker is uncertain about the costs of monitoring, we can also say that she is uncertain about the supervisor's real type. Analogously, if a party knows the payoffs of the other party, she also knows of which type the other party is.

The supervisor can observe the outcome of the random draw and knows about the level of monitoring costs that is assigned to her. The field worker can not observe this. On the basis of these considerations we can now analyze a situation of conflict with incomplete information like one with complete information. Instead of the parties themselves, their different type(s) are seen as actors in the conflict. In our case there are three actors: the field worker, the Type 1 supervisor (low costs) and the Type 2 supervisor (high costs).

In summary, to depict a situation with incomplete information as one with complete information we need to specify the following four components:

1. the parties in the situation of conflict as well as their respective types;
2. the actions or strategies that are available to each party;

3. the payoffs or consequences for each type of a party and for all possible outcomes of the situation;
4. the probabilities that each party assign to the real types of the other parties.

Like in the previous strategic form of a situation of conflict we first need to specify the parties and their possible actions. Additionally, we have to consider the different types. The set of all characteristics of a party determines the space of types available to a party. In our example the space of types of the supervisor consists of two elements: either the supervisor is of Type t_1, with low monitoring costs $c = 1$, or of Type t_2 with high monitoring costs $c = 2$. The type of a party is private information, that is it can not be observed by the other parties. As shown in Figure 2.24 the payoffs are specified for each type. We can thus describe the uncertainty about the other party's type as an uncertainty about the payoffs that result from certain interactions.

Further we have to consider the expectations of the parties about each other. Each party has a belief about the real type of the other party. We can think of these beliefs as a probability distribution over the set of the other party's types. In general, a party will be able to partially infer the other party's type from the knowledge of her own type. We assume that this is done according to the rule of Bayes:[6] before the parties' own type is assigned to them they have an expectation about the distribution of possible type combinations. After a specific type is assigned to them they use this information to update their initial belief about the other parties' types. Strategic forms of situation of conflicts under uncertainty, where expectations are updated according to this procedure, are called *Bayesian forms*.

2.3.2 Bayesian Equilibrium

What are now the implications of incomplete information on the parties' behavior in a situation of conflict? First we can conjecture that the behavior of the party with incomplete information will change. The uncertainty refers to specific payoffs to the other party resulting out of the mutual interaction. As these payoffs determine the parties' behavior we can generally assume that different types will act differently. The uninformed party adjusts her actions strategically to the behavior of the informed party and thus has to take the uncertainty about the other's type into account when deciding on her own actions.

In our example this simply means that the field worker considers the monitoring costs of the supervisor when she chooses her work effort. Of course, the degree of uncertainty influences her strategic behavior. For the extreme case of no (degree of) uncertainty, where the field worker knows the control costs of the supervisor, we have already discussed this example in connection with mixed strategies.

The question rather is, whether the introduction of uncertainty for the uninformed party changes the behavior of the informed party. At first sight it might seem that the behavior does not change. The informed party knows her own type and, as she also knows the payoffs of the uninformed party, she could behave as in a situation with complete information. However, such an argumentation would neglect the strategic component of the conflict, because the informed is in search of the best response to the behavior of the uninformed party. As the behavior of the uniformed party might change due to the uncertainty about the other party's type, the best response of the informed party might also change, despite the certain knowledge of her own type. In our example, when choosing a best response, a supervisor with low control costs would thus have to consider how a supervisor with high monitoring costs behaves in such a situation.

This requirement is a direct result of the transformation of a situation of conflict with incomplete information into one with complete information. While the actors in a situation with complete information are the actual parties, the actors in the situation with incomplete information are all types of each party in the conflict. The strategy of a party thus consists of the specification of actions for each of its possible types.

With this interpretation we are able to transfer the equilibrium concept without uncertainty to situations of conflict with uncertainty: for each party's type a *Bayesian equilibrium* determines a (mixed) strategy, which is specified on the basis of a possibly updated belief about the types of the other parties, and which is strategically stable. On this basis, each party maximizes her own expected payoffs and her equilibrium strategy. We can summarize this in another principle of strategic behavior:

Principle of Strategic Behavior V:
When confronted with uncertainty about the framework of a situation of conflict, form rational expectations of the possible characteristics and consider these in the choice of a strategically stable strategy.

In the following we will use our example of field worker monitoring to study the optimal behavior of the two parties in a situation of incomplete information. Hence, we identify the Bayesian equilibrium.

In accordance with the definition of equilibrium we have to find a strategy $(a^*, 1 - a^*)$ with $a^* \in [0,1]$ for the field worker and a strategy $(k_1^*, 1 - k_1^*)$ and $(k_2^*, 1 - k_2^*)$ with $k_1^*, k_2^* \in [0,1]$ for the supervisor's types t_1 and t_2 These strategies are in equilibrium if they satisfy the following conditions:

1. The strategy $(k_1^*, 1 - k_1^*)$ for the supervisor with low monitoring costs $c = 1$ maximizes her expected payoff, given the behavior of the field

worker. As explained before, the expected payoff of the supervisor is given by $10a^* - 2 + k_1^* (6 - 7a^*))$ if the field worker chooses a high effort level with probability $a^* \in [0, 1]$ and if the supervisor controls the field worker with a probability $k_1^* \in [0, 1]$.

2. The strategy $(k_2^*, 1 - k_2^*)$ for the supervisor with low monitoring costs $c = 2$ maximizes her expected payoff, given the behavior of the field worker. Analogous to the above explanation, the expected payoff of the supervisor is given by $10a^* - 2 + k_2^* (5 - 7a^*)$, if the field worker chooses a high effort level with probability $k_2^* \in [0, 1]$.

3. The strategy $(a^*, 1 - a^*)$ of the filed worker maximizes her expected payoff, given the behavior of the supervisor. As the supervisor can have high or low monitoring costs, the field worker has to consider in her strategy how her supervisor would behave with high or low costs. Furthermore, her behavior has to incorporate her belief about the probable type of her supervisor. As the field worker expects monitoring costs to be low with a probability $\theta \in [0, 1]$ her expected payoff is determined as

$$\theta \left[7 - 7k_1^* + a^* \left(7k_1^* - 5 \right) \right] + (1 - \theta) \left[7 - 7k_2^* + a^* \left(7k_2^* - 5 \right) \right].$$

Her expected payoff depending on the probability $a^* \in [0, 1]$ for a high work effort is determined as

$$7\theta \left(1 - k_1^* \right) + 7 \left(1 - \theta \right) \left(1 - k_2^* \right) + a^* \left[-5 + 7\theta k_1^* + 7 \left(1 - \theta \right) k_2^* \right].$$

To derive the Bayesian equilibria we can now argue as follows:

Assume that the field worker chooses her effort level such that the probability of a high work effort is smaller than $\frac{5}{7}$, $a^* < \frac{5}{7}$. From (1) and (2) it then directly follows that both types of supervisors would check the work reports with certainty. Under these circumstances and according to (3), the field worker would choose $a^* = 1$ and fulfill her duties diligently, which contradicts our assumption.

Analogously we can deduct a contradiction for the case that the field worker chooses a high effort level with a too high probability: if $a^* > \frac{6}{7}$, then both types of supervisors would conduct no monitoring at all, resulting in a low effort of the field worker. Again, this is in direct contradiction to our assumption.

Now assume that the field worker chooses her effort level such that the supervisor with high monitoring costs would be indifferent with respect to checking the work reports, that is $a^* = \frac{5}{7}$. First, we can infer that a supervisor with low monitoring costs would check the reports with certainty, $k_1^* = 1$. In order for the field worker to be indifferent between a high and a low effort, it follows out of (3) that the probability of monitoring k_2^* of the supervisor with high monitoring costs is determined by $\frac{5-7\theta}{7(1-\theta)}$. The supervisor's probability of monitoring is positive as long as the field worker expects sufficiently high monitoring costs, $1 - \theta > \frac{2}{7}$, that is $\theta < \frac{5}{7}$. If these conditions are satisfied then the specific strategies of the actors form a Bayesian equilibrium: $k_1^* = 1$, $k_2^* = \frac{5-7\theta}{7(1-\theta)}$, $a^* = \frac{5}{7}$ for $\theta < \frac{5}{7}$.

Assume that the field worker increases her effort so that $a^* \in (\frac{5}{7}, \frac{6}{7})$. Under these circumstances a supervisor with high monitoring costs would not check the work reports, $k_2^* = 0$, while a supervisor with low costs would monitor with certainty, $k_1^* = 1$. Here, the indifference of the field worker postulates that $\theta = \frac{5}{7}$. On the basis of such a belief of the field worker, the mentioned strategies are stable: $k_1^* = 1$, $k_2^* = 0$, $a^* \in (\frac{5}{7}, \frac{6}{7})$ for $\theta = \frac{5}{7}$.

In the last case that is possible, the field worker chooses a high effort level a^* with probability $\frac{6}{7}$. It follows from (2) that a supervisor with high monitoring costs would be indifferent with regard to checking the reports. The best response function of the field worker implies that the monitoring probability k_1^* is determined by $k_1^* = \frac{5}{7\theta}$. If the field worker's belief about the monitoring costs is sufficiently small, $1 - \theta < \frac{2}{7}$, that is $\theta > \frac{5}{7}$, then the supervisor will check the reports of the field worker with a positive probability, but not with certainty. Under these circumstances, the described strategies also represent a Bayesian equilibrium: $k_1^* = \frac{5}{7\theta}$, $k_2^* = 0$, $a^* = \frac{6}{7}$ for $\theta > \frac{5}{7}$.

Figure 2.25 shows how the strategically stable behavior of the parties varies with the belief of the field worker about the monitoring costs of the supervisor. If the field worker knows that her supervisor has high monitoring costs, the parties will behave as follows: for $\theta = 0$ the supervisor monitors the worker with a probability $k_2^* = \frac{5}{7}$ and the field worker chooses a high effort level with a probability $a^* = \frac{5}{7}$. If the field worker believes that the supervisor has low monitoring costs, this does not change her decision for $\theta < \frac{5}{7}$. However, the belief of the field worker has a decisive impact on the behavior of the supervisor. If the supervisor has high monitoring costs, then she will systematically reduce her likelihood of monitoring in θ. After all, a supervisor with low monitoring costs would always monitor. As the field worker incorporates this knowledge into her decision, the supervisor on her part will adapt her monitoring behavior such that she does not check the work reports at all anymore if $\theta = \frac{5}{7}$.

In the other extreme, $\theta = 1$, the supervisor with low monitoring costs decides to check the reports with a probability of $k_1^* = \frac{5}{7}$. The field worker adequately fulfills her tasks in six of seven cases, that is $a^* = \frac{6}{7}$. This relates to the behavior analyzed above. If the field worker believes that her supervisor has high instead of low monitoring costs, then this would have the following effects on the parties: if the uncertainty is not too great, $\theta > \frac{5}{7}$, there would be no change in the effort level of the field worker. The supervisor achieves this by systematically increasing the monitoring probability. Thus, by checking the reports more often, the supervisor has to compensate for the conjecture of the field worker, that the supervisor has high costs and that she therefore will not check the reports. When

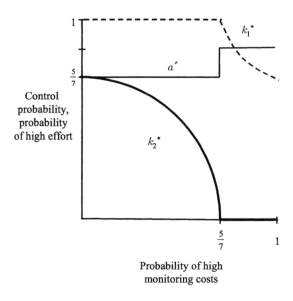

Figure 2.25. Strategically stable behavior of both parties with uncertainty of the field worker about monitoring costs

the belief of the field worker reaches the critical value of $\theta = \frac{5}{7}$, then the supervisor checks the reports with certainty.

This example shows that the Nash equilibrium is a limit case of the Bayesian equilibrium. Correspondingly, the Bayesian equilibrium concept has more requirements with regard to the knowledge of the parties in conflict. Next to rationality and common knowledge of rationality, all parties also have to know the probability distribution of all types and of each other.

2.3.3 The Interpretation of Strategic Unpredictability

In the previous section we interpreted a mixed strategy as a party's deliberate decision to make her behavior in a situation of conflict intransparent. The decision for a mixed strategy implies that the party first defines probabilities for her potential actions and then lets a random draw decide, which of the actions she really executes.

Let us look again at the situation of conflict with two leaders. The marketing and the production department both have an idea for the development of a new product. Before the first meeting they have to decide whether they want to pursue their product idea with a compromising or a non-compromising attitude. Figure 2.26 shows the consequences out of this behavior. In this situation there exist two equilibria in pure strate-

		accept a compromise	insist on own proposal
Marketing department	accept a compromise	2,2	3,4
	insist on own proposal	4,3	1,1

Production department

Figure 2.26. Conflict between the marketing and the production department

gies. The marketing department decides upon a non-compromising attitude while the production department chooses to be compromising. Or, the other way around, the marketing department decides on a compromising strategy while the production department chooses to insist on its product idea. Additionally there also exists an equilibrium in mixed strategies. Each department decides with a probability $\frac{1}{2}$ to pursue one of the two strategies.

Let us focus on the equilibrium in mixed strategies. According to our previous argumentation we could ask why a department would adopt such a random approach.at all The behavior of the other party is such that the department is indifferent between the two actions. Her payoff is thus independent of her own behavior. The consequences that are resulting from her strategically stable behavior also result from any other mixed strategy, provided the other party sticks to its own equilibrium behavior.

In the following we will advance an alternative interpretation of mixed strategies. We argue that a mixed strategy can also be seen as uncertainty about the framework of the situation of conflict. If a party chooses a mixed strategy we can argue either that this party randomly mixes between the two actions, or that the other party is uncertain about the real decision of this party. This uncertainty is then reflected in the party's payoff, as this was the case with incomplete information. We can illustrate this by using our example.

---

*Collaboration of the marketing and the production department with un-
certainty about gains in organizational status*

---

*Let us assume the marketing and the production department are uncer-
tain about the real interests of the other party. Specifically, we assume that
none of the two departments knows for sure how much organizational status
the other department gains by implementing its product idea. For, instance,
if the marketing department decides on a non-compromising strategy, then
the production department does not know how much organizational status
the marketing department would gain if the production department decides
to be compromising.*

We model this situation with the bi-matrix in Figure 2.27. The gain in
organizational status of the marketing department, if it chooses to be non-
compromising and the production department chooses to be compromising,
are given by $4 + m$. The real value of m is not known to the production
department. It knows, however, that the parameter can only lie in the
range $[0, x]$ with $x > 0$ and that every possible value of status gain in $[0, x]$
is equally likely. Analogously we specify the uncertainty of the marketing
department with regard to the gains in organizational status of the production department with the parameter $p \in [0, x]$. Again, the expectation
of the status gain of the production department is uniformly distributed.
We make the simplifying assumption that both departments have the same
maximum gain in their organizational status.

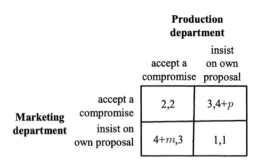

Figure 2.27. Conflict between the marketing and the production department when
both departments are uncertain about the preferences of the other party

We can describe this situation of conflict with incomplete information in
the following Bayesian form. Each parameter in the range $[0, x]$ specifies a
possible type of each of the departments. The actions of each department

and their respective payoffs are given in the bi-matrix above. Each department estimates with a uniformly distributed probability $\frac{1}{x}$ that the other department gains a certain organizational status.

In the following we will specify a Bayesian equilibrium in pure strategies, which enables the above mentioned interpretation of the equilibrium in mixed strategies. For this, let us look at the strategies of the two departments and their respective types:

- Strategy for the marketing department with a gain in organizational status of m:
  - choose compromising when $m < m^*$
  - choose non-compromising when $m \geq m^*$
- Strategy for the production department with a gain in organizational status of p:
  - choose compromising when $p < p^*$
  - choose non-compromising when $p \geq p^*$

This strategy assumes that there exist two critical values, $m^* \in [0, x]$ and $p^* \in [0, x]$, which determine the behavior of the two departments. According to this strategy, the marketing department chooses a non-compromising behavior in the meeting, if its additional gain in organizational status m is sufficiently high, $m \geq m^*$. Otherwise it would be more compromising. We will now specify the two parameters m^* and p^*, such that the two strategies above reach a Bayesian equilibrium.

Let us look at the marketing department with a real status gain of $m \in [0, x]$. If it assumes that the production department behaves according to the strategy above, it will contemplate the following. Due to the uncertainty of the marketing department about the status gain of the production department, there exists an uncertainty for the marketing department with regard to the actions of the production department. However, with a probability $\frac{x-p^*}{x}$ the marketing department can expect that the production department will opt for a non-compromising behavior. And with the probability $\frac{p^*}{x}$ the marketing department can expect that the production department will choose a compromising line in the meeting. Thus, if the marketing department chooses a compromising behavior, its status gain is $\frac{2p^*}{x} + \frac{3(x-p^*)}{x}$, ; if it decides to be non-compromising, its status gain is $\frac{(4+m)p^*}{x} + \frac{1(x-p^*)}{x}$. The marketing department therefore only opts for a compromising behavior if its status gain is sufficiently small:

$$m \leq \frac{2x}{p^*} - 4$$

The right hand side of this equation specifies m^*, that is the critical value we were looking for. Analogously we can argue out of the perspective of the production department. Due to the symmetry of the situation we find that the production department is willing to compromise if:

$$p \leq \frac{2x}{m^*} - 4$$

Again, the right hand side of the equation specifies the critical value p^*. Substituting m^* in this equation generates the condition $p^* = \sqrt{4 + 2x} - 2$.

Let us now look at the expectation of the marketing department (see Figure 2.28).

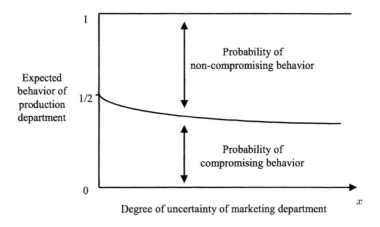

Figure 2.28. Uncertainty of the marketing department and the expected behavior of the production department

It expects with a probability $\frac{p^*}{x}$ that the production department will choose a non-compromising behavior. If the uncertainty is reduced, such that the marketing department virtually knows for sure how high the status gain of the other department is, then the probability $\frac{p^*}{x}$ converges to $\frac{1}{2}$. In other words, it converges to the probability with which the production department would choose a compromising behavior under complete information.[7] Analogously this applies to $\frac{m^*}{x}$ and a reduction of the uncertainty about the actions of the marketing department.

This example shows that we can transfer an equilibrium in mixed strategies under complete information into an equilibrium in pure strategies under incomplete information. We simply interpret the mixed equilibrium strategy of a party as a strategic uncertainty of the other parties with regard to her type. The party that has an information advantage decides on a certain action. Out of the perspective of the other parties, who have an information deficit, the informed party behaves as if she would randomize.

2.4 LITERATURE NOTES

Schelling (1960) is compulsory reading for anybody who is interested in strategic behavior. His book is hardly formal and offers ample ideas and examples. In particular, he proposed presenting the strategic form of a conflict situation in a bi-matrix.

Rapoport and Guyer (1966) offer a comprehensive classification of two-player games with two actions per party. The Prisoners' Dilemma can be traced back to a story by Alfred Tucker in the year 1950, published in Rapoport (1964) and comprehensively discussed in Poundstone (1992). The story 'Battle of Sexes' can be found in Luce and Raiffa (1957) and 'Chicken' is inspired by the film 'Rebel Without a Cause' starring James Dean. Ordeshook (1986) traces the 'Stag Hunt' story back to Jean-Jacques Rousseau.

The textbooks mentioned in this chapter provide solution concepts for non-cooperative games. The works of Bernheim (1984) and Pearce (1984) are fundamental to the concepts of dominance and iterative elimination. The assumptions that underlie the concepts of iterative elimination of dominated strategies and the Nash equilibrium are discussed in Brandenburger (1992). Brandenburger and Dekel (1990), Binmore (1992), and Geanakopolos (1992) explain the notion of common knowledge in more detail. Binmore (1990) critically reviews this notion as well as other basic concepts and assumptions in game theory.

Schelling (1960) presents the concept of focal points extensively and with many examples. Harsanyi and Selten (1988) analyze the payoff efficiency and risk dominance as criteria to select a unique equilibrium. In this book the authors also develop a general theory of equilibrium selection.

The integration of incomplete information into game theory can be attributed to Harsanyi (1967, 1968a, 1986b), also see Selten (1985). Mertens and Zamir (1985) provide a formal basis for this approach. A detailed introduction into Bayesian games and Bayesian equilibria can be found in Myerson (1985). In Brandenburger (1992) and Osborne and Rubinstein (1994) various interpretations of mixed strategies are offered. The interpretation in this chapter is based on a suggestion of Harsanyi (1973), while the formal presentation follows Gibbons (1992).

2.5 EXERCISES

2.5.1 Dominant Strategies

A static game in its normal form is given by:

Player 2

		P	Q	R	S
	X	1,0	1,2	0,1	1,1
Player 1	Y	0,3	0,1	2,2	1,0
	Z	-1,0	0,2	-1,1	2,1

Figure 2.29. Dominant strategies

1. Solve this game by iterative elimination according to the strictly dominant strategies approach. Does this lead to an equilibrium situation?
2. Determine all Nash equilibria.
3. Show that the Nash equilibrium approach is more restrictive than the strictly dominant strategies approach.

2.5.2 Weekend

It is Friday afternoon and a white collar worker is glad that she has finished her tasks for that week. She is looking forward to the upcoming weekend and is waiting for the end of her working day. At the same moment, her manager remembers that a very important assignment definitely has to be finished before next Monday. Even if the manager will help in performing the tasks, this assignment will take a large part of the weekend. Because overtime work is often the case, the worker is remaining silently in her office, not answering any phone calls from her manager. The manager's office is on the other side of the building, so it would take a while before the manager could reach the office of the worker. There is one problem, because the manager's office is next to the exit of the organizational building. If the worker left the building now, she would risk encountering her manager, who would then assign her the task anyway. However, the worker knows that before the manager would visit the worker's office to check whether she is still present, the manager would give her a call. Knowing this, the worker could reason out when the manager would be on her way to come and look after her at her office. At that moment the building's exit should be free.

The manager does not know when the worker leaves her office exactly, so she can not simply wait at the exit for the worker to come by. A map of the building is given in Figure 2.30.

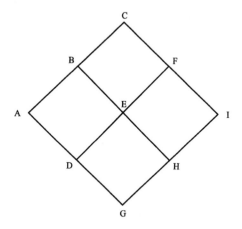

Figure 2.30. Weekend

The office of the white collar worker is at position I, while the exit and the manager's office are at position A. The routes drawn in the map are based on the present structure of the building and form the only possible routes that can be taken by the manager or worker. Both the manager and the worker walk at the same speed and the possibility of the manager taking a certain route is equal for all routes.

1. Represent this game in its normal form.
2. Is there any route that will not be taken by both the manager and the worker?
3. Give the normal form representation of the strategies and payoff that are minimally necessary to come to a decision.

2.5.3 The Electorate's Decision

Given is an electorate with an equal distribution among an ideological spectrum from left ($x = 0$) to right ($x = 1$). Two politicians stand for a top position and simultaneously present their political programs (that is a point on the ideological spectrum between $x = 0$ and $x = 1$). The voters observe both programs and then vote for the politician whose program is nearest to their own position on the spectrum.

For instance, imagine there are two candidates, politician 1 taking position $x = 0.3$ and politician 2 taking position $x = 0.6$. All voters positioned

65

on the left of $x = 0.45$ will vote for candidate 1, while all voters on the right of $x = 0.45$ will vote for candidate 2. In this example candidate 2 would win the elections with a majority of 55 percent of all votes.

It is assumed that both politicians just strive for winning the elections, so that personal preferences with respect to political issues are left out of consideration.

1. What will be the Nash equilibrium in case of an election with two political candidates?
2. Show a Nash equilibrium in case of an election with three political candidates.

(Assume that all votes on politicians with the same position on the spectrum are divided equally among them; when candidates receive an equal number of votes the winner will be determined by throwing a coin.)

2.5.4 Delegation

The manager of a certain department of a firm is assigned a specific project. She can delegate the project to one of her workers, who may carry out the task with either high or low effort. The manager can decide to let the workers' salaries depend on the level of effort supplied. However, the manager can only stop paying a worker' salary if she has incontrovertible evidence of the worker failing to supply any effort.

This leaves the manager with three options. First of all, she may monitor the worker during the performance of the task. This will lead to certain monitoring costs. Second, she may not monitor her worker. Or third, the manager may perform the task together with the worker. In the latter case, the manager can observe the worker's effort, but also entails some opportunity costs, because she could have carried out some other important tasks during the time spent on performing the task with her worker.

The utility levels resulting from choosing between the three options are given in Figure 2.31.

1. Determine all Nash equilibria of this game.
2. Depict the equilibria graphically by drawing the reaction curves of both the manager and the worker.

2.5.5 Cournot

Consider the following Cournot duopoly. Two firms are producing homogeneous products. The inverse market demand for the good is given by $P(Q) = a - 2 \cdot Q$ for $0 \leq Q \leq 30$ and $P(Q) = 0$ for $Q \geq 30$ (in which the aggregate quantity $Q = q_1 + q_2$ and $a = 60$). Both firms do not have any fixed costs of production. The variable costs per product are $c_1 = 12$ for firm 1 and $c_2 = 18$ for firm 2. This information is known by all actors on the market. Both firms simultaneously decide how much they will produce.

Worker's effort

	high	low
monitoring	7,2	4,0
no monitoring	8,2	0,7
performing task together	6,1	2,0

Manager

Figure 2.31. Delegation

1. Use the information above in constructing a Cournot game and show the corresponding Cournot-Nash equilibrium. Depict the outcome of the game graphically.
2. Suppose that the variable costs per product for firm 2 rise to $c_1 = 39$. What will be the new Nash equilibrium?
3. Continue with the original Cournot game, but now assume that the level of market demand is uncertain. The firms face a high product demand $(a = a\{H\} = 60)$ with a probability of θ and a low product demand $(a = a\{L\} = 40)$ with a probability of $(1 - \theta)$. Moreover, only firm 1 knows for sure whether the product demand is currently high or low. Give the Bayesian Nash equilibrium of this game and compare the outcome of the game with the outcome of Question 1.

2.6 NOTES

1. Also see the classification of situations of conflict according to Thomas (1976), who develops a similar taxonomy out of an organizational psychologist's perspective.
2. We would observe different behavior by the candidates if they tried to get the largest difference in the percentage of votes, or if they had the aim of simply winning the election with a majority vote.
3. The following argumentation can not only be interpreted as a thought experiment, but also as a dynamic version of the team production with two employees. If we assume that one employee always extrapolates her colleague's current behavior into the future, then our argumentation describes a tâtonnement process, which converges towards the equilibrium. In a certain sense, the equilibrium would then be the result of a learning process. However, this interpretation supposes that the parties ignore the strategic implications of their current behavior on the other party's future behavior. An alternative interpretation of this thought experiment assumes an adjustment process, where two team workers are randomly drawn out of a large group of employees. As it is unlikely that the same two employees work together again, a specific employee has no reason to consider the implications of her current behavior on the

future behavior of her colleague. When the effort spent by the production team members is observable, we can interpret a successive collaboration in new working teams as an equilibrium, provided that an employee expects that her future team mate will behave in accordance with the average of past work assignments.

4. This result is independent from the effort with which the first employee starts her strategic consideration. Suppose she plans to choose an effort e_1. Then, based on her reaction function, the second employee will decide on an effort of $\frac{1}{2}e_1 + \frac{3}{2}$ units. Hence, for the first employee it is better to choose an effort of

$$\frac{1}{2}\left(\frac{1}{2}e_1 + \frac{3}{2}\right) + \frac{3}{2} = \left(\frac{1}{2}\right)^2 e_1 + \frac{3}{2}\left(1 + \frac{1}{2}\right).$$

Based on this effort, the second employee would rather prefer an effort of

$$\left(\frac{1}{2}\right)^3 e_1 + \frac{3}{2}\left(1 + \frac{1}{2} + \left(\frac{1}{2}\right)^2\right)$$

and so on. Simple induction of the above argumentation shows that, after a finite number of n steps, the first employee chooses an effort of

$$\left(\frac{1}{2}\right)^n e_1 + \frac{3}{2}\left(\frac{1-(1/2)^{n+1}}{1-1/2}\right).$$

Hence, the (infinite) sequence of steps converges against an effort of three units, irrespective of the effort level that the employee started with.

5. For a simple theoretic explanation of the relationship between the two concepts, see, for example. Gibbons (1992, p.12). Also see Gibbons (1992, p.33) for a proof of the existence of an equilibrium in situations of conflict with a finite number of parties, each of which with a finite number of actions.

6. The Rule of Bayes determines how a party can update her previous beliefs about an unknown event on the basis of observations. Let $P(E_i)$ be the party's a priori belief about the occurrence of event E_i. Now she observes Event B. She knows that this event occurs with a probability $P(B \mid E_i)$ if the event E_i really exists. On the basis of her observation of B she can now update her belief about the likelihood of E_i. According to the Rule of Bayes her ex post belief $P(E_i \mid B)$ can be determined as

$$P(E_i \mid B) = \frac{P(E_i)P(B|E_i)}{\sum_k P(E_k)P(B|E_k)}.$$

7. According to the Rule of l'Hospital:

$$\lim_{x \to 0} \frac{p^*}{x} = \lim_{x \to 0} \frac{(4+2x)^{-1/2}}{1} = \frac{1}{2}.$$

3. The Dynamics of Conflicts

One Saturday morning, with all the summer world bright and fresh, Tom Sawyer was charged by Aunt Polly with the task of withewashing the fence.

He began to think of the fun he had planned for this day, and his sorrows multiplied. ... At this dark and hopeless moment an inspiration burst upon him! ...

He took up his brush and went tranquilly to work. Ben Rogers hove in sight presently – the very boy, of all boys, whose ridicule he had been dreading. Ben's gait was the hop-skip-and-jump – proof enough that his heart was light and his anticipation high. He was eating an apple, and giving a long melodious whoop, at intervals, followed by a deep-toned ding-dong-dong, ding-dong-dong, for he was personating a steamboat. ...

Tom went on whitewashing – paid no attention to the steamboat. ...

Tom's mouth watered for the apple, but he stuck to his work. Ben said:

Hello, old chap, you got work, hey?

Tom wheeled suddenly and said:

Why it's you, Ben! I wasn't noticing."

Say – I'm going in a-swimming, I am. Don't you wish you could? But of course you'd ruther work – wouldn't you? Course you would!

Tom contemplated the boy a bit, and said:

What do you call work?

Why ain't that work?

Tom resumed his whitewashing, and answered carelessly:

Well, maybe it is, and maybe it ain't. All I know, is, it suits Tom Sawyer.

Oh, come, now, you don't mean to let on that you like it?

The brush continued to move.

Like it? Well, I don't see why I oughtn't to like it. Does a boy get a chance to whitewash a fence every day?

That put the thing in a new light. ...

Say, Tom, let me whitewash a little.

Tom considered, was about to consent; but he altered his mind:

No – no – I reckon it wouldn't hardly do, Ben. You see, Aunt Polly's awful particular about this fence – right here on the street, you know – but if it was the back fence I wouldn't mind and she wouldn't. ...

Oh, shucks, I'll be just as careful. Now lemme try. Say – I'll give

you the core of my apple.
Well, here. – No, Ben, now don't. I'm afeared –
I'll give you all of it!
Tom gave up the brush with reluctance in his face, but alacrity
in his heart.
(Twain, 1876)

In the previous chapter we have concentrated our analysis of conflicts on situations in which the parties involved decide independently of each other. The strategic form of those situations of conflict has three elements: the parties involved, the alternatives, and the consequences for each party and each strategy combination. In the context of incomplete information of a party concerning the specific characteristics of another party we saw that situations of conflict are in general of a dynamic nature: either the informed party has an interest to disclose her private information to the other uninformed party, or the uninformed party has an interest to discover the private information of the informed party. Both cases lead to situations of conflict in which the parties are involved in a sequential course of actions.

In this chapter we will analyze the dynamics of such situations of conflict. They are characterized by sequential interdependencies between the parties. In general one party can condition her behavior on the behavior of the other party, which acts first. Therefore the previous decision of the other party is the basis for her own behavior. In dynamic situations of conflict it is typical that at least one party conditions her choice on the other's behavior.

In contrast to the strategic form of a situation of conflict with independent decisions, we have to explicitly take account of the interaction process between the parties when looking at a dynamic conflict. For each of the parties' various decisions we have to additionally specify the sequence of reactions of the parties, their possible actions, and the information that is available to them. All these strategically relevant parameters of the framework of a conflict with sequential interdependencies can be summarized in the *extensive (strategic) form* of the situation. This includes,

1. the parties in conflict;
2. the points where a party has to take a decision (decision nodes);
3. the actions that are available to each party at each of her decision nodes;
4. the information available at each decision node;
5. the payoffs or consequences for each party and for each possible outcome of the conflict, that is, for every possible sequence of the party's actions.

The extensive form displays the parameters of the framework as they are perceived by the parties in conflict. She specifies the chronological sequence of the parties' interaction and all of their possible actions. The dynamics of the conflict are depicted in a *decision tree*. Each of the parties' decisions is represented by a decision node. The decision node of the party that

70

can choose the first action is referred to as the root of the decision tree. Each decision node specifies, which party can take a decision, and which actions and information are available. The branches of the tree represent the possible actions, that a party can choose at a specific decision node.

Every path in the decision tree represents a possible sequence of interactions. Each path ends with a terminal node, which specifies the party's consequence or payoff of a certain interaction. In a conflict with two parties the left and right numbers at the terminal node display the payoffs of the first and second party, respectively.

The following example illustrates the modeling of a situation of conflict in extensive form.

Career in a consultancy

A large, international management consultancy has a vacancy for the position of senior consultant. The partners of the consultancy decide to appoint the position to an internal candidate. They also select ten consultants who are on the short list for the position.

All of these ten consultants are equally qualified for the job. The partners decide to solve the dilemma of selecting one of the ten by applying a specific assessment procedure. As one of the most important responsibilities of the consultants is to secure new projects for the firm, the partners announce they will promote the consultant who secures the highest order volume in consulting projects within a specific time frame. If several consultants happen to have the same amount, a lottery will decide between them.

How will the consultants behave in competing for the senior position? How many projects will they acquire to get promoted? And who will get promoted eventually? To analyze this dynamic situation we have to reduce the conflict to its essential strategic elements in its extensive form. This can be done as follows.

To specify the chronological sequence of the situation of conflict we assume that every project that is acquired is immediately observed by all other colleagues. We also assume that, provided the consultants are willing to put in the needed amount of acquisition effort, there are no market constraints that restrain any of the ten colleagues from securing another project at any time. However, due to time constraints, there exists a maximal acquisition capacity. This constraint applies equally to all consultants and ensures that any consultant, who secured the first project, does not enjoy a direct advantage. In this sense the consultants are 'bidding' for the senior position by securing new projects.

Each consultant knows at any time in the assessment procedure how big her own order volume and that of her competitors is. On the basis of this knowledge the consultant then decides whether she wants to go out and make the effort to secure another project or not. For simplicity we assume that all projects have the same size and that there can be no partial or joint projects. One project thus is the smallest amount with which a consultant can additionally qualify herself for promotion. As we assumed no market constraints, the absolute number of projects represents no direct advantage. We can thus assume that the consultants will increase their number of projects one by one.

To make things interesting we also assume that the consultants are interested to work as little as possible if the situation permits. Suppose that each additionally secured project requires an effort of one unit. Further we assume that each consultant would value the promotion to senior consultant as 100 units. This is the present value of the difference between the salaries of a senior consultant and a consultant.

For this situation of conflict we can now define the following extensive form. Ten consultants are on the shortlist for the position of senior consultant. Each consultant is able to secure two additional projects, once she observes that a colleague has an advantage of one project. The expected net income of the consultant depends on the number of secured projects (with effort-related costs of one unit per project) and on the fact of whether she will be finally promoted and receive a higher salary or not.

To draw a decision tree for this conflict we reduce the situation to two consultants. We assume that, due to time constraints, each consultant can secure six projects at a maximum. Figure 3.1 shows the decision tree.

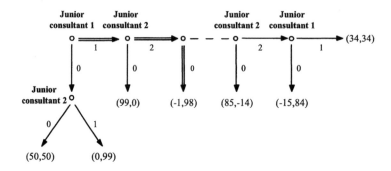

Figure 3.1. Promotion in a management consultancy

We denote the consultant who first decides on securing an additional project as Consultant 1. She is the party that decides at the root of the decision tree. She can decide between the possible alternatives 'new project' and 'no project'. Furthermore, Consultant 1 always takes another decision when she observes that Consultant 2 lies one project ahead. In this case she decides between 'two new projects' and 'no project'. If Consultant 2 has secured six projects and Consultant 1 has only five projects, the latter can still get one last project to draw level with her colleague. Analogously, we define the decision points for Consultant 2.

The payoffs of the two consultants result from the interactions in the situation of conflict. Suppose that neither Consultant 1 nor Consultant 2 secure any project at all. Then the senior consultants will let a lottery decide and each consultant can expect a payoff of 50 units $(0.5 * 100 - 0)$. Now suppose that Consultant 1 gets one new project, but Consultant 2 then secures two projects (this corresponds to the bold path in Figure 3.1). In this case Consultant 2 would get the position of senior consultant and enjoy a net difference in salaries of 98 units, while Consultant 1 would have effort-related costs without return, and thus a negative payoff of one unit.

The description of a dynamic situation of conflict requires the modeling of the information, which each party has at the time of her decision. In the next section we classify situations of conflict according to this information aspect and show how informational asymmetries of one party can be modeled. The strategic behavior of parties in a dynamic situation of conflict is analyzed in the section thereafter. According to the information a party in a situation of conflict has we derive different principles of strategic behavior.

In the last two sections we consider strategic moves. A strategic move enables a party to change the behavior of other parties to her own benefit. First, we assume that each party has complete information concerning the characteristics of the situation of conflict. In the last section we modify this assumption and consider strategic moves in situations in which parties have incomplete information.

3.1 A CLASSIFICATION OF CONFLICTS II

An important aspect in modeling situations of conflict is taking the information into account that the parties possess when making a decision. In our example of the promotion of a consultant we assumed that all consultants can immediately and directly observe the number of secured projects. In this sense they had perfect information. We denote a situation of conflict in which each party can observe the actions of all other parties as situations of *conflict with perfect information*. In such situations each party can take into account previous actions of all other parties when making her decision.

Situations of conflict in which at least one party does not know the entire history of previous actions we denote as situations of *conflict with imperfect information*. The decisions in such situations are independent. All parties act simultaneously and no party knows the decision of the other parties when making her decision.

73

From this we need to distinguish situations of *conflict with incomplete information*, which we discussed in the previous chapter. In such situations the parties do not have perfect knowledge of the general framework of the situation of conflict. This does not rule out that they know the history of previous interactions and are thus perfectly informed. Conversely, it is also possible that the parties have imperfect information while they do know all aspects of the general framework.

In a game tree we illustrate the information that a party has when making a decision by *information sets*. An information set of a party includes all decision nodes at which this party has the same information. If the party is at a non-singleton information set (including several decision nodes), then this party does not know at which decision node she actually is when making a decision.

In the following we will classify situations of conflict according to the extent of the information deficit. For this purpose we discuss an example that we will vary by different assumptions on the underlying levels of information of the parties.

Introduction of a new information and communication technology

---

The operating department of a firm is unsatisfied with the present information and communication technology. While the running system was sufficient in the past, due to the recent expansion of the firm some tasks could hardly be accomplished. Now the operating department hopes for a solution of such problems by introducing new information and communication technology (ICT).

In the course of these developments the operating department contacted the ICT department of the firm and elaborated a specification upon request. As the operating department has precise ideas about these specifications, the catalogue of requirements is very detailed. Thereby the operating department runs the risk that the ICT department does not implement the required specifications while planning the new system, due to the lack of existence of hard- and software that would satisfy those specifications. Alternatively, it is also possible that the ICT department does not want to implement the required specifications, because the specific ICT solution does not fit into the overall concept of the ICT department. For this reason the operating department reserved the right to develop an independent solution.

We will specify the situation of conflict between the operating department and the ICT department for further discussion as follows. For simplicity we assume that the ICT department has two alternative actions only: It can either be responsive to the requirements of the operating department and develop an adequate plan, or it can neglect the requirements and suggests a completely different ICT solution. Also the operating department has only two alternative actions: It can either accept the suggested solution or it can develop an independent solution. Moreover, we assume that the specification requirements possibly can not be realized from a technical perspective: With a probability of 60 percent the required specifications can technically not be realized, and with a complementing probability of 40 percent they can be realized.

The consequences from the interaction of the two departments are specified as follows. Suppose the required specifications can technically be realized. If the ICT department neglects the requirements, it saves the costs of development and also can suggest its own favorite hard- and software. This leads to an advantage of three units compared to a solution that is responsive to the requirements of the operating department. When the alternative solution is accepted by the operating department, the ICT department achieves an additional advantage of one unit due to enhanced prestige. When it is rejected, the ICT department incurs a disadvantage of two units. A solution that neglects the requirements generates only one unit for the operating department compared to four units if the solution is responsive to all requirements. If the operating department develops its own independent solution it will satisfy all its requirements but due to additional costs achieve only a total advantage of two units. For the case where the ICT department develops a solution that is responsive to the requirements of the operating department, its payoff is set equal to zero, independently of the decision of the operating department.

In case the realization of the required specifications of the operating department is technically not possible, only the alternative solution of the ICT department can be realized. If the operating department accepts (rejects) this solution, it has an advantage (disadvantage) of one unit, while the ICT department will always achieve an advantage of four units, because ultimately its favorite solution will be implemented. If a solution is planned that can not be realized technically, both departments incur a disadvantage of two units, independently from the operating departments decision.

With these assumptions a general framework is specified that allows us to depict the situation of conflict in its extensive form: The two departments are the only parties involved in this situation of conflict. The ICT department develops, on the basis of the specific request, a plan for a new information and communication technology which may either be accepted by the operating department, or substituted by an independent development. Thus, the points in time at which each party can make a decision are determined. Moreover, both parties have two alternative actions, as described, and we also determined the payoffs resulting from any possible course of action in this situation of conflict.

Except for the information available to each party we identified all relevant elements of the extensive form of this situation of conflict. In what follows we will discuss various situations of conflict, that can be distinguished only by the level of information of the two parties. This classification of situations of conflict on the basis of the level of information that the parties have when making a decision once again emphasizes how the general framework of the conflict determines the manifestation of cooperative and competitive interests of the parties.

3.1.1 Conflicts with Complete and Perfect Information

Suppose the operating department has gathered substantive information about the technical feasibility already when elaborating the specifications for the new information and communication technology. It thus knows as much as the ICT department to what extent its requirements can actually be realized. Furthermore, we assume that the operating department is not interested in a quick change-over of the information and communication technology. It rather appreciates the old technology despite its deficiencies and prefers a diligent planning and implementation of any change. We therefore assume that the operating department first awaits the extent to which the ICT department's solution is responsive to the requirements. Thereafter the operating department decides whether to adapt and reconstruct its old system.

In the illustrated situation of conflict both parties' information is complete and perfect: When making the decision, each party knows the previous decisions of the other party as well as the general framework of the situation. The first property implies that each party can make its decisions dependent on the previous course of conflict, because it could observe theprevious actions of the other party. The second property enables each party to put itself into the position of the other party and anticipate the other party's behavior when making a decision.

The decision tree in Figure 3.2 depicts the extensive form of this situation of conflict.[1] The question to what extent the requirements can actually be realized is answered at the very beginning of the situation of conflict via a random device. For this purpose we add 'nature' as an additional actor, next to the two departments, to the situation of conflict. Unlike the two other 'real' actors, nature does not decide between two alternatives. Rather one of the two options will be selected at random according to a pre-determined probability distribution. Here, we consider the case in which the requirements can actually be realized with a probability of 0.4, and can not be realized with a probability of 0.6. After nature's decision, the ICT department has to decide to either be responsive to the operating department's requirements or to neglect the requirements and suggest a different ICT solution. Since the ICT department knows nature's random decision, it can condition its own decision for one or the other alternative on the fact whether the requirements of the operating department can be realized or not.

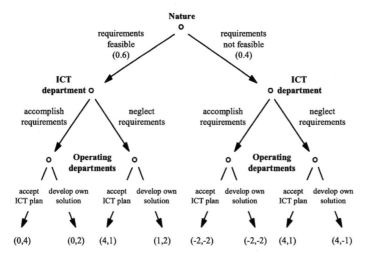

Figure 3.2. The introduction of a new information and communication technology under complete and perfect information

When the ICT department has finished its planning for the new information and communication technology, the operating department decides whether to accept this solution or whether to develop an independent solution. Its decision can be based upon nature's decision as well as upon the ICT department's decision. The department thus knows whether its own requirements actually are realizable and to what extend the ICT department's solution is responsive to those requirements. The consequences of the departments' interaction are determined according to the underlying general framework.

Each party has complete and perfect information, which is expressed in the above decision tree by the fact that each party's information set is a singleton each time this party has to make a decision. Each party knows exactly at which decision node it is. Therefore it can trace back the other party's decisions that lead to this decision node, and thus knows the exact course of conflict.[2]

The situation of conflict would also exist under perfect and complete information even if neither of the two departments knew in advance whether the operating department's requirements for the new information and communication technology could be realized or not (see Figure 3.3).

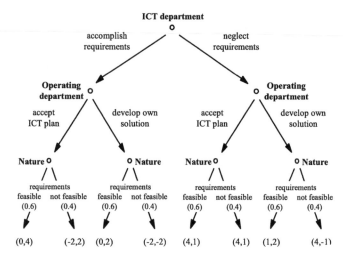

Figure 3.3. The introduction of a new information and communication technology under complete and perfect information and exogenous uncertainty

In the above situation of conflict, objections as well as possible organizational obstacles to the new information and communication technology suggested by the ICT department or developed by the operating department will only become clear after implementation. Although in this situation both parties do not know nature's random decision when making their decision, they are perfectly informed about this fact. They know the general framework of the situation of conflict and know therefore that the actual consequences of their decisions will be determined at random at a later stage. The exogenous uncertainty is thus an element of the general framework of the situation of conflict.

3.1.2 Conflicts with Complete and Imperfect Information

We now assume that the operating department is very unsatisfied with the existing information and communication technology. The old system does not meet the new requirements and the department's employees hope for an early solution. The department head tries everything to introduce a new system soon. We assume that the operating department considers the development of an own solution right after the elaboration of the specifications. More specifically, the operating department does not await the ICT department's solution, but decides in advance how to proceed. We also assume that both departments know whether the requirements of the new technology can actually be realized or not.

In this situation of conflict both parties have complete but imperfect information: Both parties know the general framework of the situation of conflict. But when making the decision, both parties do not know what the other party decided. Therefore, they can not condition their decision on the other party's decision. Figure 3.4 depicts the decision tree for this situation with complete and imperfect information.

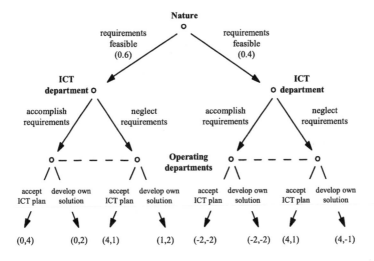

Figure 3.4. The introduction of a new information and communication technology under complete and imperfect information

In this decision tree the two left (and the two right) decision nodes of the operating department are connected by a dotted line. This line indicates that at these two left decision nodes the operating department has the same information available, and that therefore the two decision nodes belong to the same information set.

As in the situation under complete and perfect information nature decides in advance whether the requirements of the operating department can be realized or not. Nature's random decision is thus observable by both departments: In the above decision tree the ICT department knows nature's decision – its decision nodes are in a singleton information set. Also the operating department knows whether its requirements can actually be realized, since it can determine nature's decision in each of its four decision nodes: In the left information set the department knows that its requirements can be realized, in the right information set it knows that this is not the case.

Unlike a situation with complete and perfect information, when making its decision, the operating department does not know which plan the ICT departments will elaborate. This is the reason why the two decision nodes on the left and on the right, respectively, lie in the same information set. The operating department has to make its decision not knowing what the ICT department has decided. The two left and right decision nodes respectively can not be distinguished.

The situations of conflict with independent decisions, discussed in the previous chapter, were situations of conflict with imperfect information. There we already discussed that independent decisions are not equivalent to simultaneous decisions. Independency of decisions implies rather that the parties can not condition their own decisions on the decisions of other parties. Each party has to decide in ignorance of the other parties' decisions. It does in fact not matter whether the other parties' decisions are made simultaneously, or whether the other parties' decisions were made in advance but are not observable by the party. What matters is only the respective level of information at the moment of decision. The sequence in which the parties make their decisions, therefore, does not need to be interpreted as the course conflict over time.

The conflicts with independent decisions, analyzed in the previous chapter, can also be depicted as a decision tree with adequate information sets. The decision tree in Figure 3.5 shows the situation of conflict where a supervisor monitors a field worker: When monitoring, the supervisor does not know whether the field worker has invested high or low effort. She therefore is at two decision nodes: One will be reached when the field worker has invested high effort, the other when the field worker has invested low effort.

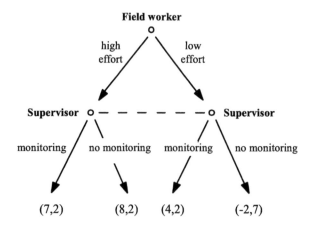

Figure 3.5. The decision tree when a supervisor monitors a field worker

3.1.3   Conflicts with Incomplete Information

Suppose the operating department could not gather substantive information about the technical feasibility before elaborating the specifications for the new information and communication technology. Unlike the ICT department, the operating departments does not know to what extent its requirements can be realized. We therefore assume in what follows that only the ICT department knows whether the requirements can be realized, while the operating department does not know this fact. The latter only has specific beliefs about the probability with which the requirements can be realized: it believes that with a probability of 60 percent the requirements can be realized, and with a probability of 40 percent it believes that this is impossible. Furthermore, we assume that the operating department is not interested in a quick change-over of the information and communication technology. The operating department first awaits the extent to which the ICT department's solution is responsive to the requirements and thereafter decides whether to adapt the new system or to reconstruct its old system.

In this situation of conflict one party obviously has incomplete information about the general framework: the operating department does not know whether its requirements can be realized or not. However, it knows that the ICT department has this information. It knows that the ICT department knows whether or not the requirements can be realized.

In a situation of conflict with incomplete information the uninformed party knows that at least one other party involved in the conflict knows those elements of the general framework that are unknown to itself.[3] Incomplete information causes a number of strategic moves and tactics: The informed party will try to use its informational lead over the uninformed party strategically, while the uninformed party will try to reduce its informational deficit through strategic conduct.

The decision tree for this situation with incomplete information is depicted in the following Figure 3.6.

In this representation we used Harsanyi's idea discussed in the previous chapter. The incomplete information of the uninformed party is taken into account as imperfect information about the previous course of the conflict. A situation of conflict with incomplete information can thus directly be interpreted as a situation of conflict with complete but imperfect information.

In our example of the introduction of a new information and communication technology this implies the following: At the beginning of the situation of conflict nature decides which information the ICT department has about the feasibility of the operating department's requirements. We can alternatively say that nature determines the type of the ICT department: either the ICT department is type 1 and knows that the requirements can be realized, or it is type 2 and knows that the requirements can not be

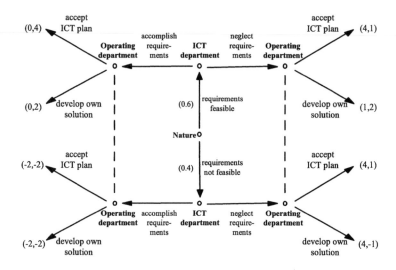

Figure 3.6. The introduction of a new information and communication technology under incomplete information

realized.

After nature has determined the ICT department's type, the ICT department decides on the planning of the information and communication technology. Thereafter, the operating department decides whether to accept or reject this planning. At that time the operating department knows which plan the ICT department wants to pursue, but does not know whether its own requirements can be realized or not. The ICT department has private information about its type. We can interpret the fact that one party does not know the other party's type as imperfect information of this uninformed party: it can not observe which type nature determined for the other party. In our example the two decision nodes of the operating department lie in the same information set.

3.2 STRATEGIC BEHAVIOR IN DYNAMIC CONFLICTS

How will the parties behave in dynamic situations of conflict? What consequences has the sequential character of the conflict for the parties' behavior? Is it in such situation advantageous to take the initiative or rather to wait, how other parties will behave?

In this section we will deal with the question of strategic behavior in situations of conflict in which each party is completely informed about the general framework. Strategic uncertainty can arise when one party can not comprehend all the actions of the other party, thus in situations of conflict with imperfect information.

In analogy to the previous chapter we will develop principles of strategic behavior that can serve as a guideline for strategic behavior in dynamic situations of conflict. We will start with simple principles of strategic conduct for situations of conflict with complete and perfect information and refine those principles successively for situations with strategic uncertainty.

Before we can analyze the behavior in different situation of conflict, we need to specify the concept of *strategy* in dynamic situations in more detail. In situations of conflict with independent decisions we specified a strategy of a party as its available alternative actions. We used the terms action and strategy synonymously. Dynamic situations of conflict are different from the situations considered so far in two aspects: first, when making a decision a party can take into consideration what others have done previously. Second, it can also happen that the same party has to decide several times between the alternative actions in one situation of conflict.

Let us reconsider the example of the promotion in a consultancy and assume now that in total only two new projects can possibly be secured, as depicted in Figure 3.7. We can fully describe the first consultant's behavior as follows. In the beginning she chooses whether to get one new project or not. When Consultant 2 secures another two projects, Consultant 1 has to decide whether to put the effort into another project or not. A full description of her behavior requires that Consultant 1 has to consider what to decide at each possible decision node she might encounter at any point in time. Her behavior in this situation of conflict is thus only then fully described, when her decisions are determined for any possible point in time, hence, for any possible course of conflict.

A strategy of a party in a dynamic situation of conflict is a complete plan of action that specifies a possible action for any point in time at which this party has to make a decision. For Consultant 1 a strategy specifies her actions at both possible decision nodes. A possible strategy for Consultant 1 would be the following: secure one new project and abstain from any additional acquisition effort if Consultant 2 also gets a new project.

At first sight it seems not really necessary to specify actions for all possible decision nodes. Why should Consultant 1 think about how many projects to secure at a later stage if she decided right at the start of the whole promotion scheme, not to put any effort into it at all? Consultant 1 could argue that she is out of the promotion contest anyhow and no longer able to later intervene in the conflict.

Now suppose the consultant's strategy does not specify what she would do at a later point in time. In this case we could not answer the question whether her behavior is strategically sensibly. If Consultant 1 wants to act strategically sensible, she has to take account of Consultant 2's reaction

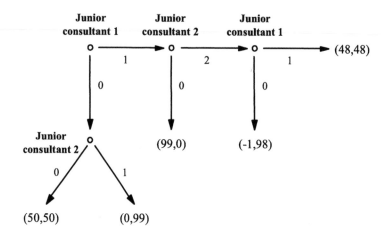

Figure 3.7. The modified promotion in a consultancy firm

to her strategy. Consultant 2 can not act a priori on the assumption that Consultant 1 does not secure any projects at the start. Rather she needs to anticipate how to react to one project of Consultant 1 when formulating her strategy. She has to plan flexibly for any possible future course of conflict. Since Consultant 1's optimal strategy depends on how Consultant 2 will react in the situation of conflict, she also has to consider how she herself would continue to act after she got one new project in the beginning. Only then will it be possible for her to adapt her behavior optimally to the behavior of Consultant 2.

With this definition of a strategy we can translate a dynamic situation of conflict into its strategic form. For this purpose let us consider the example of the field worker with the following modification: Assume the supervisor can commit herself to monitor at a later point in time, before the field worker decides about her effort. The field worker can take this announcement into account when making her decision, and can thus condition the level of her effort on it. In this situation both parties have perfect information.

If we assume the same payoffs as before, a decision tree as in Figure 3.8 can be developed. Although in this situation both parties do not know nature's random decision when taking their own decision, they are perfectly informed about this fact. They know the general framework of the situation of conflict. In other words, they know that the actual consequences of their decisions will be determined at random at a later stage. The exogenous uncertainty is thus an element of the general framework of the situation of conflict.

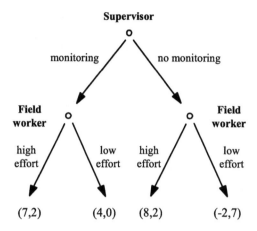

Figure 3.8. Monitoring of a fieldworker when decisions are sequential

In order to depict the strategic form of this dynamic situation of conflict we first have to identify the parties' strategies: The supervisor can, as before, monitor or refrain from monitoring. Those are her two possible strategies. A strategy of the employee specifies what she will do at each of her two decision nodes. Therefore the employee has four strategies:

- Strategy 1: Choose a high effort, if the supervisor monitors, and choose a low effort if the supervisor does not monitor.
- Strategy 2: Choose a high effort, independent of the supervisor's decision.
- Strategy 3: Choose a low effort, if the supervisor monitors, and choose a high effort if the supervisor does not monitor.
- Strategy 4: Choose a low effort, independent of the supervisor's decision.

Although the field worker has only two alternative actions, she has four strategies: There are two courses of conflict – the supervisor monitors or does not monitor – and for each possible decision node the employee has to specify her action.

With this specification of the parties' strategies we can now easily describe the dynamic situation of conflict in its strategic form: The rows in the bi-matrix refer to the alternative actions of the supervisor, the columns refer to the strategies of the employee. For each possible combination of strategies we can refer from the decision tree to the consequences in the strategic form. The outcome of this is shown in Figure 3.9.

Field worker

		strategy 1	strategy 2	strategy 3	strategy 4
Supervisor	monitoring	7,2	7,2	4,0	4,0
	no monitoring	-2,7	8,2	8,2	-2,7

Figure 3.9. The bi-matrix for monitoring of a fieldworker when decisions are sequential

3.2.1 Backward Induction

In the following we will first analyze the behavior for situations of conflict with complete and perfect information. Since each party is perfectly informed of the situation of conflict, each party can observe the previous actions of the other parties and therefore condition its own behavior on the course of conflict. Moreover, each party is also completely informed about the general framework of the situation of conflict, and is therefore also able to put itself in the other parties' position, to predict their behavior and to anticipate this when making a decision.

Cooperation with a trainee

A firm offers new employees in-house education programs to prepare them for their future tasks. By means of systematic training on the job a new entrant gets the chance to learn on the spot by dealing daily with the problems of the specific task. In order to give the new employee additionally a comprehensive overview over the field of activities and the scopes of different functions, a systematic job change has proven to be a positive aspect of the trainee program.

Recently a new trainee has been assigned for three months to a team in the production unit. After a short vocational adjustment the trainee took on a task in this team. As the team is rather small the members created a very cooperative environment. Therefore in times of high work load team members help each other, although each member has her own task and fields of responsibility. In the same manner the new employee should be integrated into the team. The team members are skeptical as to whether the entrant will be very cooperative because she announced that she will work in the purchase department in the near future.

For the analysis of the parties' behavior in this situation of conflict we
will further specify the example as follows: the trainee has problems in
accomplishing the recently delegated task. A senior member of the team
considers helping the newcomer. When helping, she would risk not finishing
her own task, since she herself has quite a heavy workload these days. She
would therefore be also dependent on the support of the trainee. Figure 3.10
depicts the simplified extensive form of this situation of conflict between
the two employees.

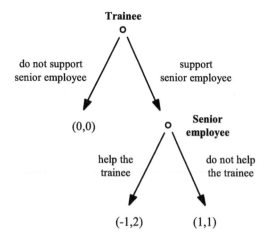

Figure 3.10. Cooperation with a trainee

The senior employee is confronted with the question whether or not to
help the trainee with her task. If she does not support the trainee, the
status quo will be maintained. For simplicity we will normalize in this case
both parties' payoffs to 0 units. If she supports her, the trainee has an
advantage of 2 units, but the senior employee incurs a disadvantage of one
unit. After the senior employee has helped her with her task, the trainee
has to decide whether to help the senior employee with her obligations.
Also here we assume that the support will bring the other an advantage of
2 units while it leads to a disadvantage of one unit for the trainee.

Apparently it is in the mutual interest of both parties to help each other,
as this leads to a payoff of one unit each as opposed to a payoff of zero if they
do not help each other. However, if both parties act in their own interest,
then it is obvious that there will be no collaboration. In her decision to help
the trainee, the senior employee will contemplate whether the trainee would
support her in her own work. The senior employee will therefore consider
what the trainee will do after she has received the help. In this situation it

is not in the self-interest of the trainee to help the senior employee. In fact, without helping the senior, the trainee would profit from the help of the senior with a payoff of two units without incurring the costs of one unit. As the senior employee knows how the trainee would react to her helping hand, the situation of conflict for the senior can be reduced to the decision tree in Figure 3.11. Here, the senior employee can directly see which consequences

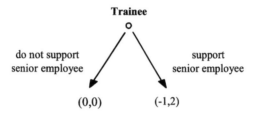

Figure 3.11. Cooperation with a trainee, reduced form

she faces when she supports the trainee. If the senior helps the trainee she would incur costs of one unit, compared to a situation in which she simply minds her own work. Thus, the senior would not support the trainee, as she expects that her help will not be returned.

We can directly transfer the procedure, which we used to analyze the behavior of the two employees, to dynamic situations of conflict with complete and perfect information and summarize it as follows:

Principle of Strategic Behavior VI:
In a dynamic situation of conflict, anticipate how the subsequent parties will behave and consider their behavior in your own choice of action.

This principle of strategic behavior is referred to in the literature as *backward induction*. The analysis of a situation of conflict starts with the party that takes the last decision, identifies her optimal response in this decision node, and then uses the anticipated behavior to predict the behavior of the party that takes the penultimate decision, and so on. Successively, we can deduce the behavior of all parties that are involved. This is possible because at each point in the situation of conflict only one party is acting, and at the time of taking a decision each party has perfect information about the history of the situation.

Let us now compare the principle of backward induction with the principle of stable strategies. We have shown above that a dynamic situation of conflict can be described in a strategic form. It therefore suggests itself to study the relationship between the concept of backward induction in dynamic situations and the concept of equilibrium for situations with independent decisions. We will do this by means of the following example.

Recommendation of an assistant

A longstanding employee is dissatisfied with her career in the company. When she started as assistant to the sales manager for the southern region four years ago, her supervisor presented her with an attractive career path within the company. However, although she performs well and although her supervisor points this out regularly, she does not get promoted. This is all the more frustrating, as two interesting vacancies in other branches have been filled recently; but every time her supervisor found a new reason why she would not be suitable for the job.

Thus, prompted by the next appraisal interview, the employee decides that it is time for a make-or-break decision. If the supervisor turns down her request for promotion again, she will make clear that she will not be prepared to passively wait for a better position. She knows that another attractive position will be vacant shortly and that her supervisor could support her greatly by recommending her as a possible candidate for the post. However, if it turns out that her supervisor is not prepared to support her, she will be on the market and have to try her luck in a different company. By openly telling her supervisor about these plans, she intends to put the apparently needed pressure on her supervisor to recommend her.

We can model the situation of conflict as follows (see Figure 3.12). The supervisor has to decide whether she should recommend her assistant for another position or not. With such a recommendation the assistant would surely get the new position. As the assistant performed very well, the supervisor would lose a good member of her team. If the assistant stays in her team this would be worth three units to the supervisor; leaving the company would lead to a negative payoff of one unit. However, if the assistant leaves the team but advances within the company, the supervisor would still be able to enjoy the benefits of an improved network within the organization, representing a positive payoff of one unit.

In the current position the assistant receives a payoff of one unit. If she was promoted to a better position, she would receive an additional payoff of two units, amounting to a total value of three units. If she left the company, a currently unfavorable situation on the job market would create high switching costs with regard to searching, mobility, and salary. In choosing this option she would therefore be worse off than today (zero units). The supervisor knows the market and her situation very well and therefore also has this information about her payoff.

Backward induction directly shows us the outcome of this situation of conflict. Irrespective of whether the supervisor recommends the assistant

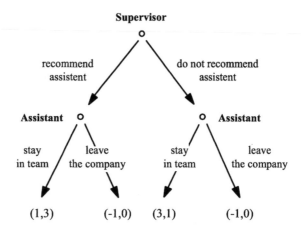

Figure 3.12. Recommendation of an assistant, extensive form

or not, the assistant will always prefer to stay in the company than to leave. As the supervisor anticipates this, the decision can be reduced to the following situation: If the supervisor supports the assistant she will have a payoff of one unit, otherwise one of three units. Thus, the supervisor will not recommend the assistant as it is clear that she will not leave the company. The threat of leaving is thus not credible.

The behavior of both parties is, of course, strategically stable. The decision to stay is a dominant strategy for the assistant, the decision not to recommend is the best response by the supervisor. A party's behavior that complies with backward induction is also strategically stable, as it represents the best response to the behavior of the other party and vice versa. However, the reverse, that is a strategically stable behavior corresponds to the outcome of backward induction, is not always true. This can be shown by modeling the example in its strategic form (see Figure 3.13).

In Figure 3.13 the strategies of the assistant are specified as follows:

- Strategy 1: Leave the company, if the supervisor offers support, and stay, if the supervisor offers no support.
- Strategy 2: Leave the company, independent of the supervisor's decision.
- Strategy 3: Stay, if the supervisor offers support, and leave the company, if the supervisor offers no support.
- Strategy 4: Stay, independent of the supervisor's decision.

In this situation of conflict there exist three equilibria. The supervisor decides to offer support and the assistant chooses Strategy 3. Or, the supervisor decides to offer no support and the assistant chooses Strategy 1 or Strategy 4. The last two equilibria lead to an outcome of the situation

Assistant

	Strategy 1	Strategy 2	Strategy 3	Strategy 4
Supervisor recommend assistant	-1,0	-1,0	1,2	1,2
do not recommend assistant	3,1	-1,0	-1,0	3,1

Figure 3.13. Recommendation of an assistant, strategic form

that is compatible with backward induction. The supervisor does not offer support and the assistant does not leave the company.

However, this does not apply to Strategy 3, which includes the threat of the assistant to leave the company. The supervisor recommends the assistant for a better position, because she expects that the assistant will otherwise leave the company. But we know that the threat of the assistant is not credible. In fact, if the assistant was be in the situation that she has to implement her threat of leaving, she would still prefer not to leave the company, as this generates a worse payoff than staying.

Thus, while backward induction excludes non-credible threats, strategically stable equilibria do not necessarily do this. In our example of backward induction, at each decision node each party knows everything about the previous process of the situation of conflict. Hence, each decision node constitutes a unique history of the previous relation, on the basis of which a party has to decide for one of the possible actions. Successive backward induction forces a party at each decision node to choose the best alternative. As the party will not be able to improve her situation by deviating from this path, she will also be prepared to implement the action that is determined with backward induction. Hence, because any behavior announced by a party is only credible if it is really implemented when the situation demands it, backward induction excludes non-credible threats.

Our example shows that non-credible threats or promises may nevertheless induce a strategically stable behavior. Thus, not every strategically stable behavior of parties satisfies the principle of backward induction.

3.2.2 Perfect Equilibrium

In the previous discussion we focused on dynamic conflicts with complete and perfect information. Here, the principle of backward induction provides plausible predictions about the behavior of the involved parties.

Now, we enlarge the class of conflicts and include those with imperfect information, where we can not apply backward induction anymore. According to the definition, at least one of the parties has the same information at different decision nodes. In at least one information set there exist several decision nodes. Therefore, at the time of the decision, at least one party does not know what the preceding party has decided. However, backward induction requires that a party knows about all the decisions that were previously taken. This concept is therefore not applicable as it can not determine which decision node the party actually has to consider.

The concept of the Nash equilibrium can still be applied in situations of conflict with imperfect information. But, as we have seen already, it can not exclude implausible predictions about the outcome of dynamic situations of conflict. We therefore combine this concept of equilibrium with the concept of backward induction in order to come to more meaningful results under imperfect information. The following example illustrates this idea.

Delegation of a dangerous task

A supervisor has to decide whether she wants to carry out a dangerous task herself or rather delegate it to an employee. The one who fulfils the task has to be diligent. This is not only necessary to ensure successful completion of the task, but also to protect the health of the one who does it.

If the supervisor carries out the task herself she could ensure diligence and thereby guarantee successful completion. However she also faces opportunity costs, as she will then not be able to use the time for other urgent matters. The delegation of the task would enable the latter, but delegation would only be of an advantage if the supervisor can expect that the employee carries out the task diligently. If the delegation ends in a failure, it will fall back onto the supervisor as the ultimately responsible decision maker. To ensure adequate diligence the supervisor has the possibility to monitor the behavior of the employee. If the employee is not careful enough the supervisor could intervene and avoid the worst. Additionally, the supervisor has the possibility to link monetary incentives to the behavior of the employee.

Figure 3.14 shows the modeling of this situation of conflict. We assume the following payoffs: If the supervisor carries out the task herself, she receives three units and the employee nothing. Delegation without monitoring increases the payoff of the supervisor by another two units provided the task is completed successfully. The employee would then receive one unit. If the supervisor monitors the employee, the supervisor incurs costs of one unit. The employee receives an additional unit as bonus if the monitoring reveals diligent work, while careless work results in a monetary sanction of one unit. Additionally, the employee would suffer a health impairment of another unit. In case of monitoring, and if the employee turns out to be careless, the supervisor could interfere and still rescue a payoff of two units.

In case of no monitoring of a careless employee the task will be a failure and the supervisor will receive a payoff of zero units.

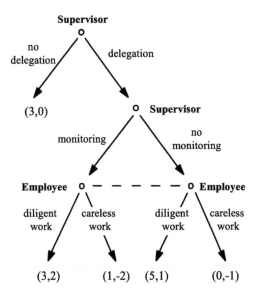

Figure 3.14. The delegation of a dangerous task

To analyze this situation we first take the perspective of the supervisor. Assume she delegates the task to an employee and now has to decide whether or not to monitor the work. At this decision node, both the supervisor and the employee are informed about the complete history of the relation. Both parties know that the task was delegated and at this point in time they both have the same information. The decisions that the parties take in the further course of conflict are therefore not dependent on their history of interactions. Rather, the parties can consider the future course of conflict as an isolated subgame. A *subconflict* in a situation of conflict in extensive form has to satisfy the following conditions:

1. The subgame starts at an isolated decision node of a party. Hence, this node does not belong to an information set that also includes other decision nodes.
2. All decision nodes and terminating nodes that follow this isolated decision node and that are directly or indirectly linked with it belong to the subgame. All other decision nodes are not part of the subgame.
3. If a decision node belongs to a subgame, then all other nodes in the same information set also belong to the subgame and have to satisfy (2).

We refer to a subgame as a real subgame if it is not identical with the whole situation of conflict. According to this definition there exists only one real subgame in our example. It starts at the decision node after the delegation decision of the supervisor. A subgame can not start at the left decision node of the employee as this node lies in a non-singleton information set. A decision that is optimal at this decision node is generally not optimal at other nodes in the information set. At the very least the employee has to consider that her uncertainty about the previous course of conflict can influence her decision.

When we look at the definition of subgames, condition (3) may first seem to be redundant. We could conjecture that this part of the definition is already incorporated in condition (2). However, this is not the case, as the following example shows:

Promotion of an employee

An employee waits for her long overdue promotion. Finally, the decision is scheduled to be taken in an interview with her supervisor and the staff executive. The employee is not sure about the attitude either of her supervisor or of the staff executive. She knows however that both have to approve her promotion. As her own supervisor has postponed her request for promotion several times, she would change her behavior towards her supervisor and be less motivated if the supervisor declines the promotion. However, if it turns out that it was only the staff executive who did not support the promotion, then the backing of her supervisor would motivate her enough not to change her work attitude.

The decision tree in Figure 3.15 depicts the two information sets of the employee. Her information set can be singleton and only contain the left terminal decision node. In this case she knows that she will be promoted and that her supervisor supported this decision. Alternatively, her information set can be non-singleton and contain the other three terminal decision nodes to the right. In this situation she will not be promoted and does not know who actually decided for or against her. She therefore can not let her work attitude depend on her supervisor's previous decision. In taking her decision about her future work effort, she can solely rely on the knowledge that she is not promoted.

The necessity of condition (3) is obvious, even without explicitly specifying the payoffs of the involved parties. In this situation of conflict subgames can not start at the decision nodes of the supervisor: conditions (1) and (2) are satisfied as both nodes belong to a singleton information set, and as all the following nodes can be incorporated, but condition (3) is violated. This

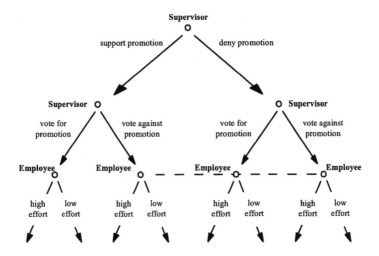

Figure 3.15. The promotion of an employee

is because in both cases not all decision nodes within one information set would belong to the same subgame.

The example shows why condition (3) is critical to isolate the behavior of the parties in the subgame from the rest of the situation of conflict. If we wanted to analyze the behavior of the employee at the two left decision nodes, we would have to assume that the employee knows that the staff executive voted against her promotion. However, whatever the behavior of the employee in this (hypothetical) subgame, we can not conclude anything from this with regard to her behavior in the whole game, because she effectively does not know how the staff executive decided. She only knows whether she got promoted or not.

To be able to analyze the subgame behavior of a party in isolation and at the same time integrate the result of this subgame into the analysis of the whole situation, condition (3) needs to be satisfied. This is also due to the fact that all parties in an isolated subgame analysis should have the same information: condition (1) just guarantees that the party with the first decision knows the history of the course of conflict. But if the analysis of the subgame is supposed to be relevant to the rest of the game then all other parties must also know this history. Otherwise they would have to make assumptions about the behavior of other parties that are simply not given in the general framework of the game. In fact, in our example, the decision of the staff executive at her left decision node is not relevant for the employee's decision, as the employee does not know whether the staff executive's decision has been taken at the left or the right decision node.

Our definition allows us to split up a complex situation of conflicts into their components and to analyze these subgames successively. As the definition guarantees that all parties' behavior in the subgames is also relevant for the whole game, we can step by step infer from the behavior in subgames to the behavior in the total situation of conflict.

Principle of Strategic Behavior VII:
Never choose a strategy that is not strategically stable in all subgames of a situation of conflict.

The requirement that a strategy has to be stable in all subgames guarantees that a party only considers strategies that are dynamically consistent. This principle of strategic behavior enables an equilibrium, which the game-theoretic literature refers to as *subgame perfect equilibrium*. This concept was developed by Selten (1965, 1975). The procedure corresponds to the principle of backward induction in combination with the principle of strategically stable strategy: we first study all subgames that can not be split up into smaller subgames anymore. For these (smallest) subgames we then determine the strategically stable behavior of the parties involved. This allows us to replace the subgame with the consequences (payoffs) of the subgame outcome for each of the parties. Like this, we can simplify a complex situation step by step.

Accordingly, we can analyze our example of the delegation of a dangerous task, by first looking at the subgame that begins after the decision to delegate (see Figure 3.16). In this subgame, the employee has a dominant strategy, that is to carry out the task diligently. If the supervisor expects this behavior, she will not monitor the effort of the employee as this saves her monitoring costs. The outcome of this subgame thus leads to a payoff of five units for the supervisor and of one unit for the employee.

		Employee	
		diligent work	careless work
Supervisor	monitoring	3,2	1,-2
	no monitoring	5,1	0,-1

Figure 3.16. Subgame within the delegation of a dangerous task, strategic form

If we insert this payoff into the original situation of conflict, then the supervisor faces the decision in Figure 3.17. Here, the supervisor will decide for the delegation of the task. The employee will not be monitored but nevertheless carry out her task diligently.

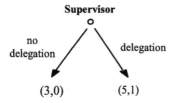

Figure 3.17. Delegation of a dangerous task, reduced form

The principle of subgame perfection excludes, like the principle of backward induction, implausible threats or promises. In contrast to the concept of the Nash equilibrium, the subgame-perfect equilibrium requires that a party's behavior is strategically stable in each subgame. This even applies to subgames that will never be reached in the course of the conflict. Nevertheless, this requirement is essential for the plausibility of a party's real behavior in the whole situation of conflict. For instance, whether the threat to leave the company has an effect on the supervisor critically depends on the employee's willingness to also implement this threat when push comes to shove.

3.2.3   Perfect Bayesian Equilibrium

We derived the concept of subgame perfection as a natural refinement of the Nash equilibrium concept for situations with imperfect information. For each subgame the strategy of one party has to induce her best response on the equilibrium strategy of the other party. With the help of this concept we can exclude implausible threats and promises, although they would be stable according to the definition of a Nash equilibrium.

In the following we will study the behavior in situation of conflicts with incomplete information. As we have seen in the previous section it is possible to transform a situation with incomplete information into a situation with complete but imperfect information. We could therefore be tempted to conjecture that the concept of subgame perfection can be directly applied to this type of situation. This is not the case: we have modeled incomplete information of the less informed party as imperfect information about the type of the better informed party. The type of the informed party is randomly determined before the actual interaction between the parties. This is why there exists no decision node at which the uninformed party knows the history of the course of conflict. In other words, she always faces a non-singleton information set. Hence, a situation with incomplete information does not really have a subgame and the concepts of subgame perfection and Nash equilibrium are identical.

To nevertheless be able to exclude implausible behavior in situations with incomplete information, we fall back on an idea that we have already used in conflicts with independent decisions. The principle of iterative elimination of dominated strategies is based on the belief that one party has about the behavior of the other. We specifically assumed that one party expects the other never to choose a dominated strategy and that the other party corresponds to this belief. Let us look at a situation with incomplete information.

The tendency to leave a company

A supervisor wants to offer one of her employees extensive training on a new business computing system. This training is not only very expensive, but can also be easily applied elsewhere. Obviously, the supervisor would like to reduce the risk of investing in an employee who might be on the brink of leaving the company anyway. Before her decision, the supervisor therefore tries to estimate the probability that the employee leaves the company.

Obviously the supervisor has only incomplete information about the possible plans of the employee to leave, but she may be able to make a prediction by studying the employee's previous behavior. The supervisor could for instance examine the employee's choice of social benefits. If she finds that the employee heavily invests in long-term benefit plans and company pension schemes, it is likely that the employee plans to stay in the company. In contrast, if the employee chooses – wherever possible – one-time benefits and lump cash payments, the supervisor can expect that the employee is more flexible and mobile. Obviously, these choices of the employee do not provide a complete picture of her attitude towards the company, but they may be clear enough for the supervisor to come to a decision about investing in the training of the employee or not.[4]

For such situations of conflict, in which the parties have incomplete information, we will include this idea of the formation of beliefs into our principle of strategic behavior. To determine strategic behavior we set up additional conditions for such a formation of beliefs. For each information set of a party we specify assessments that this party has about the previous course of the conflict. If the party acts strategically, then she will consider the previous behavior of other parties in these assessments and will behave accordingly.

Let us examine the delegation of a dangerous task again to deduce this concept. In contrast to Figure 3.14, the two individual decisions of the supervisor – delegation of a task and monitoring of the employee – are merged into a single decision, as shown in Figure 3.18.

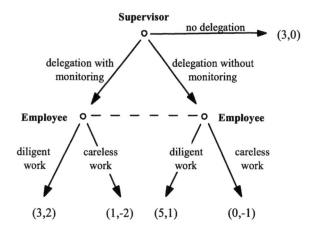

Figure 3.18. Delegation of a dangerous task, modified version

In this situation we can use neither backward induction nor the concept of subgame perfection to predict the behavior of the parties. The supervisor and the employee make their decisions independently, provided that a delegation of the task takes place at all. Thus, the parties have imperfect information. The concept of subgame perfection and the Nash equilibrium concept are identical, because there exists no real subgame in this situation of conflict. With the exception of the root of the decision tree no decision node is lying in a singleton information set.

The only principle of strategic behavior left to analyze the situation of conflict therefore is the Nash equilibrium concept. From the extensive form of the conflict we can deduce the strategic form in Figure 3.19. The conflict has two equilibria in pure strategies. In the first equilibrium, the supervisor chooses not to delegate the task, and the employee decides to execute the task without great care if it was delegated to her. In the second equilibrium, the supervisor delegates the task without monitoring the employee, and the employee carries out the task diligently.

The first of the two equilibria is based on a non-credible threat: if the task is delegated to the employee, then the diligent execution of the task dominates a careless one. In other words, the employee would always work diligently if the task is delegated to her. Unlike the previous presentation of the conflict, this behavior is subgame perfect. To exclude such an outcome of the conflict we introduce additional information for the parties to include in their decision.

Employee

		diligent work	careless work
Supervisor	no delegation	3,0	3,0
	delegation with monitoring	3,2	1,-2
	delegation without monitoring	5,1	0,-1

Figure 3.19. Bi-matrix for the delegation of a dangerous task

Which choice in an information set is optimal depends on the probability with which a party expects to reach a certain decision node in the information set. We therefore require that each party has an assessment about the previous course of conflict up to the point where it takes the decision. Thus, in each information set a party has to form beliefs about the location of her current decision node in the current information set. In a singleton information set the party knows with certainty at which node she is located. Hence, the party would assign a probability of one to this node. In a non-singleton information set this belief is represented by a probability distribution over the relevant decision nodes.

In our example this requirement implies that the employee has to form a belief about the decision node that she will be located at, provided that the task is delegated to her. This belief is represented by the probabilities p and $1 - p$. With probability p the employee expects that the execution of the task will be monitored. With probability $1 - p$ the employee expects no monitoring (see Figure 3.20).

When a party has formed such beliefs in a situation with incomplete information, then her behavior has to be sequentially rational: within each information set the party decides for optimal action, considering the probability distribution over the decision nodes in the information set and the strategies of the other parties. A party therefore does align her own behavior not only to the behavior of the others, but also to her assessment of the previous course of conflict.

In our example, this requirement of sequential rationality excludes that the task is carried out carelessly. For the alternative 'diligent execution' the employee expects a payoff of $1 + p \, [= 2p + 1(1 - p)]$ and for the alternative 'careless execution' the employee expects $-(1+p) \, [= -2p - 1(1 - p)]$. Thus, to carry out the task diligently is a dominant strategy, given the employee's

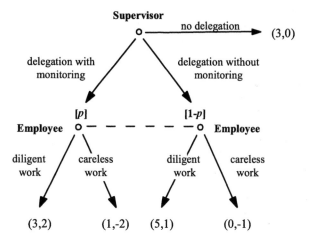

Figure 3.20. Delegation of a dangerous task including the expectation of the employee

assessment of the monitoring behavior of the supervisor.

The sequential rationality of a party guarantees optimal behavior in every information set with a given probability distribution over the decision nodes. However, we have not yet specified how the beliefs are actually formed. Here, we fall back onto the Bayesian learning model and stipulate as a requirement that each party updates its beliefs when new information becomes available. In doing this the following distinction is important. For a given strategically stable behavior of conflicting parties an information set lies *on the equilibrium path* if it is reached at some point in the course of conflict. The information set lies *off the equilibrium path* if it is not reached at all in the course of conflict.

On the equilibrium path the rule of Bayes directly determines the formation of a party's belief. On the basis of the observations of the other party, the party in question updates her previous assessment of the incomplete information. Assume, for the example of the delegation of a dangerous task, there would exist an equilibrium in mixed strategies where the supervisor would delegate the task with monitoring with a probability a_1, delegate the task without monitoring with a probability a_2, and not delegate the task at all with a probability $1 - a_1 - a_2$. Then Bayes' rule would stipulate that the employee expects the supervisor to monitor her work with $p = \frac{a_1}{a_1 + a_2}$, provided the supervisor delegated the task in the first place.

Off equilibrium path we can not apply the rule of Bayes for the formation of a party's beliefs. This is due to the fact that the information sets off the equilibrium path are never reached. Thus, the parties can not receive new information that are relevant for the updating of their beliefs. Bayes' rule therefore does not represent a restriction to a party's belief off the equilibrium path.

Principle of Strategic Behavior VIII:
Form consistent beliefs about the previous course of conflict by applying Bayes' rule and consider these when choosing a strategically stable strategy.

In the game-theoretic literature this principle of strategic behavior corresponds to the concept of the perfect Bayesian equilibrium. According to this concept, a *perfect Bayesian equilibrium* consists of strategies and beliefs that satisfy the requirements of sequential rationality and Bayesian learning. Unlike the previous principles of strategic behavior, this concept explicitly links beliefs and strategies: beliefs are consistent with strategies, which are in turn optimal under the given beliefs.

3.3 STRATEGIC MOVES AND THE ROLE OF COMMITMENT

Parties in a situation of conflict try to implement their interests with the help of strategic decisions. To achieve this, the parties' behavior may include threats, promises, provocations, step by step exploration of the others' intentions, or simply waiting what the other side does. In the following, we call such tactics *strategic moves*. With a strategic move a party tries to change another party's beliefs about her behavior. Due to this changed belief the other party will also change her behavior. The strategic move of the one party thus corrected an otherwise adverse course of conflict to her advantage.

Basically there are three different types of strategic moves (see Figure 3.21). First, a party can try to act before the other party. The advantage that the party gains out of this active strategic move the game-theoretic literature refers to as *first-mover advantage*. By pursuing such an advantage the party attempts to affect the behavior of the other parties directly. We can therefore also talk about an *unconditional strategic move*.

Second, a party can also announce how she would react to certain behavior by the other party. By committing herself to a certain action, she attempts to change the beliefs of the other party about the consequences of her actions and thus the actual behavior of the other party. As this announcement, for instance a threat or a promise, is conditioned by the the other party's previous action, we can talk of an *active conditional strategic move*. In this case the party does not act first, but she nevertheless commits herself to a specific reaction before the other party acts.

Third, in a *passive conditional strategic move*, a party deliberately forgoes acting or committing herself to react. Rather, she waits for the other party to reveal a certain behavior first, so that she can then react appropriately. In this case the party has the advantage that she can first wait and see before she has to act herself. This advantage the game-theoretic literature refers to as *second-mover advantage*.

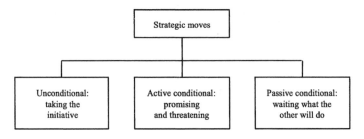

Figure 3.21. A classification of strategic moves

In the first two cases a strategic move is always an action with which one party tries to preempt another party. By doing this she deliberately restricts her room for maneuver to change the course of conflict to her advantage. In contrast to this, the third case represents a strategic move where one party allows the other to move first. Here, the strategically 'acting' party does not want to restrict her room for maneuver, but rather be able to act flexibly on the behavior of the other party.

In the following we will study the different types of possible strategic moves in more detail. To do this we will look at a specific situation of conflict and show, under which circumstances a party best uses which strategic move. We begin with situations with independent decisions and show that this type of conflict automatically obtains a dynamic character when one of the parties makes a strategic move. In the last subsection we examine under which conditions a party can not only commit herself to a specific behavior from the outset, but also actually influence the behavior of the other party by doing this.

3.3.1 Taking the Initiative

A strategic move, with which a party tries to act first, is called an unconditional move. One party takes the initiative in a certain situation of conflict in an attempt to influence the behavior of the other party directly. By doing this she acts independently of the other party. In this sense the first move is an unconditional move. In Figure 3.22, we illustrate the advantage of such an unconditional first move with the example of the situation of conflict with two leaders.

Both parties would like to coordinate their behavior, however, each party

Party B

		Alternative b_1	Alternative b_2
Party A	Alternative a_1	6,5	0,0
	Alternative a_2	0,0	5,6

Figure 3.22. Conflict with an incentive to make an unconditional strategic move

prefers a different combination of coordinated actions. In this situation, the party that takes the initiative is able to implement her interest over the interests of the other party. If, for instance, party A commits herself to action a_1, then she can expect an advantage of six units. Under these circumstances party B will only get five units with action b_1 or 0 units with action b_2. If, however, party B is able to first commit herself to action b_2 then party A will have no other option than to accept only five units by choosing a_2. Taking the initiative thus secures a first-mover advantage of one unit.

It is especially advantageous to take the initiative if a party is predictable in its behavior and the other party could exploit this for its own advantage. By taking the initiative the first moving party can foreclose this exploitation and change the course of conflict to her advantage. The following example illustrates this.

Awarding research grants

As the R&D budget of a company is restricted to fund all projects, the management decides that research teams can submit project proposals to a selection committee, which will award research grants. This selection committee includes members from all departments and awards grants according to the following system. If two teams hand in project proposals that are of equal quality with respect to costs and benefits, risks and opportunities, and utility for the company, the R&D budget is split and both teams are awarded the same grant size. If two teams submit different project proposals, then the team with the less promising proposal gets a smaller grant. If both projects are not very promising, the size of the grants depends on the additional investment requirements of other, currently running projects in the company. Also, research teams that have a track record of successful projects get a higher share of the R&D budget than newcomers do.

We assume that research team 1 has a better track record than research team 2. Figure 3.23 shows how the budget is split between the two research teams.

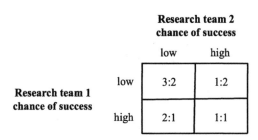

Figure 3.23. Split of the R&D budget according to the projects' chance of success

We assume that the research teams can influence the prospects of their project's success by more intensive preparation. Here they have two possibilities. Either they invest heavily into the preparation and specification of the project (and the proposal), effectively increasing the project's chance of success, or they do little front-up R&D work and thus limit their project's chance of success. For simplicity we assume that one research team can guarantee a high probability for a project's success if it invests nine units into its preparation (and the proposal). To receive a smaller grant, a preparation of two units is sufficient. Given a total R&D budget of 30 units, the payoffs for both teams are determined as shown in Figure 3.24.

| | | Research team 2 | |
		low investment	high investment
Research team 1	low investment	16,10	8,11
	high investment	11,8	6,6

Figure 3.24. R&D investments and their benefit

Clearly, research team 1 has a dominant strategy. Little preparation effort leads to a higher payoff than the alternative 'high effort', independent of the decision of team 2. If team 2 expects that team 1 will invest little then it would be optimal for team 2 to invest heavily into the preparation of the project, as this would secure a better payoff of 11 units. However, in this case, team 1 would get the second worst payoff possible (eight units).

If team 1 wants to improve its position it can do this with an unconditional first move: assume team 1 could commit itself to investing a lot into the preparation of its project proposal. Then team 1 would preempt the other team and bind itself to an action from the outset. Hence, by taking the initiative, team 1 would transfer the simultaneous interdependency into a sequential one.

In this modified situation of conflict team 1 was able to secure a first-mover advantage (see Figure 3.25). If team 1 decides on high effort, team 2 will choose little effort. Team 1 then gets a payoff of 11, which is better than the payoff it would have got in the original situation (eight units). Without this strategic move, team 2 would have believed that team 1 invests little into the preparation of its project. By taking the initiative and by committing itself to a high effort, team 1 is able to correct this belief of team 2. Accordingly, team 2 changes its behavior and makes a decision that improves the payoff of team 1.

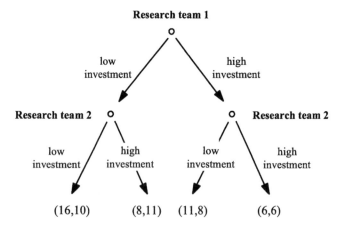

Figure 3.25. R&D investments and their benefit with sequential interdependence

3.3.2 Promises and Threats

A party can also try to influence the behavior of another party with conditional moves. With an active conditional move the party commits herself from the outset to a certain reaction function. By announcing how she will react to the behavior of the other party, she wants to provoke the latter to re-evaluate the consequences of her actions and change her behavior accordingly. As with unconditional moves, the active party deliberately limits her room for maneuver also with conditional moves. Conditional moves are basically threats and promises.

By making a promise a party announces a reaction that will reward a certain behavior by the other party. Of course, the party that acts first will only get the reward if she behaves as required by the promising party. The central element of a promise is the circumstance that the promising party has an incentive to break the promise as soon as the other party behaves to the advantage of the promising party. Thus, only if the promise is credible it does have strategic implications for the other party.

The following example illustrates this.

Financing of a joint advertising campaign

Two divisions of a company individually plan product-oriented advertising campaigns. Division A produces refrigerators and Division B produces ovens. As the products of the two divisions both target similar segments within the kitchen equipment market, a joint campaign would also be possible. In comparison to the product-oriented advertising campaigns by the two divisions, a joint campaign could promote the image and the brand of the company and would lead to a similar increase in turnover, but with significantly less costs for each division.

We model the question whether the two divisions finance an individual or joint advertising campaign as a situation of conflict with independent decisions. Assume that the two divisions can only decide for or against an advertising campaign, irrespective of whether they conduct it jointly or individually. If both divisions choose for a campaign, then they would plan this jointly as an image campaign and split the costs. If only one division chooses to invest in an advertising campaign and the other does not, then the former will conduct a product-specific campaign. For simplicity, the total costs of a joint campaign are not higher than the costs for a product-oriented campaign of one of the divisions. Assume that both types of advertising campaign cost two units. The returns of a joint image campaign are three units for each division. If one division conducts a product-specific campaign the returns are also three units, but due to interdependencies in the market segments the other division also profits from this campaign with returns of two units. Figure 3.26 shows the payoffs in this conflict.

This situation is a typical cooperation dilemma. Each division has an incentive not to invest in advertising. If the other division conducts a campaign, then it is advantageous to free ride on this advertising without own

Division B

	invest in campaign	do not invest in campaign
invest in campaign	1,1	-1,2
do not invest in campaign	2,-1	0,0

Division A (row labels)

Figure 3.26. Financing of a joint advertising campaign

investment. If the other division decides not to advertise, then it is still advantageous not to invest in an own campaign, as the costs of an individual campaign exceed the benefits. As this argumentation applies to both divisions, the company will have no advertising campaigns, despite a collective interest to share the costs of a joint image campaign.

In this situation a unilateral promise could improve the situation of both divisions. If, for instance, Division B has the possibility to commit to a promise, then the following strategic move could enable a joint image campaign. Division B commits herself up-front to investing in an advertising campaign, provided that the other division decides likewise. Figure 3.27 depicts the structure of the respective decision tree.

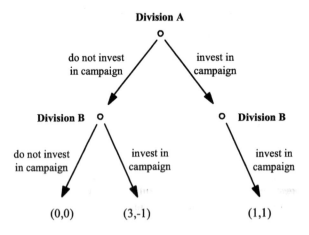

Figure 3.27. Financing of a joint advertising campaign after announcing a credible promise

108

If Division A decides against an advertising campaign then Division B will also not invest. However, if Division A chooses for advertising, then she can be sure that Division B will join forces. As this is an improvement for Division A, when compared with the previous case where none of the divisions invested in advertising, we find that the existence of Division B's promise enabled a mutually improved outcome.

Next to promises, threats are a second fundamental form of active conditional moves. In contrast to a promise, a threatening party announces a reaction with which she will punish the other party for undesired behavior.

As with a promise, the active (threatening) party commits to an action which would be to her disadvantage if it were not for the purpose to sanction the other party. Without the commitment to stick to her announcement, the active party would have no incentive to implement her threat. Thus, a threat is a successful move for the threatening party only if she does not have to act upon it. If the threat fails and the other party does not act as expected, then the active party experiences a disadvantage by executing the threatened action.

In contrast to a promise the general magnitude of the threat is not important.[5] A successful threat is a threat that does not have to be carried out. If a party announces a threat that is more severe than necessary to change the behavior of the other party, then this is needless but it also does not harm the threatening party. This is different when we look at promises. A promise is linked to costs when they are successful. If a party promises more than necessary to change the other party's behavior, then this is detrimental, as she has to fulfill her promise.

The following modified example of the joint advertising campaign illustrates this aspect of threat as an active conditional move.

Financing of a joint advertising campaign, modified version

Assume that one of the two divisions was established during a recent diversification of the company. Division A is new and has just started to produce and sell ovens, while Division B has already produced refrigerators for a much longer period. Again, as both divisions have partly similar customer groups, a joint image and branding campaign would generally be possible.

As Division A is still relatively small, she can not conduct an advertising campaign on the scale of Division B. Accordingly, Division B profits only relatively little from A's campaign. However, Division B is able to finance a much bigger own campaign. In this case Division B's return from the campaign is also higher than that of the smaller Division A.

Division B

		invest in campaign	do not invest in campaign
Division A	invest in campaign	1,3	-1,1
	do not invest in campaign	3,1	0,0

Figure 3.28. Financing of a joint advertising campaign, modified version

If Division B conducts its own advertising campaign or is part of a joint campaign, its payoff will always be five units, while the payoff of Division A will be three units. A campaign in which Division B is involved always costs four units. In case of a joint campaign these costs are split evenly. If Division A conducts its own campaign, then this costs two units and generates a return of one unit per division (see Figure 3.28).

As investing in advertising is a dominant strategy for Division B, Division A will decide against it. By doing this Division A can profit fully from the indirect advertising effects of the other division without sharing the costs involved. In other words, it is profitable for Division A to free ride on the investment of Division B, which ends up with a payoff of one unit (instead of three units if both divisions had invested in a joint campaign).

In this case, Division B can solve the dilemma by announcing a credible threat. If Division B threatens that it will not invest in advertising unless Division A also contributes to the costs, then a joint campaign is in reach. If Division A decides against any investment, then Division B will follow through with its threat and also refrain from any advertising investment. Thus, both divisions will receive no additional return. If, however, Division A decides to invest in a joint image campaign, then it would be the best response of Division B to also invest in this campaign. In this case Division A would have a positive payoff of one unit (compared to no units otherwise) and it would carry some of the costs of the campaign, which generates three units payoff for Division B (see Figure 3.29).

As with a promise, a threatening party also commits herself to an action which she would not choose without the benefits of a strategic move. This characteristic differentiates a threat from a warning and a promise from an assertion. A warning or assertion merely informs a party about the consequences of her actions. By this a party clarifies how she would react to the actions of the other party. The reaction does not change because of a warning or promise. As this does not change the belief about the actions

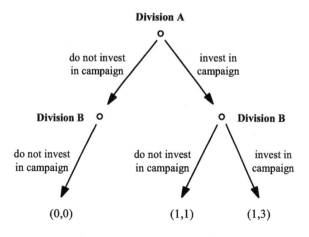

Figure 3.29. Financing of a joint advertising campaign after announcing a credible threat

of the warning party, the other parties also do not change their behavior.

Promises and threats can also be announced together. We illustrate this by changing our example such that the bigger Division B benefits from the advertising campaign of the smaller Division A with five units (see Figure 3.30). In this situation Division A has the dominant strategy not to

		Division B	
		invest in campaign	do not invest in campaign
Division A	invest in campaign	1,3	-1,5
	do not invest in campaign	3,1	0,0

Figure 3.30. Financing of a joint advertising campaign, second modified version

invest in advertising. Division B will decide for an individual advertising campaign. The only strategically stable behavior leads to a payoff of three units for Division A and of one unit for Division B.

An isolated threat by Division B, not to invest in advertising unless the other party does so, would not change the behavior of Division A. If the latter decided for a campaign, it would have to expect that Division B

111

chooses not to invest. Here, Division A would have a disadvantage of one unit compared to a payoff of no units when deciding against any investment at all.

However, a threat, combined with a promise, could lead to an improved outcome for Division B. It threatens not to advertise if Division A decides against campaigning, but at the same time promises to reciprocate an investment from the other division. If Division B can announce this credibly, then both divisions will finance a joint image campaign. In comparison to the previous outcome, Division A would lose two units and Division B would gain two additional units (see Figure 3.31).

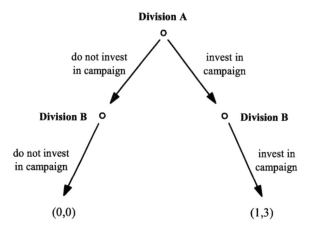

Figure 3.31. Financing of a joint advertising campaign after announcing a credible promise and threat

3.3.3 Waiting to See What the Other Will Do

The strategic moves we analyzed thus far had in common that one party wanted to preempt the other with her actions. However, in certain situations of conflict it can also be of an advantage not to actively intervene in the course of action, but rather to leave the initiative to the other party. With such a passive conditional move a party does not limit her room for maneuver from the outset. Rather, she allows another party to decide on a strategic move herself. The commitment of the other party to a certain behavior can allow the passive party to react more appropriately to the action of the other party. In this way she is able to change the outcome of the situation to her own advantage.

For illustrative purposes let us look at a passive conditional move in the above example of the selection committee that awards research grants. We modify the selection procedure as follows: if both teams propose research projects with equal probability of success the size of the grant depends on the track record of the teams' previous projects. As team 1 had more successful projects in the past, the budget will be split 3:2 in favor of team 1. Apart from this modification, the conditions for the distribution of the budget remain as in the previous example. Thus, maintaining possible investments of nine and two units for high and low project success probabilities, respectively, we have a modified situation of conflict with the payoff matrix in Figure 3.32.

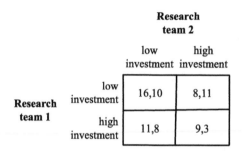

Figure 3.32. R&D investments and their benefit, modified version

In this situation there exists no equilibrium in pure strategies. If research team 1 invests a lot into the preparation of the project, then it is best for team 2 to invest little. However, in this case team 1 would also invest little in order to utilize its reputation with the selection committee. But with a low effort from team 1, the alternative to invest more into the preparation of the project becomes more attractive again for team 2. However, if this is anticipated by the other team, then team 1 would also invest more so that it can secure itself an additional payoff of one unit.

Assume that one party first makes an unconditional move, because she maybe wants to speed up the selection process (see Figure 3.33). Then the passive party can always exploit this action to her advantage and to the disadvantage of the active party. If team 2 moves first, then team 1 can use this first move to reach its maximum budget of 16 units. If we compare this with the expected payoffs in the situation of independent decisions, then this means $6\frac{2}{3}$ more units for team 1, as in the mixed equilibrium team 1 chooses little effort with a probability $\frac{5}{6}$ and team 2 decides on high effort with a probability $\frac{5}{6}$.

In contrast to the exploitation of another party's unconditional first move to one's own advantage, the toleration of another party's conditional first

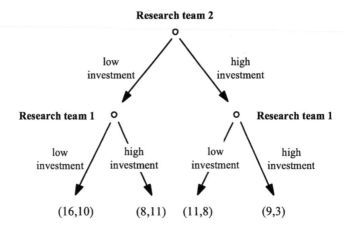

Figure 3.33. R&D investments and their benefit with sequential interdependence, modified version

move is less straightforward. In the latter case we have to differentiate between the announcement of a promise or a threat. As in our example of the Prisoners' Dilemma, it is always beneficial to allow the other party to make a promise. In fact, a promise always rewards a party for deviating from her original strategically stable behavior. However, it is never advantageous to allow another party to announce a threat. After all, the threatening party does nothing but demand a behavior that could always be chosen voluntarily.

3.3.4 The Role of Commitment

Strategic moves aim to change the beliefs of other parties in the conflict. A party that, for instance, announces a threat, tries to change the behavior of the other party to her own advantage. The party deliberately announces a reaction to undesirable behavior from the other party, which she would not choose otherwise, that is without announcing a threat. The other party will only consider the threat if she assumes that the threatening party will really act as announced.

Thus, the threatening party can only influence the behavior of the other party to her own advantage, if she can credibly communicate her strategic move. The pure announcement is not enough. If a party can withdraw her threat effortlessly then it will have little effect. After all, the threatening party would simply harm herself if she acts on her threat without being committed to do so.

A communication that aims to increase the credibility of the strategic move must therefore be more than just verbal communication. The other party must have absolute certainty that the announcement of the active party is credible. To create such credibility, the active party must first of all complete another action that makes the strategic move effective. Only then can the other party be sure that the active party will also implement her announcement, if needed. In this sense credibility demands a commitment from a party to her strategic move. Furthermore, this commitment also has to be communicated to the other party.

Using the example of financing an advertising campaign, we will discuss several possibilities as to how a party can bind herself credibly to a certain strategic move. Which of these probabilities is most effective will be determined by the general framework of the situation of conflict.

Signing a contract is a simple form to create commitment. In this contract the active party can commit herself to a penalty clause, which effectively prevents any deviation from the announced behavior. Consider the above example with investments in advertising campaigns. If Division B signs a contract that commits it to its promise to invest in a joint image campaign, then she will be penalized if she does not deliver as promised. If this penalty more than compensates for the benefits of breaching the contract, then she has no incentive left not to deliver on her promise. In our example the contractual penalty would have to be at least two units.

With contractual solutions there always arises the question about the enforcement of the contract. There must be a neutral party that is responsible for the compliance with the contract. This neutral party may have no personal interest whether the parties in conflict breach the contract or comply with it. Further, the neutral party must always judge rightfully and breach of contract must be verifiable. On the other hand, the costs that arise for the plaintiff in the case of contractual breach may not overcompensate for the penalty. Otherwise the plaintiff would not turn to a neutral party to claim fulfillment of the contract, that is payment of the penalty for not delivering on the promise.

The reputation of a party can also guarantee a commitment to a strategic move. If a certain behavior is bound to the reputation of a certain party, then this party would lose her reputation if she deviates from her announced behavior. Let us look at Division A again, which has made a commitment to invest in a joint image campaign. Assume that this is not the only project of the two divisions, but that there will be repeated situations in the future in which both divisions can individually decide whether to engage in joint (profitable) projects. If Division A does not deliver on its promise, then this will lead to a lack of trust by Division B. Thus, in the following similar situation Division B will not rely on the promise of Division A. The potential benefits from future joint projects will therefore not be realized to the fullest possible extent. If Division A's long-term disadvantages of losing reputation overcompensate for the short-term benefits of breaching the promise or contract, then it has no incentive to deviate from the announced behavior. It would rather invest in its reputation and credibility.

The build-up of trust is often done in small steps: the subject of the conflict is split into several pieces. Hence, the consequences of each interaction are less severe, as are the disadvantages that an active party has when it delivers on its promise. Consequently, the other party's trust in the active party's promises is greater. The announcements are more credible. For illustrative purposes let us assume that the decision for or against joint advertising is split into several decisions about smaller campaigns, each of which offer lower benefits of breaching a promise. Then the divisions can proceed step by step and successively coordinate each other in their decisions. As the advantage to betray the other party's trust is smaller for each of these decisions, the incentive not to cooperate is also smaller. Each party will probably be prepared to invest a little into each of these steps to build up mutual trust. Successively this induces a cooperative mutual decision to invest in a joint image campaign.

Another possibility for a party to commit herself to a strategic move is to use a supporting action to deliberately make an announced reaction irreversible. This supporting action can have an investing or divesting character. In both cases a party incurs additional costs if she does not really execute the announced reaction. Let us look at the example where Division B, independently of the decision of Division A, always invests into an advertising campaign (Figure 3.34). Division B's threat, that it will only invest in advertising if the other division carries some of the costs, can be made credible, if ithad no advantage from its own campaign.

In contrast to the previous situation, the supporting action of Division B generates a negative payoff of one unit, if Division B conducts the advertising campaign on its own. This additional action makes the threat credible as it really commits Division B to its announcement. If Division A does not invest in advertising, then the supporting action of Division B will alter its best response such that it will also not invest. Such a supporting action could, for instance, be that Division B terminates the contract with the advertising agency, which was responsible for all previous campaigns.

3.4 STRATEGIC MOVES AND THE REVELATION OF INFORMATION

In the last section we analyzed strategic moves in a situation in which the parties had complete information about the framework of the situation of conflict, taking into account that they possibly were not informed about all the decisions of the other parties. In this section we analyze strategic moves in situations of conflict with incomplete information.

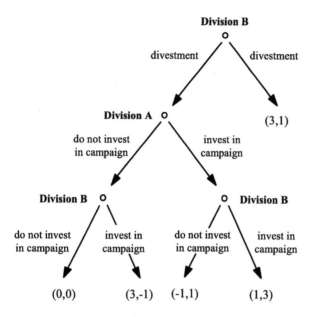

Figure 3.34. Financing of a joint advertising campaign after announcing a threat with a supporting action

A party having an informational lead over another party will try to use this for her advantage and to strategically assert her own interests in the situation of conflict. Similarly, the uninformed party will strive to learn the missing information through adequate strategic moves. The degree to which information is asymmetric therefore has a determining influence on the manifestation of cooperative or competitive interests of the parties, and thus also on the course of conflict.

The extent to which a party can strategically use her informational lead over the uninformed party depends mainly on the type of information. We distinguish *verifiable* information from *non-verifiable* information: Information is verifiable if it can be certified as soon as it is received. The board's decision on the construction of a new plant, for example, is verifiable information. By means of the meeting's minutes it can clearly be determined whether the plant will be constructed or not.

Other information however is not verifiable, as it can not be certified. A supervisor can not be sure whether the employee really suffers from a headache or whether she is just simulating in order not to come to work. This information will be important for the annual assessment of the employee. Her private information in this context is not verifiable, because

117

the supervisor can not check the validity of the statement. In such cases the supervisor will try to draw conclusions on the private information from other actions of the employee.

In situations of conflict in which one party has non-verifiable private information we distinguish the following two strategic moves:

On the one hand the informed party can try to use actions that signal her private information to the uninformed party. Signaling takes place when the informed party can communicate her private information to the uninformed party by means of actions. In this case the uninformed party takes the initiative. In the game-theoretic literature these situations of conflicts are called *signaling games*.

On the other hand also the uninformed party can, by the means of her own actions, try to induce the informed party to choose actions that reveal her private information. The informed party acts first, aiming to early learn the private information and to use it later in the course of conflict to her own advantage. In the game-theoretic literature these situations of conflicts are called *screening games*.

3.4.1 Voluntary Disclosure of Information

Let us first consider an example of a situation of conflict where one party has private information that is verifiable by the other party as soon as it is revealed:

The appointment of a new employee

An insurance company has a job opening for a regional sales manager. He or she should lead a group of sales representatives and take care of the continuous development of the selling capacity. The company expects profound knowledge of the direct insurance business from a candidate.

Suppose it would be possible to classify all skills of a candidate concerning the insurance business according to a one-dimensional scale. Now consider a potential candidate. She knows how to classify her skills: she was trained as an insurance specialist and thereafter worked for three years as a sales representative for an insurance company. Both can be documented. The degree from the college of higher education certifies her general knowledge of the insurance business, a number of awards document her success in her current position.

The human-resources director of the insurance company who is responsible for hiring the new regional sales manager does not know the expertise of the candidate. He rather knows that the candidate knows her knowledge of the insurance business. The candidate therefore has private information.

We assume that any misinformation about the candidate's skills will be detected after employment and that this would result in dismissal. However, the insurance company can not release an employee who did not fully report on her skills.

In these circumstances we can conclude that it is a strategically stable strategy for every candidate to voluntarily reveal his or her knowledge of the insurance business truthfully, independently of the real level of his or her specific skills. Consider first a candidate with maximum possible skills. Of course this candidate would reveal her skills and would present respective certificates to the human-resources director. This will significantly increase her chances to get the position. Moreover the candidate has no incentives to lie about her skills and risk dismissal, since she is perfectly skilled. The candidate also has no incentive to conceal any skills. This would only reduce her chances to get the position. The candidate with maximum skills would therefore report truthfully and voluntarily all her private information.

Now consider a candidate with skills that are only second-best for this position. First we can argue that this candidate would also not conceal any skills: She would only have an incentive to conceal her private information if this would lead the human-resources director to believe she is confronted with a maximally skilled candidate. In equilibrium she can not count on that because a candidate with maximum skills would report her skills truthfully and voluntarily. Not to reveal her skills would thus imply that the human-resources director assumes she is confronted with a less skilled candidate, possibly even less skilled than the candidate really is. To forestall this, the second-best candidate will reveal her skills. She will do this truthfully because the information is verifiable and she would otherwise risk being dismissed soon.

The argument for the next-best candidate is analogous and holds up to the penultimate candidate, who would also reveal her knowledge on the insurance business truthfully and voluntarily. It is only the least qualified candidate who does not care whether she reveals her skills or not: in both cases the human-resources director can, in equilibrium, infer her skills.

We can summarize the general logic of these considerations as follows: A party who possesses advantageous information for a situation of conflict will reveal this voluntarily, since she can distance herself from those who have disadvantageous information.

For this result it is not important whether the private information can immediately be checked or is only verifiable in the course of the interaction. If it is of importance for the appointment whether the candidate would like to have children, then this would not be verifiable during the job interview. The candidate could thus always pretend not to wish to have children. Because the employer would always verify the truthfulness of this statement later in the employment, every candidate would truthfully reveal her private information on her wish to have children during the job interview, provided that the employer could dismiss her on the basis of a wrong assertion. If she does not have the possibility to sanction a wrong assertion by the candidate, the statement not to wish forchildren is not credible any more. Either candidates will not provide any information concerning their wish to have children, or this information does not reveal any information to the employer. Any question by the human-resources director regarding this topic would be meaningless.

Next to the verifiability of the information the above discussed solution presumes that the privately informed party knows the relevancy of this information. Suppose that for a specific position the candidate's health is of importance, but that a law forbids the employer to ask about it. If the healthy candidates know about the legal restrictions, they will voluntarily provide the information about their good health if this information is verifiable: the candidate with the best health condition will undergo a medical test and reveal the results. As argued above also the candidate with slightly less good health will do the same, and so on. In this case the legal restriction forbidding to ask about health conditions is completely irrelevant. Every candidate will reveal his or her health conditions voluntarily to the employer. This however is only true if the healthy candidates know the legal restrictions and the relevance of their health for the position.

This example also shows that there are situations in which a party can choose to acquire and to reveal private information. A candidate who did not undergo the medical test does not know his or her health condition and, given possible consequences for a wrong assertion, will not make any statement concerning his or her health. From the fact that a party does not want to reveal private information it is thus not possible to conclude that this party's information is concealed because it is disadvantageous. Our result, saying that advantageous private verifiable information will be revealed voluntarily and truthfully, does not hold without restrictions in such cases. The following example illustrates this.

For simplicity we assume that a candidate can either have good or poor health. The prospects of being appointed for the position are better with good health than with poor health. More importantly, we assume that the employer will hire a candidate with good health for sure, while she will hire a candidate with poor health with a probability of 80 percent. The position therefore has an expected value of 100 units for a healthy candidate and a value of 80 units for a candidate with poor health. The employer has no possibility to gain information directly about the health status of the candidate. But the candidate can undergo a medical test, for which she pays out of her own pocket, and then show the test results to the employer. Without such test results the employer can not infer on the health status of the applicant.

In the following we want to analyze the perfect Bayesian equilibria in this situation of conflict. We assume that 50 percent of the candidates have a good health, while the other half has poor health. Further we assume that one half of the candidates has high costs for medical tests while the other half has low costs. A reason for this could be that the two groups of candidates have a different medical insurance. This is all common knowledge. We do not specify the absolute magnitude of the costs for the medical tests, because we would like to show how the different equilibria depend on this variable.

At first we study under which conditions there exists an equilibrium, where all candidates are prepared to not only bear the costs of medical tests, but also to report the results of these tests to the employer. In such equilibrium the employer assumes that all candidates undergo a test. If a candidate does not report any information on her health condition, the employee will infer poor health. The following explains the voluntary disclosure of information: a healthy candidate gains 100 units if she discloses her good health condition. A candidate with poor health only receives 80 units. Before the candidate undergoes the medical examination, the expected payoff is 90 units.[6] Hence, being examined and knowing about her health condition is in the interest of the candidate, because if she does not undergo the medical examination, the employer will assume a poor health, which leads to a payoff of only 80 units. This is less than the candidate's expected payoff before an examination. The information about the state of health has thus a value of ten units. The equilibrium discussed above can therefore only exist if the costs for a medical test for any candidate do not exceed ten units. If this is not the case and just one candidate has higher costs there does not exist a perfect Bayesian equilibrium in this situation of conflict, in which all candidates bear the costs for the medical test and reveal the result of this test to the employer.

We can further analyze whether, for some constellation of costs, only one type of candidate will have the test performed. Now suppose that in equilibrium only candidates with low costs will undergo the test. Since only half of the tested candidates have good health the following behavior will be observed: $\frac{1}{4}$ of all candidates will present a medical test certifying their health and. $\frac{3}{4}$ of all candidates will not present a test. Of those not presenting a test $\frac{1}{3}$ is informed about their poor health, $\frac{1}{3}$ will not be informed about their poor health and $\frac{1}{3}$ will not be informed about their good health. The employer will therefore not be able to conclude unambiguously from the absence of a test to the candidate's health condition. Nevertheless, she should revise her beliefs over the candidate's health if no test is presented: If she a priori assumed that half of all candidates have good health, she should now revise her belief to $\frac{1}{3}$. If a candidate does not present a medical test, Bayes' rule leads to a probability of $\frac{1}{3}$ that this candidate has good health and high costs for testing. The value that the employer attributes to a candidate who does not give any information about health conditions is $86\frac{2}{3}$.[7] A candidate with low testing costs can expect a value of either 100

121

units or $86\frac{2}{3}$ units, provided he or she has a test performed, thus on average $93\frac{1}{3}$ units. From this the costs have to be subtracted. Hence, the candidate will undergo a medical test provided that the advantage of $93\frac{1}{3}$ exceeds the value of $86\frac{2}{3}$ that he or she would receive without the test. An equilibrium in which only half of all candidates has a medical test performed only exists if their costs for the test are less than $6\frac{2}{3}$ units while for the other half of the candidates the costs exceed $6\frac{2}{3}$ units. Under these conditions only $\frac{1}{4}$ of all candidates will inform the employer voluntarily about their health conditions.

Finally we will analyze a perfect Bayesian equilibrium in which no candidate will present a medical test: In this case the employer will pay an average value of 90 units to every candidate. If a candidate decided to undergo the test he or she could expect a payment of either 100 or 90 units. If the test certified good health he or she would get the former, if the test certified poor health he or she would not reveal this fact to the employer and receive the latter. On average the candidate can expect an advantage of 95 units. It is thus not beneficial for the candidate to undergo a medical test if the costs are higher than five units. An equilibrium in which no candidate will undergo a test therefore only exists if the costs for all candidates exceed five units.[8]

3.4.2 Imitating Others and Distancing Oneself

Until now we assumed that a party's private information in a situation of conflict is verifiable as soon as it is revealed. We saw that the informed party in such situations has an incentive to reveal her advantageous information voluntarily and truthfully.

In many situations of conflict the private information is not verifiable. An uninformed party is then in the following dilemma: She can not directly assess whether the informed party reveals her information truthfully or not. If for example a candidate's health condition is not verifiable, her announcement to be of good health is meaningless for the employer. The candidate could always claim this independently of his true health condition. The revelation of non-verifiable information has no informational value for the uninformed party.

An uninformed party in such a situation often has just one option: She observes the behavior of the informed party and tries to draw conclusions about the other party's private information. The underlying idea is that a party's decisions may allow for conclusions about her information. At the same time the uninformed party has to account for the fact that the informed party may act strategically:

If the informed party's information would have negative consequences, she will try not to reveal this information. On the contrary, the informed party will try to suggest by her action that she has advantageous information instead. She will try to imitate a party for which the revelation of information would have positive consequences. For example a candidate, who wishes to have children, could try to conceal this by an adequate appearance in the interview. She could act as if the job gives her fulfillment and emphasize being unattached and mobile.

A party will try to reveal her information through her actions if the revelation of her private information would have positive consequences. She knows that the pure announcement of this information to the uninformed party would not be credible. She will thus endeavour to signal her information through her actions. A candidate who really wants to remain childless would therefore try to make this clear by her appearance. The informed party has here an incentive to choose a behavior that differentiates herself from a party who has disadvantageous information.

The extent to which the uninformed party can indeed infer the other party's private information from her behavior depends on the 'costs' for this behavior. The uninformed party will be able to draw unambiguous conclusions if the informed party, who has advantageous information, chooses an action that is too costly for the informed party with disadvantageous information.

In the following we will analyze possible strategic moves of the informed party. In particular, we will see to what extent the possibility to imitate or to differentiate depends on the general framework of the situation of conflict. We will consider the following example for illustration:

The training of an unmotivated employee

An employee is dissatisfied with her current position in a company as a consequence of her negative work attitude. Until now she could conceal her low motivation from her supervisor. Now she considers leaving the company. She has not yet informed her supervisor about her intention, because on the basis of her career development plan she can possibly participate in further training. This training is advantageous for her as it will significantly increase her chances to find a new position later on the job market.

The supervisor would not permit the further training if she detected that the employee is about to leave the company. The employee therefore intends not to raise any doubts about her motivation when executing the recently assigned project. On the one hand she does not want the employer to infer her motivation from her effort and then cancel the training program. On the other hand, due to her low motivation, the execution of the project leads to considerable personal costs.

How will the employee behave in this situation of conflict, and on what factors will her behavior depend? On the basis of what has been said so far it is obvious that an unmotivated employee has to have a notion of how a highly motivated employee in her place would execute the project. Because if she does not want to reveal her low motivation, she has to behave as a highly motivated employee. Thereby the employee would also support the employer's expectation that she will stay in the company.

To make then the situation of conflict more concrete, consider the game tree in Figure 3.35. In this situation of conflict the supervisor assumes, on the basis of past experience with the employee, that the employee's motivation is more likely to be high. She thus assumes that with a probability of $\gamma = 0.2$ the employee is unmotivated. The employee can prove her motivation when executing a project. She has two alternative options: she can decide to provide either high effort or low effort. A highly motivated employee enjoys an advantage of one unit when providing high effort due to her intrinsic motivation, while she receives only zero when providing low effort. When providing high effort she incurs costs of two units. The training would have a benefit of ten units for an employee, independent of her motivation. The payoff for the employer in this situation relates to the advantage she has from training the employee. She would not offer training to an employee if she knew about that employee's low motivation and the fact that she intends to leave the company soon after the training. In this case the employer would have a disadvantage of one unit, as the costs for the training would be larger than the resulting benefits. She would only pay to offer training to a highly motivated employee who stays in the company afterwards. In this case the training would result in a higher productivity of one unit and would thus be beneficial.

We will show in the following that under this basic framework the unmotivated employee will imitate a highly motivated colleague.[9] The corresponding equilibrium is called *pooling equilibrium*: The informed party chooses the same strategy independent of this party's type. The uninformed party can thus not infer anything from the informed party's behavior. In equilibrium the information remains private and the uninformed party does not learn anything.

Let us first consider the case in which both types of employees choose to provide a high effort level. The employer can not draw any conclusions about the employee's motivation from observing high effort. Applying Bayes' rule the employer will not change her prior belief about the motivation of the employee: in the left information set of the employer her posterior belief is $p = \gamma$. On the basis of this positive assessment of the employee's motivation $(1 - \gamma = 0.8)$, the supervisor will choose to offer her training. For $p = \gamma$ the expected benefit from training the employee is larger than from not offering any training: $p(-1) + (1 - p) = 0.6 > 0$. The unmotivated employee would receive a payoff of eight units, while a highly motivated employee would receive 11 units.

Is this behavior strategically stable, or do the parties have an incentive

124

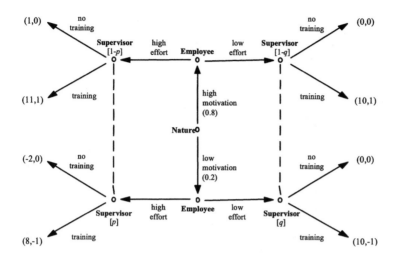

Figure 3.35. The training of an unmotivated employee

to deviate? To answer this question, we have to completely characterize the Bayesian equilibrium, and thus specify the employer's beliefs out-of-equilibrium – when the employee provides low effort. Since Bayes' rule can not be applied in this case, we can, for example, assume that the employer supposes that the employee is unmotivated. Her posterior belief in the right information set is therefore $q = 1$. The employer's belief would imply that she would not offer any training as otherwise this would lead to negative consequences.

Let us now consider the parties' incentives to deviate from the suggested behavior: If we consider the suggested behavior of the two types of employees as given, then the employer's beliefs are consistent with their behavior and her training decision is optimal given those beliefs. On the other hand would it not be beneficial for the employee to deviate, independent of her type? If an employee chose low effort, then her supervisor would not offer her training and her payoff would be zero units. This would be less than what she would get for choosing high effort, independent from her motivation. The supervisor's (implicit) threat not to offer training after observing low effort, leads to the stability of the employee's strategic behavior.

Next to this perfect Bayesian equilibrium there exists a second equilibrium in this situation of conflict, in which the highly motivated employee imitates the employee with low motivation: both employees choose low effort and the employer offers training after observing low effort, but not after observing high effort. The employer's beliefs are such that she infers low motivation with certainty when observing high effort, while when observing low effort she concludes that the employee is highly motivated with a probability of 80 percent. She will offer training when observing low effort but not when observing high effort.

It directly follows from the previous discussion that this is a perfect Bayesian equilibrium: For given behavior of the two types of employees the beliefs of the employer are consistent. When observing low effort she can not conclude anything about the employee's motivation. Therefore her posterior belief coincides with her prior belief. Thus, $q = 0.2$ and the employer will offer training since this leads to a higher expected payoff for her. But when observing high effort, she will not offer training since she assumes that she is facing an employee with low motivation ($p = 1$). The beliefs are therefore consistent with the employee's behavior and the employer's training decision is sequentially rational given those beliefs. Similarly, the employee does not have an incentive to deviate from her behavior, given the employer's behavior. When choosing low effort, both types of employees would get a payoff of ten units, while providing low effort would lead to a lower payoff as the employer would not offer training (one unit for the highly motivated employee, minus two units for the employee with the low motivation).

This last equilibrium is of course not plausible: the employer threatens not to offer training when observing high effort. We can not exclude this behavior when applying the concept of a perfect Bayesian equilibrium, since it gives us are no restrictions concerning the parties' beliefs off the equilibrium path. But we can use our example to deduct plausible predictions also for such situations.

Let us consider the employer's beliefs at the left information set. Suppose she observes that the employee provides high effort. How can she plausibly correct her prior beliefs over the employee's motivation? She knows that an unmotivated employee would in this equilibrium receive a payoff of ten units. This payoff is the maximum such an employee could receive in this situation of conflict. Choosing high effort would make her worse off in any case. Therefore it is dominant for her to choose low effort. On the other hand, a highly motivated employee would have an incentive to choose high effort. Due to her intrinsic motivation she would receive a payoff of 11 units if she would be trained. Only for this type of employee does there exist the possibility of improving her payoff by choosing a different behavior than the equilibrium behavior. On the basis of these considerations the employer should assume that when observing high effort this could only imply she is confronted with a highly intrinsically motivated employee. Her belief of $p = 1$ is thus implausible and leads therefore to an implausible equilibrium.

We can use this reasoning to refine the concept of the perfect Bayesian equilibrium as follows: when forming beliefs, the uninformed party should exclude the possibility that one type of the informed party deviates to get a payoff that is even under the best circumstances lower than her equilibrium payoff. As with the concept of dominant strategies, the party should not expect that the other party will choose a strategy that always leads to a lower payoff than the considered equilibrium strategy. This refinement is called the *intuitive criterion* in the literature.

Let us go back to the perfect Bayesian equilibrium that we analyzed first and apply the intuitive criterion to it. This equilibrium came about because the employer inferred low motivation when observing low effort. The intuitive criterion establishes the plausibility of the belief: a highly motivated employee would always be worse off compared to her equilibrium payoff, when choosing low effort. Therefore such an employee would not have an incentive to deviate from her strategically stable behavior. Thus, observing low effort, the employer can conclude she is confronted with an unmotivated employee.

So far, we have discussed extensively how the informed party can strategically imitate another type, to avoid the possible negative consequences of her private information. In what follows we will shift the perspective to the opposite case: the informed party wants to signal her private information with her behavior to benefit from the possible positive consequences. We will shows this by means of the following example:

The training of a motivated employee

An employee is very satisfied with her current position in a company. Specifically, she is very happy about the fact that her supervisor has announced further training. This would allow her to gain new skills and to further qualify herself for future tasks. Unfortunately, in the past the supervisor has had the unpleasant experience that previous employees participated in the training and resigned immediately afterwards, because they had been dissatisfied with the company for quite some time. This behavior leads to significant costs for the company. The employee would therefore like to prove to the supervisor that she sees her future in the company where she acquired the new skills.

In Figure 3.36, in contrast to our previous example of the training of an unmotivated employee, we have changed two parameters in the framework of the situation of conflict. Let the probability that the supervisor assigns a negative work attitude to her employee be $\gamma = 0.8$. And let the value of the training only be one unit.

In this general framework we can show that a highly motivated employee will distance herself from an employee with a lower motivation to work. The associated equilibrium is called a *separating equilibrium*. Each type of the informed party chooses a different strategy. Thereby, each type credibly signals her private information. The uninformed party can uniquely iden-

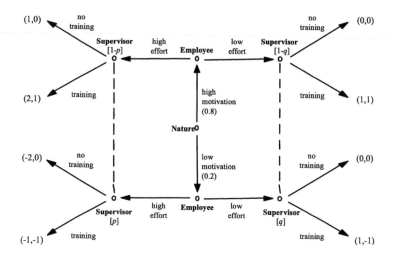

Figure 3.36. The training of a motivated employee

tify the information of the informed parties by observing their respective behavior.

We will show that there only exists a single perfectly separating Bayesian equilibrium in our example. The highly motivated employee chooses a high work effort, the employee with the low motivation decides for a low effort, and the supervisor only offers further training to the employee if she showed a high work effort. Thanks to the rule of Bayes and under certain circumstances, the belief of the supervisor is uniquely defined. In the left information set the supervisor knows that the employee has a positive work attitude, $p = 0$, in the right information set she expects a negative work attitude, $q = 1$.

We can directly conclude that this behavior and these beliefs describe a perfect Bayesian equilibrium. The beliefs of the supervisor are consistent with the behavior of the types of the employee, and the supervisor's decision about further training is fully rational, under these beliefs. Furthermore, none of the employees' types has an incentive to deviate from the described behavior. In fact, the employee with a high motivation would receive no further training if she would work less, and her payoff would decrease by two units. An employee with a negative work attitude would also suffer from a deviation, as she would indeed get further training in the case of a high work effort, but the work costs incurred overcompensate for the advantages of the training.

Further we can argue very easily that this is the only possible conflict behavior. Let us first examine a separating equilibrium where the unmotivated employee shows a high effort and receives no training ($p = 1$), while the motivated employee chooses a low effort and receives further training ($q = 0$). For the unmotivated employee this would result in a disadvantage of two units. She could, however, improve her situation by choosing a low effort, which, in combination with the associated training, would generate an advantage of one unit. Hence, for her the proposed behavior is not strategically stable.

We can also exclude the existence of a pooling equilibrium in this situation of conflict. If both types of the employee chose the same effort level, then the supervisor would not be able to update her belief about their work attitude. As she assumes that the employee has a rather low motivation, $\gamma = 0.8$, she will never offer further training: $0 > \gamma(-1) + (1 - \gamma) = -0.6$.

Assume that both types of employee were to choose a high effort. Then an employee with a low motivation could always improve her situation by deviating from this behavior, irrespective of the supervisor's decision about further training.

And when we assume that both types of employee choose a low work effort, then the highly motivated employee always has an incentive to deviate from this behavior. In fact, faced with a payoff of zero units, she would always receive a positive payoff if deviating, again, irrespective of the supervisor's behavior.

This example shows under which conditions an informed party can differentiate herself from other types. According to the general framework of the situation, in equilibrium, it is possible either to differentiate oneself from another type or to imitate this type. However, it may also happen that both are possible. In such situations of conflicts pooling as well as separating equilibria coexist.

3.4.3   Screening What the Other Knows

In the previous section we have analyzed how an informed party can strategically use her private information vis-à-vis an uninformed party. We have seen that the informed party can hide her information under certain circumstances. She will especially try to do this when the revelation of information has negative consequences. But exactly then the other party has a special interest in this information. As the information is relevant for the action of the uninformed party, she would behave differently under complete information than under information uncertainty. Due to her information deficit the uninformed party has to make a choice, which does not necessarily generate the payoff she would have under complete information.

Hence, in such a situation the uninformed party thus is interested to influence the course of conflict to her own advantage. She will try to reveal the private information of the other party as soon as possible so that she can integrate it in her choice of behavior. With a conditional strategic move the uninformed party wants to induce the informed party to a reaction that reveals her private information. The idea is as follows: the uninformed party offers the informed party several 'contracts'. Each contract specifies the consequences that result from the actions of the informed party. The aim is to design the contracts in such a way that different types of informed parties accept different contracts by which they reveal their private information. In the game-theoretical literature this is referred to as the design of a *screening mechanism*.

We illustrate the revelation of private information by an uninformed party by using our previous example of the decision for further training of a motivated employee. Assume that the supervisor can freely determine the value s of the training for the employee within a certain range $s \in (0, \bar{s}]$. Before the assignment of the project the supervisor informs the employee of her decision about further training, which she makes dependent on the effort of the employee in the project. If the employee invests a lot of effort into the project she will receive further training worth s; if the employee shows little effort, no further training will be granted. The supervisor offers these two 'contracts' to the employee. By choosing one of them the employee implicitly determines whether she will receive further training or not.

The goal of the supervisor is to specify the value of the training in such a way that the employee reveals her motivation to work. An employee with a negative work attitude is meant to choose the contract without further training, while an employee with a positive work attitude ought to choose the contract that guarantees further training.

We can easily calculate the appropriate value of the training. Based on a high effort and subsequent further training, the motivated employee can expect a payoff of $1 + s$, while an unmotivated employee expects a payoff of $-2 + s$. On the other hand, the decision to invest only little effort, which effectively waives further training, generates a payoff of no units. Therefore the employee with the positive work attitude will always invest a lot of effort into the project, while the employee with a negative attitude will prefer a low to a high effort if $-2 + s < 0$. Hence, the value of further training must be smaller than the work effort that the employee has to invest in order to receive the training, $s < 2$.

3.4.4 Building a Reputation

We have discussed the possibility that a party can credibly announce a strategic move if she has built up a respective reputation. The build up of reputation for a certain behavior presupposes that the party has been involved in a series of similar events. If the party has repeatedly shown the same behavior in previous situations, then the other parties will expect the same behavior also for the future. They will therefore take the previously observed behavior as a given and attune their own actions to it.

In the following we want to examine in more detail, whether and how a party can build up such a reputation in a situation of conflict. For example, if the board of a company has always kept its promise to save as many jobs as possible, if the works council agrees to a business-friendly operation agreement, should the works council then believe that the board always sticks to this behavior?

We now model the possibility of building up reputation in a situation of conflict with incomplete information. For this we assume that one of the parties in conflict does not know the type of the other party. If the uninformed party expects that the types of the informed party will behave differently, then the reputation of the informed party can be interpreted as the belief of the uninformed party about the informed party's type. Assume for the above example that the works council is uncertain about the trustworthiness of the board that it always keeps its promises. Then the belief of the works council about the type of the board is a reflection of the latter's reputation. The higher the reputation of the board to really save jobs, the higher the works council will estimate the probability that the board is trustworthy.

Intuitively it is clear that the informed party enjoys greater advantages of reputation the longer the relation with the uninformed party is. A board that slashes jobs after a business-friendly agreement with the works council, will trade off the short-term advantages of this behavior with the long term disadvantages of less reputation. Reputation is a valuable resource in which the board has to invest. The willingness to invest in this resource will be the higher the more often an informed party can use her reputation to her own advantage. In a repeated situation of conflict, the party will invest in her reputation at the beginning rather than at the end. Let us study this situation with the following situation of conflict.

Authority of a team leader

A smaller company recently introduced the production in teams as a new organizational concept. One of the teams quickly established an older employee as team leader. She is widely respected by the other team members, because she generally has longstanding experience, diverse contacts in the company, and a lot of detailed knowledge about the relevant work processes. The other team members respected her authority and never seriously questioned her leadership.

However, a few weeks ago a young colleague entered the team. Before she came into this team she was trained in a bigger company with newer production technology and work processes. Of course, she is now eager to implement this knowledge in the new company. However, her attempts to convince the team of the benefits of these new methods has already led to

131

some frictions with some of her colleagues. Consequently, the team leader expects that sooner or later the new employee will question the authority of her leadership and challenge her position in the team.

We model this situation as a conflict between the informal team leader and the younger employee as follows (also see Figure 3.37). The younger employee first has to decide whether she really wants to challenge the authority of the informal leader. If the younger employee decides to accept the position of the older employee then the team leader gains two units as her position in the team is strengthened. The younger employee receives no units. If the younger employee decides to question the team leader's authority, then the success of this challenge depends on the reaction of the older employee. The informal leader then has two alternatives. If she reacts compliable and searches for a compromise, then she largely maintains her authority in the team and receives a payoff of no units. In this case the younger employee gains some respect of the other colleagues and thus gains 0.5 units. If the informal leader is not compliant and accepts the challenge, she will be the (relative) loser, because the subsequent confrontation will inflict a loss of one unit onto the older employee and a loss of only 0.5 units onto the younger employee.

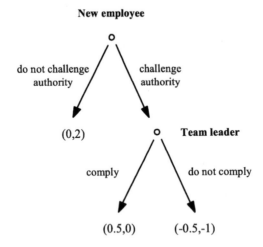

Figure 3.37. Employee challenges a team leader

The behavior of both parties is obvious. By applying the principle of backward induction we can directly infer that the informal leader will be compliant and willing to find a compromise with the new employee in order to avoid the negative consequences of a challenge that she will lose. If the new employee anticipates this behavior then she will challenge the informal leader to increase her own authority in the team. The principle of backward induction excludes a threat of the informal leader that she will stand up to any challenge, because this threat would not be credible. The younger employee will simply not care about this threat when deciding on her actions.

Thus, compliant behavior on the side of the informal leader and a corresponding loss of authority is the result of the above modeling of the situation of conflict. We have modeled this conflict as a unique incident or one-shot game. By doing this we neither considered the possibility that the younger employee may challenge the informal leader again some time in the future, nor did we include possible reactions of the other team members. We could expect that a loss of authority by the informal leader prompts other members in the team to question her leadership. The informal leader thus faces several conflicts and the above decision tree would have to be extended so that it includes the long-term relationship between the informal leader and the team members. In the game-theoretical literature this extension was first discussed and referred to by Selten (1978) as a *chain-store paradox*.

First we will show that the long-term perspective of the relationship does not constitute a sufficient condition for the build-up of reputation. Assume we would model the situation in such a way that each team member decides once whether to challenge the informal leader or not. If the team consists of N members then the informal leader faces N possible conflicts. The team members decide sequentially about challenging the leader and in each of these individual conflicts the informal leader decides whether she will take up the challenge in the form of a straightforward confrontation or rather settle on a compromise (see Figure 3.38).

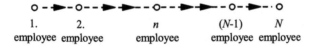

| 1. | 2. | | n | | $(N\text{-}1)$ | N |
| employee | employee | | employee | | employee | employee |

Figure 3.38. Several employees challenge a team leader

If the payoff in each of these conflicts between the informal leader and one of the employees correspond to the original decision tree of this example, then we are able to conclude the parties' behavior for the whole situation. Each team member will challenge the team leader's authority and every time the team leader will avoid a direct confrontation and rather compromise.

As in the one-shot game, this directly results from the application of the principle of backward induction. To understand this, let us first look at the behavior of the team leader in the very last conflict with employee N. If this employee decides to challenge the team leader, then the latter will try to avoid a confrontation, which would incur an even higher loss of authority than a compromise. Hence, employee N will challenge the leader's authority. Exactly the same argumentation can now successively be used for each of the preceding conflicts right up to the very first employee. Each team member will anticipate the compliant behavior of the leader and thus decide to challenge her authority.

At first sight this result may be surprising. We might expect that the informal leader confronts at least some of the challengers in order to discourage further attempts. However, this would not be consistent with the general framework of our example. In the last conflict a confrontation would not pay off for the team leader, as she can not discourage anyone anymore. In the last but one conflict a confrontation would only make sense if this would effectively discourage the last employee from challenging the leader. But as the leader will never be able to keep the last employee from challenging her, it is also not beneficial to enter into a confrontation with the last but one employee. In our example, employee $N-1$ can fully anticipates this, and thus she and all the other team members before her will also challenge the leader.

On second thoughts this result is not so surprising anymore. According to our argumentation above, the informal leader has no opportunity whatsoever to build up a reputation of unaccommodating behavior. As all team members have complete information about the preferences of the leader, her behavior is completely calculable and foreseeable. Our idea to interpret the reputation of a party as beliefs of the other parties about the preferences of the more informed party, must fail in a situation of complete information. The parties simply can not learn anything about each other that they do not already know.

In order to explain that a team leader confronts early challengers in order to discourage others from doing this, we have to include incomplete information about the preferences of the group leader in our situation of conflict. Figure 3.39 depicts a situation of conflict between a younger employee and a team leader. In contrast to the previous example of a rather conciliatory team leader, the leader here is of a more aggressive type.

As the payoffs in Figure 3.39 show, the leader will always react with direct confrontation if her authority is challenged by one of her team members. Unlike the conciliatory team leader, the aggressive leader can announce this reaction as a credible threat. In a situation of conflict with such a leader, no team member would ever question the authority of the leader, as this would certainly not lead to a compromise but rather to the far worse (negative) consequences of a direct confrontation.

New employee

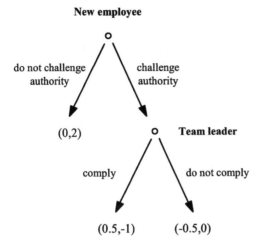

Figure 3.39. Employee challenges an aggressive team leader

Assume that the team members are not quite sure whether their informal leader is of a conciliatory or aggressive type. Let δ be the probability that the leader really reacts aggressively to a challenge. Then the situation of conflict out of the perspective of the employee is as shown in Figure 3.40.

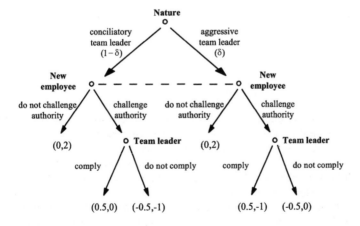

Figure 3.40. Employee challenges an aggressive or conciliatory team leader

For a situation of conflict with N team members, let us now look at the behavior of the parties in the last conflict, that is between employee N and the team leader. An aggressive leader would always react with confrontation, a conciliatory leader always with a compromise. A challenging employee would receive a payoff of -0.5 with an aggressive leader and 0.5 units with a conciliatory leader. As long as it is more probable that the leader is conciliatory, the employee will challenge her authority. The conciliatory leader has no incentive to react with confrontation as this is the very last conflict with a team member.

However, this changes when we analyze the one but last (or an even earlier) conflict. Should a team member decide to challenge the leader, then it can be useful for the leader not to compromise, as this would enable her to build up a reputation of aggressive behavior. This could make sense, if the advantages of discouraging subsequent employees overcompensate for the disadvantages of the current conflict. In fact, if the leader compromises, then every employee would know for sure that she is of the conciliatory type. The leader would have revealed her private information and subsequent employees would definitely challenge her authority. An aggressive behavior, however, would preserve the team member's uncertainty about the leader's real type. They simply can not read from her behavior, whether she only imitates an aggressive type or whether she really is aggressive.

But why do the employees know for sure that the leader is conciliatory if she only once reacts with a compromise, while reacting with confrontation does not provide this certainty? The answer can be found in the argumentation that leads to the following Bayesian equilibrium. As long as nobody challenges the authority of the leader, the team members will not change their belief about the leader's type. A challenge which the leader stands up against with confrontation, induces an update of the team members' beliefs so that they see their leader as more aggressive. This behavior prevents another member from attempting to question the authority of the team leader. It is thus optimal both for a conciliatory and for an aggressive leader to react to the first challenge with direct confrontation. However, in the course of the whole situation of conflict, as the advantage of reacting with confrontation decreases for a truly conciliatory type, the probability that one of the remaining team members challenges the leader increases. This behavior by a team member is consistent with a possible compromising behavior by the team leader. Thus, as soon as a leader does not react to a challenge with confrontation, it is absolutely clear that the leader is actually of the conciliatory type as only this type would have an incentive to deviate from a confronting behavior at some point in time. Consequently, all subsequent team members will also challenge the leader's authority and the leader will always make a compromise.

Figure 3.41 shows how the parties behave in the whole situation of conflict in the explained Bayesian equilibrium. The dotted lines depict the

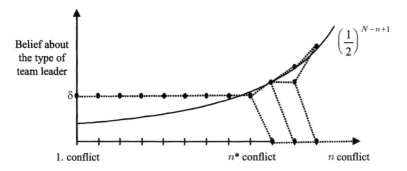

Figure 3.41. Development of the reputation of a team leader and of the behavior of the parties in equilibrium

behavior of the parties on the possible paths to equilibrium. Figure 3.41 also shows the development of the beliefs of the team members at the beginning of each individual conflict. Here the points indicate the consistent beliefs on the possible paths to equilibrium.

We can now understand the perfect Bayesian equilibrium as follows. The curve $(\frac{1}{2})^{N-n+1}$ provides the marginal belief of the team members about the type of the team leader. If there current belief lies above this marginal belief, then they will not challenge the authority of the leader; however, above the marginal belief this will happen with certainty. Let n^* be the first individual situation of conflict in which the original belief of the team members δ is smaller than the marginal belief. In all individual conflicts before n^*, the employees will not challenge their leader. Thus, their belief about their leader's aggressiveness is not updated. As the marginal belief in the conflict n^* is smaller than the original belief, the team member in this individual conflict will definitely challenge the leader. The conciliatory leader reacts with some incalculability. She chooses a probability of confrontation such that the belief of the team members about her type corresponds to the marginal belief. If her reaction to the challenge of the employee in n^*-* is a compromise, then all subsequent team members know that the leader is not really aggressive. Thus, the next member in (n^*+1) will challenge her again. However, if the leader reacts with confrontation, then the belief of the team members about her aggressive type increases to $(\frac{1}{2})^{N-n^*+1}$. Therefore the behavior of the team member in the individual conflict n^*+1 is also somewhat incalculable. The employee randomizes between challenging the leader and not challenging her. If the employee in n^*+1 refrains from a challenge, the belief about the leader will not be updated and the subsequent employee will definitely decide for a challenge. If the employee in n^*+1 decides to challenge the leader in that individual

137

conflict and the team leader reacts with confrontation, then her reputation increase to $4(\frac{1}{2})^{N-n^*+1}$. Of course, a compliant reaction at this point would lead to an irreversible revelation of her type. This behavior continues up to the end of the whole situation of conflict.

Our example has shown that a long-term relationship alone is not sufficient to motivate the development of reputation. In fact, for this we also need the possibility of a learning process. This again implies that one party has incomplete information, so that the informed party has a chance to invest in reputation and also benefit from it.

3.5 LITERATURE NOTES

Kreps (1990b) offers an illustrative introduction to the modeling of dynamic games under various assumptions with regard to the information that is available to the players. Holloway's (1979) introduction to decisions under uncertainty can be regarded as fundamental literature to this.

The textbooks mentioned in this chapter provide solution concepts for non-cooperative games with sequential interactions. The sequential equilibrium, which is closely related with the perfect Bayesian equilibrium, was first studied by Kreps and Wilson (1982a). Fudenberg and Tirole (1991) discuss the differences between these two equilibrium concepts. Van Damme (1987) offers further refinements of the Nash equilibrium. Different assumptions about players' beliefs off the equilibrium path are discussed in McLennan (1985), Banks and Sobel (1987), Cho and Kreps (1987), and Kreps (1990a).

Schelling (1960) studies strategic moves in great detail and provides a number of illustrations and examples that correspond to the respective explanations in this book. The role of information and communication is also considered in Schelling's seminal work, although our explanations in this book refer to the following, subsequent literature.

Grossman (1981) and Milgrom (1981) analyze the voluntary disclosure of verifiable information. Jovanovic (1982) considers a situation in which the disclosure of information is costly. Okuno-Fujiwara, Postlewaite and Suzumura (1990) theoretically analyze the conditions, under which information is voluntarily disclosed.

The literature on signaling games originates with Spence (1973). He analyzes to what extent the training of an employee is a signal of productivity. Grossman (1981) transfers this idea to guarantees that are offered by a producer as a signal for product quality. Milgrom and Roberts (1986) discuss marketing strategy as signal for a company's product quality. Fudenberg and Tirole (1991) and Myerson (1991) are just a few of the previously mentioned textbooks that provide a comprehensive introduction with regard to signaling games.

Rothschild and Stiglitz (1976) were the first to study screening mechanisms by looking at insurance policies and the identification of the insurant's risk propensity by the insurer. Again, this idea can be applied to a number of other economic problems. Guasch and Weiss (1981), for instance, study to what extent we can interpret an applicant's willingness to pay for an entry test reflects her qualification for the position. Salop and Salop (1976) propose a payment scheme that reveals an employee's probability of leaving. The differences between screening mechanisms and signaling games are discussed in Stiglitz and Weiss (1983).

Selten's (1978) work on the chain store paradox represents the starting point of the literature on reputation. Milgrom and Roberts (1982), Kreps, Milgrom, Roberts, and Wilson (1982), and Kreps and Wilson (1982b) are the first to analyze the build-up of reputation under incomplete information.

3.6 EXERCISES

3.6.1 Taking a Vote

According to the following procedure, three players have to choose between three alternatives (A, B and C). First, player 1 proposes one of the alternatives. If player 2 agrees with this proposal, the alternative will be chosen. However, if player 2 does not agree with the proposal, player 3 can decide on her own which of the other two alternatives will be chosen. The utility levels of each player derived from each alternative are given below.

$$u_1(A) = u_2(B) = u_3(C) = 2$$
$$u_1(B) = u_2(A) = u_3(B) = 1$$
$$u_1(C) = u_2(C) = u_3(A) = 0$$

1. Draw the game tree corresponding to the ballot described above.
2. Determine the subgame perfect equilibrium of this extensive form game. Which alternative will be the equilibrium outcome?
3. Are there any Nash equilibria in this game that are not subgame perfect? If so, please give one and explain how this equilibrium can be reached.

3.6.2 Two Projects

A manager (principal) can choose between two projects; project 1 and project 2. After choosing one of the projects, she assigns the project to one of her workers (agent). After being assigned to one of the projects, the worker decides whether she will invest a high or low effort in finishing the task.

If the principal chooses project 1 and the worker decides to invest a high level of effort, the principal gains a return of three units, while the worker gains only one unit. If instead the worker decides to put in low effort, both the principal and agent get a return of two units.

If the manager chooses project 2, she can subsequently decide whether she will monitor the worker's effort or not. The worker will not be able to tell whether her manager is monitoring her or not. If the manager decides to monitor her worker and observes a high level of effort, the principal gains four units and the agent three units. However, if a low level of effort comes to light, the principal's return remains four, but the worker only gets a return of only 1 unit.

If the manager decides not to monitor her worker in carrying out project 2 and high effort is chosen, the returns remain the same for the agent, but the principal gets a return of six units. If the invested effort is low, the principal gains four units and the worker gains three units.

1. Model this game in its dynamic, extensive form. First, the principal decides which project to assign to her worker and subsequently, the worker decides whether to put in high or low effort.
2. Now, model the game above in its normal form and determine its Nash equilibria.
3. Are the Nash equilibria subgame perfect? Explain your answer.
4. Define the concept of 'information set'.

3.6.3   Inspection

A firm receives an announcement about an inspection that will be carried out next week. When the firm asks the inspector on which day she will come by, the inspector answers that it will certainly be on a day on which the firm has not anticipated her coming. Suppose that the firm acts completely rationally.

1. Elucidate the considerations of the firm with respect to the moment of inspection. On which day will the firm prepare itself for the inspection?
2. Discuss the case in which the inspection indeed takes place on Monday. Is this situation in correspondence with the inspector's claim that the inspection would take place on an unanticipated day? Clarify your point of view.

3.6.4   Two Research Teams

A firm employs two research teams, working on different projects. When a new research project has to be assigned to one of the teams, both research teams have to submit a research design to a committee, which then will decide which team can perform the task. By increasing the effort supplied in carrying out the project, the research team may raise the chance of obtaining a higher budget. Before the end of this year, the two research teams will submit two more research designs. The committee will judge the designs sequentially. Assume that both teams will carry out the project with either high effort (hA) or low effort (nA). Taking into account the effort supplied in performing the project, both teams face the payoffs in Figure 3.42 and Figure 3.43.

Team 2

		nA	hA
	nA	1,1	6,0
Team 1			
	hA	0,6	5,5

Figure 3.42. Two research teams - Project 1

Team 2

		nA	hA
	nA	5,5	-3,6
Team 1			
	hA	6,-3	0,0

Figure 3.43. Two research teams - Project 2

1. Model the complete situation of conflict for both teams concerning the decision about both projects. Assume that both research teams decide independently about the level of effort supplied to projects 1 and 2. When deciding about the second project, the behavior of the other team in deciding about the first project is assumed to be known.
2. Determine all equilibrium outcomes of the total game and elucidate the adequate concept of this equilibrium. Additionally, define the concept of a subgame.
3. Now, suppose that both teams have decided about the level of effort supplied to the first project and that both teams know each others decision. Analyze whether team 1 can influence the outcome of the total game, after the decision about the first project, in favour of its own interest by making a strategic move.

141

3.6.5 Hiring a New Computer Programmer

The software company Fastwork is considering the hiring of a new programmer, Mrs McIntosh. However, because her actual program skills and productivity are not known to the firm, Fastwork can only estimate the productivity of Mrs McIntosh. The firm faces two possibilities; on the one hand, Mrs McIntosh may be a very skilled programmer and has a value for the firm of 1 million Euro. On the other hand, Mrs McIntosh may only have average program skills, so that additional programmers have to be hired and the value for Fastwork of hiring Mrs McIntosh is only 50.000 Euro. It is known that in the computer programming industry, a more or less equal division of good and bad performing programmers is present. Moreover, Fastwork is risk-neutral.

1. Mrs McIntosh requests a salary of 250000 Euro p.a. Given this request, will Fastwork decide to hire Mrs McIntosh?
2. An assessment centre offers to test the productivity of Mrs McIntosh in return for 5000 Euro. In expert circles it is known that the services of the assessment center are inexpensive, but it is also known that their test results represent the true productivity in only half of all cases. Will Fastwork accept the offer of the assessment center?
3. Assume Fastwork has commissioned the assessment center to perform the test. Explain whether Fastwork will change its opinion about hiring Mrs McIntosh, based on the test results.

3.6.6 Training

A manager (M) wants to train her employee (E). Only if the employee is highly motivated the training will lead to a substantial increase of her labor productivity. Therefore, the manager decides to let the decision about whether the employee may join the training depend on the employee's working effort. In order to determine the worker's motivational level, the manager gives away an assignment.

To carry out the assignment successfully, the worker has to supply a high level of working effort. Supplying much effort is, however, costly to the employee. For simplicity, we assume that supplying a high level of effort is twice as costly for a low-motivated worker as it is for a high-motivated worker.

The situation can be sketched as follows. In carrying out the assignment, the worker must decide whether to supply a high or low level of effort. A worker with a high motivational level faces costs of three units when supplying a high level of effort. For a low-motivated worker these costs amount to six units. Both high- and low-motivated workers face zero costs if they decide to supply a low level of effort. Assume the manager is able to observe the level of effort supplied by her worker.

If the worker has finished the assignment, the manager has to choose whether she will offer her worker training or not. Each worker (independent of her motivational level) derives a utility of ten units from the training program. For a worker who supplied much effort and who was offered the training, this implies a net return of ten minus the costs of supplying effort. In the case where the worker supplied a high level of effort, but was not offered any training, her (negative) net return amounts to her costs of supplying effort.

The manager faces a payoff of training her worker of 1 (or -1) for a high- (or low-) motivated employee. If the manager decides not to train her employee, she faces a payoff of zero. The manager estimates the a priori probability of encountering a low-motivated worker to be 0.4.

1. Describe this conflict situation in its dynamic form. Briefly elucidate the equilibrium concept that has to be used to describe the behavior of the players correctly.
2. Determine the strategically stable equilibrium of this conflict situation resulting from the adequate equilibrium concept.
3. Based on the level of effort supplied by the worker, can the manager determine the motivational level of her employee? If not, determine what cost level of the assignment is needed to enable the manager to determine the worker's motivational level correctly.

3.6.7 Chain Store

Selten described the so called 'chain store paradox' as follows: chain stores are monopolists in n geographically distinct markets. In each of the n markets the monopolist has to compete with one potential entrant. Those n potential competitors decide on entering the markets sequentially. At time $i(i = 1, \ldots, n)$ competitor i knows what has happened in the $(i-1)$ preceding markets up to that moment. Based on this knowledge she decides whether to enter the market (I) or not $(-I)$. If the competitor enters the market, the monopolist may decide to start a price war (K) or to come to an agreement with the competitor and collaborate $(-K)$. The payoffs in the market i are presented in Figure 3.44 (the top payoff is the one of the monopolist).

The total payoff of the monopolist is the sum of the payoffs earned in n markets.

1. How do the actors relate to each other when there is only one market $(n = 1)$? How do the actors relate to each other when the number of markets is arbitrary?
2. Now, assume that the competitors do not know for sure the payoffs of the monopolist. Assume that they face a probability of $(1 - x)$ that the payoffs correspond to those described above. Moreover, they face a

Competitor

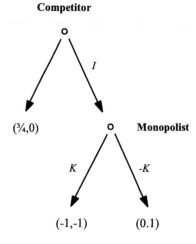

Figure 3.44. Chain store

probability of x that the monopolist's payoff is $\frac{1}{2}$ instead of -1 in case she decides to start a price war. The other payoffs remain unchanged. First, solve this game for a potential competitor i. Then determine the equilibrium outcome for competitor i by backward induction, assuming a posteriori beliefs of $x\{i\}$ at the beginning of period i. What value should $x_1 = x$ have to induce competitor i to remain outside the market?

3.7 NOTES

1. We encountered such a situation of conflict with complete and perfect information in the earlier example of the promotion of a consultant to senior consultant. Each consultant knows at each point in time how many projects the other colleagues have secured. At the point of choosing a specific action. the consultant possesses all information about the complete history of all prior interactions. Further. every consultant knows that the present value of a promotion is 100 units and that the costs for securing a new project are one unit for everybody. Hence, every consultant knows the exact payoff of every other consultant at any point in the conflict.
2. As a singleton information set only has one decision node, such an information set is not emphasized in the presentation of a game tree.
3. We have already discussed the case in which both departments do not know the random draw of nature in connection with conflicts under complete and perfect information.
4. Certainly an employee with long-term prospects in the company can still prefer short-term benefits, for example, because she has just bought a new home and wants to pay off the mortgage quickly. The information that a supervisor can get about the employee's future plans and prospects do not provide a complete picture of her

motives. The supervisor still has to consider the strategic behavior of the employee. The latter could, for instance, choose a social benefit plan just to pretend to stay with the company, although she already knows that she will leave soon.

5. Moderate threats have advantages over excessive threats if, for instance, costs are incurred with the threat or if when the threatening party is uncertain about the effect of her threat.

6. $\frac{1}{2} \cdot 100 + \frac{1}{2} \cdot 80 = 90$.

7. $\frac{1}{3} \cdot 100 + \frac{2}{3} \cdot 80 = 86\frac{2}{3}$.

8. The analysis shows that two Bayesian equilibria can exist for certain cost constellations: one where no applicant undergoes medical testing, and one where all applicants undergo medical testing. In general. one of the two equilibria can be excluded with the help of additional plausibility checks.

9. In this example there exists no Bayesian equilibrium where the effort of the employee is type-dependent. These equilibria will be discussed in the following example of further training for a motivated employee.

PART II
Conflict Management

4. Vertical Conflict Management

> ...the prince ... must imitate the fox and the lion, for the lion
> can not protect himself from traps and the fox can not protect
> himself from wolves. One must, therefore, be a fox to recognize
> traps and a lion to frighten wolves. Those who wish to be lions
> do not understand this.
> (Machiavelli, [1532] 1950)

In the first part of this book we have defined conflict management as the appropriate influence of interdependencies and conflicts of interest of organizational units in a conflict situation. This definition leads to the following tasks for a conflict manager: First, she has to design the structure of conflict situations according to the organizational aim. Second, she has to coordinate the behavior of the organizational units accordingly.

In the following we will discuss the structural and personal actions of conflict management in the framework of a game-theoretic analysis. The starting point is the strategic behavior of parties in conflict as discussed in the first part of this book. We will now analyze how this conflict behavior can be influenced by the appropriate actions of the conflict manager so that the modified conflict situation is in line with the aims of the organization.

In this chapter we will discuss those instruments of conflict management which are available for managing vertical interdependencies. *Vertical conflict management* is concerned with situations in which a principal tries to make sure that the agent fulfills his duty. The literature discusses those situations as the *principal-agent relationship*: An agent acts on behalf of the principal when doing his job. He should act in accordance with the interests and aims of the principal. The principal therefore has to design an incentive system so that the agent actually acts in his interests. An incentive system covers all instruments for motivating the agent. Moreover the principal can also use structural actions to influence the behavior of the agent.

The following analysis of conflict management in vertical interdependencies therefore is covered by our previous analysis of the behavior of parties involved in a conflict: The principal and the agent are the only parties in the conflict situation. The principal has the possibility of designing the framework of the conflict situation to induce adequate acting by the agent. He has to take into account the consequences of the agent's behavior.

Principal-agent relationships are always dynamic conflict situations. Moreover information asymmetries to the costs of the principal are characteristic for these situations.[1] The analysis of a principal-agent relationship can therefore be considered as a game-theoretical analysis of different contract forms under asymmetric information. The principles of strategic behavior derived in the previous chapter can be used to answer the question how the principal should design the structure of the conflict situation in his interest.

In the next section we consider how the principal can influence the behavior of the agent by using incentive instruments. The design of incentive systems is derived under different assumptions about the information the principal has at the time of designing the incentives. In section 4.2 we consider the use of coordination instruments. Here, the principal will design the structural framework of his relationship to the agent so that the agent acts according to the principal's interest in the modified situation.

4.1 THE DESIGN OF INCENTIVE SYSTEMS

A supervisor can employ a number of incentive instruments to manage the behavior of an employee. For instance, a supervisor can offer further training to advance the knowledge and competence of employees and to meet their desires for further development and enlargement of job responsibility. Social preferences of employees may be satisfied by introducing the possibility of a more team-oriented work environment.

For the employee, all these instruments change the payoff that is linked to the outcome of a situation of conflict. This is independent of the fact as to whether the incentive is a direct or indirect one. The announcement of a possible promotion or the introduction of a more performance-oriented wage system change employees' payoffs in a similar way as the introduction of new corporate values or goals would.

If the instruments are meant to influence the decisions of the employees, then the supervisor has to consider their strategic reaction to the introduction of theses measures. The goal of the supervisor therefore is to design the incentive system in such a way that the strategic reactions of the employees are compatible with the goals of the organization as a whole. Achieving this aim largely depends on whether the changes in the payoffs are significant enough to induce the desired change in the employees' behavior.

For each incentive we could analyze under which circumstances it would produce the desired behavioral changes. As this would go beyond the scope of this book, we will focus on employees' payment as an incentive. After all, performance-oriented payment is one of the most important incentive instruments in practice. In the following example we will look at the specific problems that can arise in the design of such an incentive system.

Payment of a Biochemist

A pharmaceutical company decides to extend its current product range by developing a new drug. For this, the company needs to recruit an additional biochemist who will work exclusively on this project. After the first round of job interviews it is clear that the pool of applicants can be divided into two groups, that is excellent and average biochemists. The excellent candidates have a good knowledge of their field and are prepared to work at a high effort level. The average candidates also have good knowledge but are primarily interested in a job with moderate effort requirements. Within each group of applicants the salary requirements are quite similar. However, the salary requirements in the group of excellent applicants are significantly higher than those in the group of average biochemists. Due to a tight labor market, all biochemists know that they will be able to realize their salary requirements within a reasonable time frame.

The future supervisor of the new biochemist has to decide whether she wants to employ an average or excellent candidate for the development of the new drug and which kind of contract she should offer. From the perspective of the supervisor it would be optimal if the employee shows the highest possible effort for a given payment. However, from the perspective of the biochemist a high effort would be suboptimal when she receives fixed pay, because the employee also faces effort-related costs. As the effort level directly determines these costs, the biochemist will try to increase her combined utility from payment and cost.

In designing an incentive system, the supervisor has to take into account that she can not directly infer from the project's success whether the employee's effort level was high or low. For a large part the development of the new drug is based on a trial-and-error process, where the medical success or failure of a certain active pharmaceutical ingredient, let alone its commercial success, is hard to predict.

To find a solution to this problem, we assume the following recruitment procedure and work relationship between the supervisor and the potential employee:

1. The supervisor offers the potential employee a contract which stipulates the responsibilities in developing the new drug and the payment.
2. The potential employee decides whether to accept or reject this contract.
3. If the potential employee accepts the contract, she will start with the development of the new drug.
4. The project will either be successful or fail.
5. The employee will be paid accordingly.

This procedure forms the basis of any principal-agent model. The contract offer in the first stage depicts the incentive with which the supervisor wants to motivate the employee to execute her task adequately.

The information available to the parties in this situation of conflict determines which possibilities the supervisor has in drafting the contract, that is which factors she can use to make the payment dependent on. From a

151

strategic perspective, the relationship between the principal and the agent is only interesting, if at least one of the parties has an information deficit. If this is not the case, and if both parties have complete information about all aspects of the relationship, then we can find a very simple incentive system: The supervisor knows about the interests of the employee and can observe her performance within the project. Therefore, the supervisor is able to design an incentive system which considers all the possible reactions of the employee. In delegating the task, the supervisor can therefore implement the most advantageous solution: the employee receives her payment only when the task is executed adequately; otherwise she will receive no payment or will even be sanctioned. Due to the assumption of complete information, the employee has an interest to act in accordance with the intentions of the supervisor. This is also to the employee's advantage as the payment complies with the requirements of the employee. Any deviating action would therefore not only constitute a disadvantage for the supervisor, but also for the employee.

In a world of complete information, the supervisor is thus able to link the payment to the employee directly to her effort in developing the new drug. If the supervisor determines a low payment for a low effort, then the biochemist will have no incentive to work with a low effort.

However, in general, the supervisor will not have complete information about the employee. She may, for instance, not be able to directly observe the behavior of the employee. In this case the above incentive system is not optimal anymore. The employee now has discrete action sets, which she can exploit to her advantage and to the disadvantage of the supervisor. Hence, if the supervisor is less well informed about the situation of conflict than the employee, she has to take this information deficit into account when designing the incentive mechanism. There are three reasons why the supervisor can have an information deficit with regard to the employee.

1. The supervisor can not directly observe the behavior of the employee in the third stage of the relationship delineated above. Further, the costs for monitoring the employee may be prohibitively high, so that the supervisor is also not able to indirectly infer from ex post inspections the employee's prior behavior or actions. This situation might be given if, for example, the supervisor can not directly or indirectly observe whether the employee carries out certain test series systematically and diligently or not. In the literature this type of information asymmetry is referred to as *hidden action*.

2. The supervisor might be able to observe the actions of the employee, but she can not appraise them appropriately. In fulfilling the task, the employee might gain information that the supervisor does not have. Due to this informational advantage the employee may be able to appraise the project's probability of success more accurately. For example, in her

studies for the development of the drug, a biochemist may have found out that a certain component of the active pharmaceutical ingredient is already successfully applied in another drug. This increases the probability that the new drug will successfully complete the clinical trials. Hence, the employee has private information about a higher probability of success of the project. This form of information asymmetry is typically referred to as *hidden information*.

3. The supervisor may be able to observe the actions of the employee, but she can not appraise the execution of the task. In contrast to the previous information deficit, the employee now has private information about some of her own characteristics and abilities that are non-observable to the supervisor. In our example this would be the case if the supervisor does not know whether the employee is a very good or average biochemist. In the literature this type of incomplete information is referred to as *hidden characteristics*.

Normally, the different types of information symmetry exist concurrently in situations of conflict. In the following we will nevertheless focus on one of the three types separately. This allows us to explain how a certain type of information asymmetry affects specific structures of incentive systems. But even when several types of information asymmetry coexist, the idiosyncrasy of these structures remains.

4.1.1 Conflicts with Hidden Action

Let us assume that the supervisor can not observe the actions of the employee. As exogenous factors may also influence the performance of the project, next to the behavior of the employee, there is no clear-cut relation between the actions of the employee and the success of the project. The employee may be able to explain a bad performance by exogenous factors, although it may actually result from a low effort. This is the reason why the supervisor can not reliably infer the real behavior of the employee from the project's success. Accordingly, the behavior of the employee can not be a subject of the contract.

The employee thus has the possibility to decide on an action that is not in the interest of the supervisor, without an automatic forfeit in payment. The risk that the employee exploits her private information to her own advantage is generally referred to as *moral hazard*.

The goal of the supervisor is to design a contract that limits moral hazard. She will draft the contract in such a way that her own advantage is maximized when considering the employee's reaction on such a contract. To illustrate the implications of hidden action on the design of the incentive mechanism, we use the example as specified in Figure 4.1. In developing the new drug, the biochemist can chose between a high or low effort. If she opts for a low effort she limits herself to routine work with a disutility

Effort	Probability of success	Effort-related costs
low	50%	1
high	90%	3

Figure 4.1. Effort, probability of success, and effort-related costs of the biochemist

or effort-related cost of one unit. A high effort is associated with a cost of three units. The project's probability of success depends on the effort of the biochemist. With a high effort there will be 90 percent chance of success, routine work reduces this probability to 50 percent. We also assume that the profit of the company, and thus of the supervisor, will be ten units if the projects is successful and zero if the project fails. The desired payment of the potential employee, after deducting her effort-related costs, is three units. This can be interpreted as a *reservation payment* (corresponding to a reservation utility).

Before we look at the design of an incentive system that appropriately deals with hidden action, let us first briefly look at the optimal contract in a situation of complete information, that is in a situation where the supervisor can observe the behavior of the employee. In such a case the supervisor could directly relate the payment to the employee's effort.

If the biochemist developed the new drug with a low effort, then the supervisor would have to offer her a payment of at least 4 units (3 units as reservation payment plus one unit to compensate for effort-related costs). As routine work generates an average company profit of five units (10 units with a 50 percent chance), the supervisor's advantage of this payment will be one unit (average profit of five units minus payment of four units).

If the biochemist worked with a high effort, then her payment would have to amount to at least six units $(3 + 3)$. On average, her effort would generate a company profit of nine units $(10 * 0.9)$ such that the supervisor's advantage would be three units $(9 - 6)$.

From the perspective of the supervisor it would be optimal to offer a contract that leads to a high effort by the employee. Such a contract could, for instance, guarantee a payment of six units for a high effort and a payment of three units for a low effort. (Note that the payment offered for a low effort is lower than the minimum payment of four units as calculated above.) However, the biochemist would nevertheless accept this contract as it enables her to realize her requirements of at least three units if she works with at a high effort level (and nothing less).

In a situation where the behavior of the employee is not observable anymore, the supervisor can not link the payment to the effort of the employee as a subject of the contract. But the supervisor can condition the contract on the observable outcome of the project, that is on the success or failure of the new drug. As the employee can influence the project's success with her own behavior, such a contract can work as an incentive system.

Let us denote w_E and w_M as the payment for the employee if the project is successful or unsuccessful, respectively. Then we can describe the contract between supervisor and employee as (w_E, w_M). Figure 4.2 depicts the extensive form of the situation of conflict between the two parties.

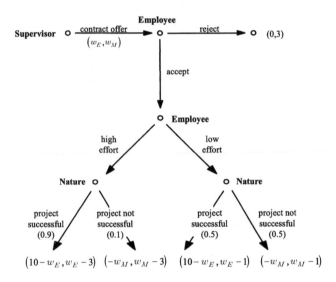

Figure 4.2. Principal-agent relationship with hidden action

The supervisor offers the potential employee a contract (w_E, w_M). If she declines the offer then the supervisor can not conduct the project without delay, leading to a payoff of zero. However, the biochemist is able to get her payment requirements from another company and receives a reservation payment of three units. If the potential employee accepts the contract then she must choose between a high or low effort in the project. After this decision, the success of the project will be determined by a random draw of nature. The payoffs to both parties are then determined according to the contract.

In order to determine the optimal incentive system (w_E, w_M) in this situation of conflict, the supervisor has to solve the following two-stage problem with the principle of backward induction. In a first step, she designs a contract (w_E, w_M), for each of the employee's possible effort levels, which maximizes her own payoff while giving an incentive to the employee to not only accept the contract, but also to choose the effort level that is in the supervisor's best interest. In a second step, the supervisor will pick and offer the contract that secures her the highest payoff.

Let us first look at the case where the supervisor wants to give the employee an incentive to choose a low effort. The optimal contract would always provide the employee with a payment of four units, irrespective of the success of the project. In this case the expected payoff for the employee is three units for routine work and only one unit for a high effort. The employee would therefore accept the contract and then choose the intended (low) effort level. Accordingly, the expected payoff for the supervisor is then one unit.

Let us now assume that the supervisor wants to draft a contract (w_E, w_M) that motivates the employee to contribute a high effort. If the supervisor succeeds in doing this, she can expect a payoff of $0.9 (10 - w_E) - 0.1w_M$ For this to happen, two conditions have to be fulfilled: (a) the employee must accept the contract, and (b) it has to be in her own interest to work at the required high effort level. To determine the optimal contract we take a closer look at these two conditions.

The employee will accept the contract if her expected payoff is at least equal to her reservation payment of three units.

$$0.9w_E + 0.1w_M - 3 \geq 3$$

This condition is called *participation constraint*. If this is satisfied, the employee accepts the contract (w_E, w_M). The second condition specifies that it is in the interest of the employee to put a high effort into the project:

$$0.9w_E + 0.1w_M - 3 \geq 0.5w_E + 0.5w_M - 1$$

This condition is commonly referred to as *incentive compatibility constraint*. It ensures that the employee works with the effort level that was anticipated by the supervisor.

As the expected payoff of the supervisor is negatively related to payment of the employee, the supervisor will try to keep w_E and w_M as small as possible. In the optimum, the supervisor will therefore offer a contract that only ensures the reservation payment of the employee. Thus, the participation constraint is binding in the optimum. Following from this the expected payoff of the supervisor is exactly three units, provided she can motivate the employee to decide on a high effort: on average, the supervisor receives nine units (ten units with a 90 percent probability), while she pays six units to the employee.

The question is how the incentives have to be designed such that it really is in the best interest of the employee to choose a high effort level. To find the answer we have to look at the success bonus, which is the difference between the payments for a successful and for an unsuccessful project. A high effort of the employee increases the probability of receiving this bonus. The higher the success bonus of the employee, the greater is her incentive to choose a high effort level. In our example the success bonus has to be large enough that the additional payment can compensate for the additional effort of two units. As the probability of receiving this bonus is 40 percent greater than with routine work (90 percent-50 percent) the success bonus must be at least 5 units $(0.4 * 5 = 2)$.

Based on this we can now define the optimal contract that not only fulfills the payment requirements of the employee, but also provides an optimal incentive for contributing a high effort. The employee receives a fixed payment of $w_M = 1.5$. If the project is successful, she receives a bonus of five units so that the total payment amounts to $w_E = 6.5$. In our example, this incentive system can not be improved anymore: both the participation constraint and the incentive compatibility constraint are satisfied and, on average, the supervisor receives a payoff of three units. Despite an information deficit, the supervisor does not have to accept a lower payoff.

In our argumentation we implicitly assume that the employee is *risk-neutral*. This means that she is indifferent between a certain payoff and a lottery that would provide her with the same expected payoff. In our example the biochemist considers a payment consisting of 1.5 units with a 10 percent probability and of 6.5 units with a 90 percent probability perfectly equal to a guaranteed payment of six units.

A risk-averse employee would not accept the contract as specified above. Rather she would prefer the secure payment of six units over a lottery with the same expected payoff. Although the contract in our example guarantees an expected payoff of six units, the risk-averse biochemist would nevertheless decline the offer, because the contract can be seen as a lottery that includes a 10 percent probability to receive less than expected six units.

In the case of risk aversion, the supervisor does not only have to compensate the employee for a high effort, but also for bearing some risk. The supervisor can modify the incentive system in two ways. First, she can pay the employee a higher bonus. The higher the risk the employee bears, the higher the additional bonus that is needed to compensate for this. Second, the supervisor can reduce the risk for the employer by offering a higher guaranteed payment for the case that the project fails. The higher the risk the supervisor takes, the less fluctuation the employee experiences in her payment. However, the employee must bear at least some risk. The more risk the supervisor transfers from the employee, the smaller are the incentives left for the latter to work to the satisfaction of the former. Thus, risk-aversion leads to a trade-off between risk allocation and incentive compatibility. An optimal incentive system has to deal with this trade-off. As a result the risk-averse employee would bear less risk than the supervisor and/or receive a higher bonus than a risk-neutral employee. Moreover, the average effort of a risk-averse employee and the expected payoff of the supervisor would also be relatively lower than in the case of risk-neutrality.

4.1.2 Conflicts with Hidden Information

We now look at situations of conflict in which the supervisor can observe the behavior of the employee, but after signing the contract the employee gains access to private information. This is information about the realization of exogenous factors that determine not only the behavior of the employee, but also the results of her actions.

Although the supervisor can observe the behavior of the employee and make it a subject of the contract, she can not properly appraise the observed behavior. In general, an employee will let her optimal effort depend on the realization of exogenous factors. As the supervisor has an information disadvantage with regard to the impact of exogenous factors, she can not determine whether the employee's effort was adequate, or whether the observed outcome was an exogenously produced result. As in the situation with hidden action the supervisor is confronted with the problem of moral hazard: in the case of underperformance the employee can, for instance, defend a low effort with the argument that this was the only choice, because an unfavorable development of exogenous factors doomed the project to failure. However, in reality the exogenous factors may have been favorable and the employee was simply speculating on success despite little effort.

To illustrate this, we modify the above example and assume that both the supervisor and the biochemist are uncertain about the project's chances of success when they sign the contract (see Figure 4.3). The project can have good or bad prospects to be successful. Let $\delta \in (0,1)$ be the chance that a component of the active pharmaceutical ingredient in the new drug turns out to be successfully applied in another drug. This probability is common knowledge. If the component is indeed successfully used in another drug, then there is a 90 percent chance that her own project will be successful if the biochemist puts in a high effort. Routine work creates a 50 percent success probability. If it turns out that the component is not successfully used in another drug, then the prospects for the own project's success are 50 percent, provided the biochemist puts in a high effort. Routine work reduces this probability to 40 percent. All other parameters in this situation of conflict are assumed to remain equal.

Assume the supervisor has reliable information about the successful application of the component in another drug. Then she would offer a contract that manages the effort from the biochemist accordingly. With knowledge about a successful application in another drug the supervisor would prefer

Effort	Project success with good prospects	Project success with bad prospects
low	50%	40%
high	90%	50%
prospect assessment	δ	$1-\delta$

Figure 4.3. Effort and project success with good and bad prospects

a high effort of the biochemist. With knowledge about a failure in another drug the supervisor would like the biochemist to limit her efforts, because otherwise she would face a negative payoff of one unit. If the biochemist only does routine work, the supervisor would receive no units and thus at least avert a loss.[2]

Let us now analyze a situation in which the biochemist (but not the supervisor) gains information about the application and performance of the component in another drug after the contract has been signed. From the perspective of the supervisor, the biochemist can then be of two types. Either she is a type that knows that the component is successfully applied elsewhere or she is of the type that has information about the failure of the component. The private information of the biochemist about the realization of the exogenous factor determines her type.

Obviously it would be beneficial for the supervisor to know about the type of biochemist she is facing. Let us therefore assume that she asks the biochemist about her type, that is about her knowledge of the component's performance in the other drug. If she could rely on an honest answer from the biochemist, the situation would be straightforward. In this case she could determine the optimal effort of the biochemist and pay her accordingly.

Under normal circumstances it would be naïve to assume that the biochemist is always honest. In other words, it is prudent to assume some moral hazard, where the biochemist only shares the information that serves her own end. Hence, the supervisor will try to design the contract with the biochemist in such a way that she will work with a high effort if the component's application in the other drug is successful, and with a low effort if the application is a failure. In the latter case it would be in the interest of the biochemist to inform the supervisor truthfully, as she would otherwise have to reckon with a lower payoff. The optimal design of the incentive system thus guarantees that moral hazard is limited as much as possible.

In principle, the supervisor could offer the biochemist a contract, which indirectly inquires her private information. Or the supervisor drafts a contract that motivates the biochemist never to tell the truth. If the supervisor anticipates that the biochemist always lies, then she would offer incentives for a high effort if the biochemist reports bad news about the component's application and vice versa. In both cases the supervisor would be able to design a contract on the basis of the biochemist's information.

The *revelation principle* guarantees that the supervisor is able to draft a contract that induces the biochemist to openly and truthfully share her private information. For every incentive system that allows cheating to be a stable strategy for the biochemist, or that allows the indirect revelation of information, there exists an alternative incentive system which does not put the supervisor into a worse position, and which motivates the biochemist to reveal her private information directly and truthfully.

Figure 4.4 shows the situation in extensive form. The supervisor offers the employee a contract that consists of four components $w_E(G)$, $w_M(G)$, $w_E(S)$, $w_M(S)$, where $w_E(G)$ and $w_M(G)$ specify the employee's payoff if she reports that the prospects of the project are good, and if she puts a lot of effort into the project that turns out to be successful or unsuccessful, respectively.

Analogously $w_E(S)$ and $w_M(S)$ specify the employee's payoff if she informs the supervisor of bad prospects and if she works with little effort in a successful or unsuccessful project, respectively. If the employee accepts this contract, she observes the random draw of nature that determines the project's chances of success. Subsequently she informs the supervisor of the prospects for the project and determines her effort level. After the project is finished the employee receives her payment.

An optimal incentive system $[w_E(G), w_M(G), w_E(S), w_M(S)]$ has to fulfill several requirements. First it has to correspond to the payment requirements of the employee, so that she is willing to accept the contract. First consider the case where the project's prospects for success are good. As the employee receives the payment $w_E(G)$ with 90 percent probability and the payment $w_M(G)$ with a 10 percent chance, her expected payment is $0.9w_E(G) + 0.1w_M(G)$. On the other hand, if the project's prospects are bad she receives the payment $w_E(S)$ with a 40 percent probability and the payment $w_M(S)$ with a 60 percent chance, resulting in an expected payoff of $0.4w_E(S) + 0.6w_M(S)$. To satisfy the participation constraint, the employee's required payment may not be higher than the expected payment minus her effort-related costs.

$$\delta\left[0.9w_E(G) + 0.1w_M(G) - 3 + (1-\delta)0.4w_E(S) + 0.6w_M(S) - 1\right] \geq 3$$

Further, two incentive compatibility constraints have to be satisfied as well. An employee who observes good prospects for the project must have an incentive to report this information truthfully and to work on the project

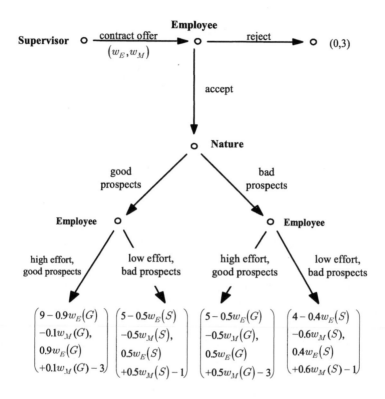

Figure 4.4. Principal-agent relation with unobservable information

with a high effort. And for an employee who observes bad prospects it must be advantageous to report the bad news and decide for routine work.

The first incentive compatibility constraint specifies the corresponding incentives for an employee who observes good prospects:

$$0.9w_E(G) + 0.1w_M(G) - 3 \geq 0.5w_E(S) + 0.5w_M(S) - 1$$

The supervisor has to prevent a situation in which the employee pretends to be confronted with bad prospects, only to justify a decision to do routine work, because the actually good prospects still give her a 50 percent chance to finish the project successfully. Thus, the employee's expected payment minus her effort-related costs must be greater than the payoff she could expect if she pretends to observe bad prospects.

The second incentive compatibility constraint aligns the employee's behavior to the supervisor's goals when the prospects are bad:

$$0.4w_E(S) + 0.6w_M(S) - 1 \geq 0.5w_E(G) + 0.5w_M(G) - 3$$

Here, the supervisor has to make sure that the employee does not pretend to observe good prospects. The payment that the employee receives when reporting truthfully therefore has to be greater than under false pretense, after considering the corresponding costs.

The expected payoff for the supervisor, given an optimal incentive system, is determined by the project's expected payoff $9\delta + 4(1 - \delta)$ minus the expected payment to the employee. The supervisor's expected payoff is the higher the lower the payment to the employee. In an optimal contract, the supervisor will therefore define the components $w_E(G)$, $w_M(G)$, $w_E(S)$, $w_M(S)$ in such a way that that the employee merely receives her reservation payment. The participation constraint is binding, such that the supervisor can expect a payoff of 3δ units under an optimal incentive system.[3]

When drafting an optimal contract, the supervisor has to keep the two incentive compatibility constraints in mind. The first condition implies that the employee receives a success bonus that is high enough to make a high effort attractive. In our case the success bonus has to be big enough that it compensates for the additional two units of effort, compared with the expected net payment under the false pretense of bad prospects for the project. The second incentive compatibility constraint is satisfied when an employee does not have an incentive to choose a high effort level when the project's prospects are bad. The lower her success bonus under good prospects, the more it will be in her interest to choose a low effort level. However, considering the first incentive compatibility constraint, this success bonus may not be too low. When we compare the two incentive compatibility constraints, then we find that the increase in payment due to a 40 percent higher success bonus under good prospects and a high effort has to be at least equal to the increase in payment that is due to a 10 percent higher success bonus under bad prospects and a low effort level.

The following contract provides an example of an optimal incentive system that satisfies the payment requirements of the employee and specifies the right incentives for each type of employee. If the employee reports good prospects, she receives (as in our earlier example above) a fixed payment of $w_M(G) = 1.5$ units, and, in case of a successful project, a bonus of five units, resulting in $w_E(G) = 6.5$. If the employee reports bad prospects, she will receive a fixed payment of four units. This payment is completely independent from the project's performance. This incentive system fulfils the employee's payment requirements under good and bad prospects. Further, the system stays optimal, irrespective whether the employee confronts the supervisor with hidden information or with hidden action.

4.1.3   Conflicts with Hidden Characteristics

As a third case we now want to analyze a situation of conflict where the employee has characteristics that are unobservable to the supervisor. The employee thus possesses private information about her ability to fulfill the task. In contrast to the previously discussed conflict, where new information comes up after signing the contract, here the employee possesses private information before signing the contract. As the supervisor does not know which type of employee she is dealing with, she has incomplete information.

With this form of information asymmetry the supervisor risks *adverse selection*. If the supervisor offers a contract that is designed for the average type of employee, then she has to fear that a less able employee imitates a highly able employee, while the latter type does not accept the offer. Therefore the supervisor risks systematically attracting and selecting less able employees for the job.

As we already have discussed in the previous chapter, in such a situation the supervisor will try to reveal the private information of the employee by means of optimal contract design. In particular, she will offer different contracts to each potential employee, in the hope that different types of employees chose different types of contracts. Hence, the optimal design of two or more separating contracts is at the centre of interest, and not, as in the previous situation of hidden information, the design of a single contract with an optimal incentive system for a specific effort level. For further illustration we will again use the example of the biochemist as depicted in Figure 4.5.

Effort	Effort-related costs of an able type	Effort-related costs of a less able type
low	1	1.5
high	3	6
probability of employee's ability	ρ	$1-\rho$

Figure 4.5. Effort and costs of an able and of a less able biochemist

Irrespective of her ability to do the job, the biochemist can work with either a high or a low effort when doing research for the new drug. Let $\rho \in (0,1)$ be the probability that the biochemist is highly able and thus well suited for the job. If the able type works with a high effort, she has

163

costs of three units, as opposed to one unit when doing routine work. A less able biochemist experiences costs of six units when putting a lot of effort into the project, while the costs for routine work are 1.5 units. All other parameters are equal to the previous analysis.

With complete information about the ability of the biochemist, the supervisor would condition the optimal effort of the employee on her costs. If the biochemist is of the able type, the supervisor would prefer a high effort to routine work. However, with a less able type she would rather want to scale activities down, because a high effort of this type would require the compensation of such high costs that the supervisor's profit is reduced to zero units. However, routine work by the less able type would still allow a small but positive profit of 0.5 units for the supervisor.[4] Hence, in this case the supervisor would not want to offer the less able biochemist any incentive to do more than the routines.

If the supervisor does not know about the biochemist's real abilities, she can not condition the contract on these costs. But she can try to reveal the biochemist's private information. In order to do this, the supervisor has to offer two contracts, each of which is tailored to a specific type of biochemist, $[w_E(N), w_M(N)]$ and $[w_E(H), w_M(H)]$. It must be in the self interest of the respective type of biochemist to choose and accept the one contract that is tailored to her abilities. The able type picks the contract $[w_E(N), w_M(N)]$ and the less able type decides to sign $[w_E(H), w_M(H)]$. To accomplish this, the design of an optimal incentive system has to fulfill the following requirements.

First of all, both types of employees have to at least receive their reservation payment. Since the less able type is supposed to do routine work while the able type prefers to choose a high effort, the following two participation constraints have to be satisfied:

$$0.9w_E(N) + 0.1w_M(N) - 3 \geq 3$$

$$0.5w_E(H) + 0.5w_M(H) - 1.5 \geq 3$$

If both of these conditions are met, both, the able and the less able biochemist will principally accept a contract. Further, in an optimal incentive system it should be in the interest of the biochemist to pick the contract that was designed for her type:

$$0.9w_E(N) + 0.1w_M(N) - 3 \geq 0.5w_E(H) + 0.5w_M(H) - 1$$

$$0.5w_E(H) + 0.5w_M(H) - 1.5 \geq 0.9w_E(N) + 0.1w_M(N) - 6$$

The first incentive compatibility constraint refers to the able biochemist. Her payoff for a high effort has to be higher than the payoff she would receive when she imitates the less able type. Analogously, the second incentive compatibility constraint has to be satisfied to prevent the less able type from imitateting the able type. If both these conditions are met, the supervisor can expect that either type of employee will work with exactly the effort level that is in the supervisor's best interest. Furthermore, the employee will reveal her private information by signing the contract, that is by picking one of the two offers. Figure 4.6 summarizes this.

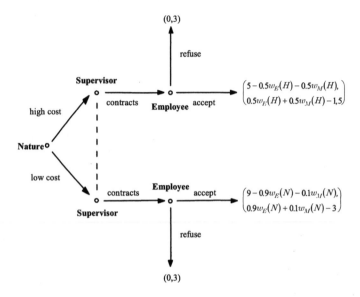

Figure 4.6. Principal-agent relationship with unobserved characteristics, provided the incentive compatibility constraints are satisfied

Which of these four conditions are binding for an optimal incentive system? Let us first look at the participation constraint and let us assume that this just meets the desired payment of the less able biochemist. If the more able type decides to sign the same contract she would enjoy the same expected payment, but with fewer costs than the less able biochemist. Hence, by imitating a lower ability, the former would receive a higher payoff than her reservation payment. Accordingly, the supervisor has to offer the more able biochemist a contract that grants her more than her reservation payment. This additional payment is called an *information rent*. Note that therefore the participation constraint of the able biochemist is not binding.

Let us now look at the two incentive compatibility constraints. It is never advantageous for a less able biochemist to accept a contract that was designed for an employee with superior abilities. If she imitated the more able type, then she could not reach her required payment anymore, because the contract is based on a lower effort-related cost basis and payment.

165

Hence, the incentive compatibility constraint is non-binding for the less able biochemist. But this does not apply to the more able biochemist. As shown above, she has an incentive to pretend to be less able. The supervisor will have to pay an information rent in order to align the biochemist's effort, but she will also try to keep this rent as low as possible. In the optimum, the biochemist will be indifferent between the contract tailored to her type and that designed for the other type.

We now have delineated the most important aspects of optimal contract design. The participation constraint of the less able type and the incentive compatibility constraint of the more able type are binding. For our example we can infer from the first property that the less able biochemist gets an expected payment of 4.5 units. In combination with the second property the expected payment of the more able biochemist is 6.5 units. The difference between the payments exactly corresponds to the increase of two units in effort-related costs. This effectively renders the able biochemist indifferent between the two contracts. By deducting the expected payment to the biochemist $6.5\rho + 4.5(1-\rho)$ from the project's expected return $0.5 + 2\rho$ we can then calculate the expected profit or payoff for the supervisor $(0.5+2\rho)$.

On this basis we can specify the following optimal incentive system. The supervisor offers two contracts. One contract offers the biochemist a fixed payment of $w_M(N) = 1.5$ and, if the project is successful, a bonus of $5\frac{4}{9}$ units, such that $w_E(N) = 7\frac{1}{18}$. The second contract includes no bonus and guarantees the employee a payment of $w_M(H) = w_E(H) = 4.5$ units, independent of the success of the project. This incentive system perfectly separates the two types of biochemist. This is commonly referred to as separating equilibrium. Both types of biochemist accept the offer. The able biochemist signs the performance-related contract, while the less able biochemist picks the contract with the fixed payment. The supervisor's information deficit reduces her expected payoff in relation to a fully informed situation where she would know about the abilities of the applicants. As the latter is not the case, the supervisor has to transfer an information rent of 0.5 units to the more able biochemist.

4.2   DESIGNING THE STRUCTURAL FRAMEWORK

In managing a vertical conflict not only personnel measures, but also structural measures are available. Generally, the following parameters in the general framework of a conflict situation can be starting points for structural measures: the number and identity of parties in a conflict, their information about the subject, the course of the conflict, and the actions that are available to the parties.

To vary these parameters a supervisor can employ numerous coordination instruments. She could, for instance, ensure that an employee fulfills her task adequately by giving her access to a specialist in the field. Or the supervisor could ask a third party to monitor the employee's efforts. In order to receive better information about the employee's behavior a supervisor could also introduce improved reporting systems. Alternatively, the supervisor could also improve the employee's information status, for example, by asking a fellow employee to provide her with specific information about the task at hand.

Two coordination instruments are of special importance for the design of the structural framework of a situation of conflict. Changing the employee's rights to access certain resources, and to reformulate certain codes of behavior, for example, to explicitly rule out certain actions, or to define minimum requirements for certain actions. For the employee both of these measures affect the availability of actions with which she can fulfill the task.

Which concrete structural measures the supervisor can employ depends on the specific structure of the situation of conflict. In principle, all coordination instruments can be considered. Depending on their mode of functioning, these instruments do not only modify the structural framework of the situation of conflict, but also the employees' payoffs.

Whether and to what extent the use of coordination instruments positively affects the employee's task fulfillment depends on how the employee reacts on these measures. As with the design of an incentive system the supervisor has to define the structural framework in such a way that the employee's behavior supports the goals of the organization.

In analyzing the optimal design of a situation of conflict between a supervisor and an employee we should ideally consider all possible structural measures. Such an approach goes beyond the scope of this book. In the following we therefore focus on a specific relationship between a supervisor and employee. By way of example we show how the supervisor can strategically influence the behavior of the employee with specific designs of the structural framework.

Monitoring and payment of a depot master

In the logistics department of a company a depot worker is responsible for the high rack storage of finished products. Next to the consignment of orders and respective stockpiling and stock removal, she is also responsible for the rearrangement of stock to utilize the available space optimally. Due to the array of tasks the depot worker's productivity can not be directly determined, which effectively rules out strictly performance-related pay. However, it is possible to design incentives on the basis of output variables. To do this the head of logistics, who is the supervisor of the depot worker, introduces a monitoring system. By checking the consignments and by directly inspecting

167

some of the other tasks of the depot worker, the supervisor hopes to reveal and prevent shirking. Further, the results of these inspections affect the depot worker's remuneration.

Hence, the goal of the head of logistics is to design a monitoring and remuneration system that sets optimal work incentives for the employee in the depot. This example links the analysis of an optimal monitoring strategy, as discussed in the first part of this book, with the above design of an optimal payment system.

4.2.1 Influencing the Course of Conflict

Before we analyze how the superior can influence the behavior of the agent with structural measures, let us first specify the situation of conflict in more detail.

The depot worker has two alternatives. She can work either with a high or with a low effort. Compared to a low effort, a high effort leads to additional effort-related costs of two units. However, a high effort also increases productivity by nine units. The head of logistics is able to monitor the effort of the worker. This monitoring costs one unit. If the supervisor finds that the employee works with a high effort, she pays the depot worker a bonus b on top of her fixed payment. This bonus is not paid should the supervisor reveal shirking. If no monitoring takes place, the supervisor gives the depot worker the benefit of the doubt and also pays the bonus b.

How should we determine the optimal monitoring and payment system for the depot worker? And which incentives does it specify for her effort? To answer these questions we first assume that both parties chose their actions without knowing about the behavior of the other. As both parties decide independently from each other, we can illustrate the situation of conflict in a bi-matrix (see Figure 4.7).

		Head of logistics	
		monitoring	no monitoring
Depot worker	high effort	b-2,8-b	b-2,9-b
	low effort	0,-1	b,-b

Figure 4.7. Monitoring and pay of a depot worker with independent decisions

To ensure that the depot worker even contemplates a high effort, the bonus b must at least compensate for the affiliated increase in effort-related costs. If this is not the case, then the alternative 'low effort' is a dominant strategy and the supervisor will always monitor. In the following we thus assume that the bonus will always be larger than the additional costs of the depot worker, that is $b \geq 2$.

In the first part of this book we explained that one party should not be able to anticipate the behavior of the other. Accordingly there exists no strategically stable behavior in pure strategies; rather each party will choose a mixed strategy. Let $k \in [0, 1]$ be the probability that the supervisor monitors the employee and let $a \in [0, 1]$ be the probability that the depot worker chooses a low effort. Then we can infer the following equilibrium behavior.

To make sure that the supervisor can not anticipate the behavior of the depot worker, the latter must be indifferent between a low and a high effort. Hence, the advantage of shirking in the magnitude of two units must be equal to the expected loss of payment if she gets caught. The latter is kb units, which yields an optimal probability of monitoring by the supervisor of $k^* = \frac{2}{b}$. This indifference of the supervisor with regard to her monitoring strategy requires that the monitoring costs of one unit are equal to the expected savings in bonus payments. As these are ab units the optimal strategy of the depot worker is $a^* = \frac{1}{b}$. Further, by assumption, $k^*, a^* \in [0, 1]$.

On the basis of this strategically stable relationship between the two parties we can now derive the optimal payment system. The supervisor will choose a bonus b such that her expected payoff is maximized, given the equilibrium behavior in the course of the working relationship. The expected payoff is determined as follows. With a probability $(1 - a^*)$ the supervisor enjoys an increased productivity of nine units, with a probability k^* she will have to incur monitoring costs for this, and with a probability $(1 - k^* a^*)$ she has to pay the depot worker a bonus of b units. This yields the following expected payoff:

$$9 (1 - a^*) - k^* - b (1 - k^* a^*) = 9 \left(1 - \frac{1}{b} \right) - b.$$

We can now calculate the optimal bonus as $b^* = 3$. And we have everything we need to fully characterize the optimal monitoring and payment system. The head of logistics pays the depot worker a bonus of three units, except when she reveals shirking. The supervisor will monitor the worker in $\frac{2}{3}$ of all cases. Thus, her expected payoff is three units. The depot worker will work with a low effort in $\frac{1}{3}$ of all cases.

In the following we will explain how the supervisor can influence the course of conflict to her advantage by changing the structural framework of the situation. For this we assume that the supervisor can bind herself credibly to a certain monitoring strategy when signing the contract. Hence, the contract consists of two components: a payment system in the form of a bonus b and a monitoring system in the form of a monitoring probability k.

In the previous chapter we referred to this approach as an unconditional strategic move. Before we come to the question as to how credible such a strategic move can be, we will first discuss its advantages for the supervisor (see Figure 4.8).

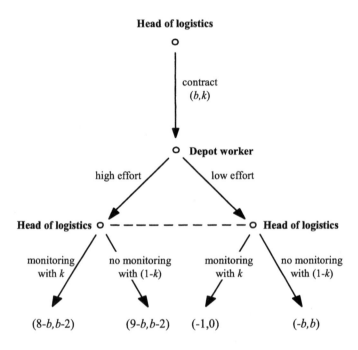

Head of logistics

contract
(b,k)

○ **Depot worker**

high effort   low effort

Head of logistics ○ – – – – – – – – – – ○ **Head of logistics**

monitoring   no monitoring   monitoring   no monitoring
with k with $(1\text{-}k)$ with k with $(1\text{-}k)$

$(8\text{-}b,b\text{-}2)$ $(9\text{-}b,b\text{-}2)$ $(-1,0)$ $(-b,b)$

Figure 4.8. Monitoring and payment of a depot worker with sequential decisions

Let's assume that the head of logistics is able to credibly bind herself to her monitoring strategy when signing the contract. In order to motivate the depot worker to work with a high effort the optimal monitoring and payment system (k^*, b^*) has to satisfy the following incentive compatibility constraint:[5]

$$b - 2 \geq (1 - k^*)\, b$$

The left-hand side of the inequation describes the expected payment of the depot worker for a high effort. She receives the bonus irrespective of monitoring by the supervisor, but she also has to bear the additional costs of two units. The right-hand side of the inequation shows the expected payoff for a low effort. Here, the depot worker only gets a bonus if the supervisor forgoes monitoring, otherwise she receives no bonus.

The optimal monitoring probability for any given bonus $b \geq 2$ is $k^* = \frac{2}{b}$: In this case the depot worker is indifferent between a high and a low effort and would thus decide against shirking for any infinitesimal but positive number ε with a monitoring probability of $\frac{2}{b} + \varepsilon$. Under these circumstances the head of logistics could count on an additional productivity of nine units. Since the employee always works with a high effort, the supervisor is forced to always pay the bonus b, irrespective whether she actually monitors the depot worker or not. Hence, the expected (approximated) payoff of the supervisor is $9 - b - \frac{2}{b}$.

In fact, the expected payoff for the head of logistics is greater than three units (as in our original example), that is $5\frac{1}{3}$ units, provided she always pays the depot worker a bonus of three units. Hence, the supervisor can improve her payoff compared with the situation with independent decisions if she changes the structural framework of the conflict and takes the initiative.

However, given this new situation, a bonus of three units would not be optimal for the supervisor. If she maximizes her expected payoff then she will pay the depot worker a bonus of two units and thus keep six units to herself. This implies that she monitors the depot worker with certainty and just compensates her for the costs of working with a high effort. We implicitly assume that the supervisor is able to commit herself to this monitoring strategy without any cost. As this is probably not possible under normal circumstances, the commitment costs in this system may not exceed three units.

4.2.2 Delegating Decision Rights

In the last section we did not enter into the question of how the head of logistics can commit herself to her monitoring strategy when signing the contract.[6] In the following we explain how the head of logistics can use delegation order to make sure that her announced monitoring activity is also implemented.

In this sense delegation is a structural change in the situation of conflict. A third party is introduced into the conflict. She has the task of attending to the interests of the head of logistics and acting on her behalf. By delegating the monitoring decision to a third party, the supervisor changes the direct conflict between the depot worker and herself in such a way that it does not come to a manifestation of competing interest.

In the following we discuss this aspect of the delegation of decision competencies using the monitoring and payment system for the depot worker. We assume that delegation of the monitoring is advantageous for the head of logistics. Thus, the additional payoff, which results out of the credible an-

171

nouncement of a monitoring strategy, exceeds the costs that are associated with delegating the task to a third party.

As in the previous section, we further assume that it is to the benefit of the head of logistics to commit herself to a monitoring strategy k^* that motivates the depot worker to a high effort. Then the problem of credibility can be solved by delegating the monitoring task to, for instance, the manager of the depot in the following way.

The head of logistics provides the depot manager with a budget, which can be used to effectively monitor the depot worker. As the monitoring costs in our example are one unit, the budget has a size of k^* units. In addition to this budget the head of logistics offers the depot manager an incentive system, which specifies her payment w for her monitoring activities γ. This is equivalent to monitoring costs of γ, as follows:

$$w = \begin{cases} w_0 + b & \text{if monitoring reveals shirking by the depot worker} \\ w_0 - (\gamma - k^*)^2 & \text{if monitoring does not reveal any shirking} \end{cases}$$

This incentive system has a simple interpretation. The depot manager should maximize the sum of bonuses b that are not paid to the depot worker. If the manager successfully reveals shirking, then she will receive, next to a fixed payment w_0 for her monitoring activities, the bonus b that is not paid to the depot worker. However, if the monitoring reveals a high effort by the depot worker, then the payment for the depot manager depends on the budget that she spent on the monitoring activities. In fact, she has an incentive to use up the budget k^* completely and to choose a monitoring strategy $\gamma = k^*$. The depot worker knows about the size of the budget and about the manager's payment system (also see Figure 4.9).

How will the depot manager behave in the subconflict between herself and the depot worker? And which effort will the depot worker choose within this changed situation of conflict? To answer this we look at the strategy combination $(\gamma, a) = (k^*, 1)$, that is the depot manager decides to implement the monitoring strategy k^*, while the depot worker chooses a high effort with the probability 1. This strategy represents a strategically stable behavior in the subconflict of the two parties.

Assume that the depot worker believes that the depot manager decides on a monitoring strategy $\gamma = k^*$. Then a high effort would be her best response to this strategy, because with monitoring of k^* she would never shirk. Assume that the depot manager believes that the depot worker will choose a high effort with certainty. Then she would have no incentive to deviate from the strategy k^*, because any other monitoring probability would lead to a lower payoff than w_0 With this we have shown that $(k^*, 1)$ constitutes an equilibrium in the subconflict.

This equilibrium is furthermore the only strategically stable strategy combination. To show this, assume that the depot worker would choose a

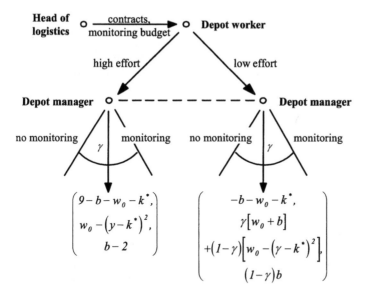

Figure 4.9. Monitoring and payment of a depot worker under delegation of monitoring activities

low effort with a positive probability. Due to the incentive system of the depot manager it would then be beneficial for her to monitor the worker with certainty. By doing this she would maximize her payoff, because she receives the depot worker's foregone bonus of two units, in addition to the fixed payment w_0 . Also, in order to reveal shirking, she would be able to exceed her budget k^*. But if the depot manager monitored with certainty, it would not be optimal for the depot worker to shirk. In this situation she would rather always work with a high effort.

In equilibrium, the depot manager will 'only' receive her fixed payment w_0. This payment must be high enough for the depot manager to accept and do the job. The fixed payment w_0 also determines whether monitoring via delegation is beneficial for the head of logistics. Her payoff with the delegation of monitoring must be at least equal to the payoff without any commitment to a monitoring strategy. In our example the head of logistics receives a payoff of three units without commitment. With costless commitment the payoff maximum lies at six units. Hence, the fixed payment w_0 of the depot manager should not exceed three units.

In our considerations we implicitly assumed that the depot manager reports any revealed shirking to the head of logistics. In reality this may not always be the case. The head of logistics should therefore account for a possible collusion between the depot manager and the depot worker. The latter could, for instance, agree on no monitoring at all, but report to the head of logistics that monitoring took place and that it revealed no shirking. Under these circumstances the depot worker could receive the bonus despite shirking, and the depot manager would receive the monitoring budget without really spending it. To exclude such collusion the head of logistics has to either monitor the depot manager or create additional incentives. In both cases her benefits of delegation are reduced.

4.3 LITERATURE NOTES

The principal-agent models in this chapter belong to the foundation of the economic incentive theory. Their applicability exceeds the work relationships between supervisors and employees as presented in our book. Mathewson and Winter (1985) study the incentives that a franchisor can give a franchisee in order to assure quality. Grossman and Hart (1982) discuss how shareholders can motivate managers to invest in their interest. Holmstrom and Ricart i Costa (1986) study incentive systems that motivate managers to invest in their human capital, and Lambert (1986) discusses how an incentive system can motivate managers to also invest in risky projects.

Harris and Raviv (1979), Holmstrom (1979), Shavell (1979), and Grossman and Hart (1983) contributed significantly to the literature of principal-agent models. The papers of Ross (1973), Arrow (1986), Pratt and Zeckhauser (1985), and Sappington (1991) are helpful introductions to this topic. Interesting extensions to the basic models in this chapter can be found in, for example, Radner (1985), who studies long-term principal-agent relationships, in Holmstrom (1982) as well as Demski and Sappington (1984), who analyze incentive systems with several agents, or in Dye (1986) and Jost (1988), who examine the possibility of monitoring and control as an additional incentive instrument.

The revelation principle for Bayesian games can be traced back to Myerson (1979), although it was previously mentioned in other contexts by a number of authors; for example, Gibbard (1973), Green and Laffont (1977), or Dasgupta, Hammond, and Maskin (1979).

The question to what extent a principal is able commit herself to monitoring activities is discussed in Jost (1996). Schelling (1960) first proposed delegation as a possibility for the principal to commit herself to a monitoring strategy. Melumad and Mookherjee (1989) provide a formal treatment of this topic. The collusion problems that can arise when a monitoring task is delegated to a third party are studied in, for example, Tirole (1986), and Kofmann and Lawarree (1993).

4.4 EXERCISES

4.4.1 Safety Goggles

Suppose a worker can decide whether to wear her safety goggles or not. The glasses, however, do not protect the worker's eyes with 100 percent probability. The employee works alone, so that no one knows whether she wears her glasses or not. If the eyes of the employee are damaged, the present value of the worker's future income is reduced by 1 million Euro. The probability of damaging an eye when wearing the safety goggles is 10 percent, while when not wearing any glasses this probability is 15 percent. An insurance company considers offering an insurance against eye damage. The insurer can not check on whether the worker wears her safety goggles or not. Wearing safety goggles brings along psychological costs to the worker corresponding to a (present) value of 10000 Euro. The worker's utility function is given by $U(Y) = ln(Y)$ and (the present value of) her current income amounts to 2 million Euro.

1. Draw the corresponding game tree of this game.
2. Suppose the insurance company offers an insurance policy with a premium of (a present value of) 100000 Euro and a payment of 1 million Euro. What would the rational worker decide? Is this a fair insurance policy? Explain your answer.

4.5 NOTES

1. In the following discussion we assume that the employee is always better informed about the situation of conflict than the supervisor. This is a basic assumption in most of the principal-agent literature. Some studies also discuss the situation where the supervisor has private information. see for example Myerson (1983), Maskin and Tirole (1990, 1992), or Jost (1996).
2. The supervisor must pay the employee at least six units for a high effort, and at least four units for a low effort. Suppose the supervisor knows prior to signing the contract that the subcomponent is not successful. Then the supervisor's payoff is at most $5 - 6 = -1$ units if the employee chooses a high effort resulting in a 50 percent success chance for the project. For the case that the employee works with a low effort (project success probability at 40 percent), the supervisor's payoff is at most $4 - 4 = 0$ units.
3. If the participation constraint is binding, then the expected payment for the employee $\delta [0.9w_E(G) + 0.1w_M(G)] + (1 - \delta) [0.4w_E(S) + 0.6w_M(S)]$ is identical with $3 + 3\delta + (1 - \delta)$. The supervisor's payoff then is $9\delta + 4(1 - \delta) - [3 + 3\delta + (1 - \delta)] = 3\delta$.
4. Assume the supervisor knows that the effort-related costs of the biochemist are high. Then she has to pay a hard-working biochemist at least nine units, and a routinely working biochemist at least 4.5 units. As the project's probability of success is 90 percent in the first case and 50 percent in the second case, the payoff of the supervisor is 0 and 0.5, respectively.
5. In the following discussion we do not consider the participation constraint. It can be satisfied by appropriately determining the payment of the depot worker.

6. Also see the discussion in this book on commitment possibilities. The supervisor could, for instance, built up reputation in a long-term relationship with her employee.

5. Lateral Conflict Management

> ... a general sense of common interest; which sense all the members of the society express to one another, and which induces them to regulate their conduct by certain rules. ... When this common sense of interest is mutually express'd and is known to both, it produces a suitable resolution and behavior.
> (Hume, 1888)

Vertical conflict management considers the interdependencies between a principal and an agent. In the following we will consider situations between organizational units without hierarchical order. In such lateral interdependencies we will analyze different instruments of conflict management.

In the case of lateral interdependencies the interaction between organizational units is not influenced by direct actions of the principal. Instead, *lateral conflict management* concerns the appropriate design of conflict situations so that the interaction between the parties involved corresponds to the organizational aim. The principal is not directly involved in these interactions. After designing the conflict situation she leaves the parties to self manage within the given structure.

Lateral conflict management therefore implies higher requirements for the conflict manager than vertical conflict management does. The conflict manager not only has to consider the strategic behavior of each subordinate agent but also the interdependencies between the organizational units by the choice of their actions. In such situations, strategic conflict management is generally done in two steps: First, for a given structural framework, the conflict manager has to anticipate the behavior of the parties. Depending on how the parties interact with regard to the organizational aim the conflict manager then has to systematically modify the characteristics of the conflict situation. This requires that she anticipates the change in the parties' behavior that is caused by her structural modifications. The final design of the conflict situation is the one which supports the organizational aim.

In the next section we consider situations in which the parties involved can self manage their conflict of interests within a predetermined situation of conflict. We discuss different instruments of lateral conflict management. In particular we analyze under which circumstances self management leads to favorable results for the organization.

In the second section we then discuss what additional actions a conflict manager can take in order to create a favorable situation for cooperation between parties. She can be a mediator when this is demanded by the parties, but also act as a designer. In the latter case she designs the institutional framework of the relationship between the parties such that their interactions are in line with the organizational goal.

5.1 SELF MANAGEMENT WITHIN PREDETERMINED STRUCTURES

How do parties behave that are supposed to align their actions with a common corporate goal? To what extent can parties manage existing conflicts of interest by themselves?

In the following we assume that the situation of conflict is predetermined. The conflict manager as a superior authority leaves it to the parties in conflict to self manage into a mutually beneficial collaboration. Without a reliable anticipation of the parties' behavior in a certain situation of conflict the authority risks that the parties' self management does not lead to the desired outcome.

In this section we want to analyze, which general frameworks of conflict situations enable a self management that corresponds to a corporate goal. We discuss three instruments of self management: trust between parties in their future collaboration, communication between parties about their present collaboration, and bargaining between parties when communication alone is not enough to settle their conflicting interests.

5.1.1 Trust

In the first part of this book we studied situations of conflict in which the parties involved interacted only once. This may be justified for the collaboration in innovation projects, but in general it is prudent to assume that the same parties interact repeatedly, especially when they are part of the same organization. An employee might negotiate with her supervisor about her wage on a regular basis; the sales department probably contacts the production department more than once to convince them to deal with the order of an important client immediately; or two colleagues routinely work together on the same task.

Situations in which the parties interact more than once in the same general framework are referred to as repeated situations of conflict. The following example illustrated such a situation.[1]

Daily collaboration of two colleagues

Two colleagues in a branch office of a bank are responsible for advising small investors. Both are working at the bank for many years and sit virtually next to each other, only separated by a cubicle wall, in the service hall of the branch. All of the branch's small investors are personally assigned to one of the two colleagues. Despite a fair 50:50 allocation it happens at least once a day that one of the colleagues has customers waiting, while the other has little to do. As both colleagues work equally well, this backlog has nothing to do with their efficiency. Unfortunately, this situation mostly occurs shortly before the service hall closes.

We can interpret this work relationship between the two colleagues as a repeated situation of conflict. On a daily basis, both colleagues are confronted with the decision whether they cooperate and help their colleague with advising her clients, or rather not cooperate and go home in time. With taking this decision each of the colleagues will probably consider the previous behavior of the other.

We can describe repeated situations of conflict as recurrences of a basic situation. The sequence of the interaction, the point in time at which each party can take her decision, the actions that a party can take, ... all these parameters of the general framework do not change from repetition to repetition. The only aspect that changes with each recurrence of the situation is the parties' information about the previous behavior of the other player.

Repeated situation of conflicts are required for the development of trust between the parties involved. The fact that the parties interact more than once can lead to the manifestation of joint interests. If the parties' interactions are embedded in a long-term relationship, they obviously will also consider the long-term effects of today's behavior. If one side pursues her own short term interests, she risks that the other side adapts to that behavior and also decides not to cooperate any more. If the long-term disadvantages from such uncooperative behavior are greater than the short-term benefits, then the recurrence of the situation of conflict can have a collaborative effect.

We therefore expect that the behavior in long-term relationships is very different from that in a one-shot situation, where parties only interact once. Also, cooperation, promises and threats, as well as retaliation can be used as strategic moves. In order to explain and clarify this intuition let us specify the example used above in more detail. We assume that the two bank colleagues take their decision independently and on a daily basis. Figure 5.1 depicts the basic situation of the two colleagues.[2] The basic situation of conflict constitutes a cooperation dilemma. Although it is beneficial for both parties to help each other, there will be no cooperation in equilibrium. Here, uncooperative behavior is the dominant strategy for both parties. In a one-shot situation it is therefore individually rational for both colleagues, not to help each other, although this leads to the worst outcome of the conflict.

In general the colleagues will not know when their work relationship will end. Career changes that may end the direct relationship are possible, but uncertain, and they only come up in the course of time. To take this into account, we include a probability $(1 - p)$ that the relationship will

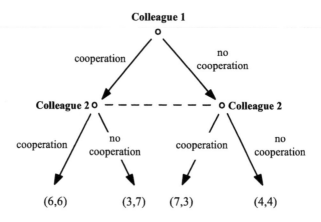

Figure 5.1. Basic conflict situation of the daily work relationship between two colleagues

not be continued at the end of the working day. At the beginning of each day, the colleagues know that they will still work together tomorrow with a probability p. The probability that the work relationship still exists the day after tomorrow is p^2, and for T days into the future this probability is p^T. As shown in Figure 5.2, the relationship between the two colleagues presents itself as an infinite situation of conflict: on each day the continuation of the relationship is possible. In the pertinent literature such a situation is referred to as a *super-game*.

To fully describe the situation we still have to specify the payoffs of the parties. This requires that we establish a link between the payoffs in the basic conflict and those in future recurrences of the situation. We assume that the colleagues value a payoff in the future less than the same payoff today. A discount factor determines by which amount a future value has to be corrected to establish its present value. Thus, a discount factor of δ means that the present value of one unit tomorrow is δ today.[3]

Which strategic possibilities do the parties now have in this repeated situation of conflict? In each repetition of the basic situation the two colleagues can choose between one of the alternatives. When they observe the decision of their colleague at the end of the day, they can then use this information on the following day, that is they can condition their decision in the situation T on the previous course of conflict.[4] If we denote the history of the relationship up to T with h_T, then the strategy of colleague i, $i = 1, 2$, is determined as follows:

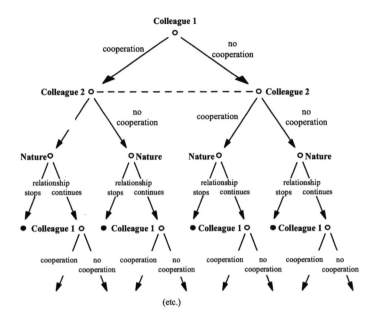

Figure 5.2. Situation of conflict of two colleagues when continuation is uncertain

1. On the first day choose an action s_{i1}.
2. If the relationship still exists on day 2, choose the action $s_{i2}(h_2)$, which may depend on the previous course of conflict $h_2 = (s_{11}, s_{21})$.
3. If the relationship still exists on day 3, choose the action $s_{i3}(h_3)$, which may depend on the previous course of conflict $h_3 = (s_{11}, s_{21}, s_{12}, s_{22})$.

$\vdots$

T. If the relationship still exists on day T, choose the action $s_{iT}(h_T)$, which may depend on the previous course of conflict $h_T = (s_{11}, s_{21}, s_{12}, s_{22}, ..., s_{1T-1}, s_{2T-1})$.

$\vdots$

   A pure strategy s_i for the colleague i is then a sequence of decisions $\{s_{i1}, s_{i2}(h_2), s_{i3}(h_3), ..., s_{iT}(h_T), ...\}$. For example, the strategy 'cooperate on each even day and do not cooperate on each uneven day', or 'cooperate on the first day and after that always do what the other colleague did on the day before' are both plans of actions, which determine the behavior for each party in each information set (that is, on each day) of the repeated situation.

   We can not use the principle of backward induction to analyze the parties' behavior in this repeated situation of conflict. There is no predetermined

181

last round and thus no last decision of any party to start with. We will therefore determine the behavior of the party by using the concept of subgame perfection. For a party's given strategy we will analyze whether it induces a strategically stable strategy in each subgame.

On each day in our infinitely repeated situation of conflict a new subconflict starts. This subgame on day T does not only include the conflict on that specific day, but also the infinitely repeated relationship between the colleagues in the future, starting on that day. The subconflict is thus always identical to the original, infinitely repeated situation of conflict. Further, for any possible history of the previous relationship another subconflict starts on day T. As this relationship exist for already $(T - 1)$ days and as each party can choose between two actions, on each day there exist altogether $2^{2(T-1)}$ subconflicts.

We will argue that cooperation, in contrast to the one-shot situation, can be a strategically stable behavior for both colleagues on each day of their work relationship. For this let us look at the following *trigger strategy* of colleague i:

1. On the first day of the relationship decide to cooperate.
2. On the T-th day of the relationship decide to cooperate if nobody deviated from the cooperative behavior up to that day. Otherwise choose not to cooperate.

The trigger strategy is a strategy that retaliates. A party cooperates until the collaboration breaks down and then switches to uncooperative behavior. Here, cooperation can be understood as an implicit agreement between the parties. As soon as the other party does not honor this agreement the rest of the relationship will be uncooperative. Hence, any deviation from the implicit agreement is punished immediately and irreversibly, such that the long-term disadvantage of retaliation stands against any short-term benefit of uncooperative behavior. Each party will abide by the implicit agreement if the costs incurred by retaliation exceed the benefits of deviation.

The trigger strategy is strategically stable in every possible subconflict, provided the discount factor and the probability for a long-term relationship are sufficiently high. To see this, note that if a party contemplates the pros and cons of a specific strategy, she will discount tomorrow's payoffs with a factor $\tilde{\delta}$ and the probability p that the interaction will be continued into the next day at all. The payoff on the day after tomorrow will be discounted with $\tilde{\delta}^2$ and p^2 and so on. Each day, the party will evaluate all her payoffs with $\tilde{\delta}p$. This allows us to interpret a situation of conflict with an uncertain end as an infinitely repeated conflict with a discount factor $\delta = \tilde{\delta}p$ that is corrected by the probability of a premature end. We restrict our further explanation to this discount factor.

First, we check under which condition the trigger strategy constitutes an equilibrium strategy at all. For this we take the perspective of Colleague 1 and assume that Colleague 2 plays trigger. In the following we will show that this strategy will also be the best response of Colleague 1, provided she has a sufficiently high valuation of future payoffs. As both colleagues are in a symmetric position, the trigger strategy is strategically stable. Subsequently we will explain why this equilibrium also is subgame perfect.

As Colleague 1 knows that Colleague 2 will never cooperate anymore, as soon as she stops helping even once, her best response then is to also react in an uncooperative way. Assume that both parties helped each other during the last $(T-1)$ days. If Colleague 1 also adheres to the trigger strategy, then both parties will also collaborate in the future. Every day, Colleague 1 would receive a payoff of six units, resulting in a present value of $\frac{6}{1-\delta}$ units.[5] What would happen if Colleague 1 decides to be uncooperative on day T? On this day she would receive a payoff of seven units, but on all subsequent days only four units. The present value of her uncooperative behavior on day T would thus be $7 + \frac{4\delta}{1-\delta}$. units. Consequently, a cooperative behavior on day T is only beneficial for Colleague 1 if

$$\frac{6}{1-\delta} > 7 + \frac{4\delta}{1-\delta}.$$

The discount factor δ must be greater than $\frac{1}{3}$ so that the benefits of a cooperative behavior exceed those of an uncooperative behavior. The greater δ, the smaller is the incentive of the colleague to be uncooperative, because her future payoffs become more important. If the condition $\delta > \frac{1}{3}$ is satisfied, Colleague 1 will cooperate on the first day and on each further T-th day of the previously cooperative relationship. In our numerical example the trigger strategy is strategically stable, when $\delta > \frac{1}{3}$.

To show that the trigger strategy also induces a strategically stable behavior in all subconflicts, we group the infinite number of subconflicts into two classes. In the first class we only look at subconflicts with perfectly cooperative histories. The second class contains subconflicts with at least one day of uncooperative behavior. Remember, that all subconflicts, irrespective of their class, are identical to the total conflict, because each subconflict represents an infinite situation of conflict.

Let us now assume that on day 1, both colleagues decide to pursue the trigger strategy. Then, the induced strategies in each subconflict in the first class are also trigger strategies. These are, according to our argumentation above, strategically stable. The induced strategies in the second class of subconflicts stipulate an uncooperative behavior. But this is already a strategically stable behavior in the basic situation of the conflict. Hence, the trigger strategy is strategically stable not only for the total situation of conflict, but also for each possible subconflict, and thus constitutes an equilibrium strategy.

Although this enables a long-term relationship with the manifestation of cooperative behavior, we should be careful not to overrate this result.

1. The proposed trigger strategy is not the only behavior that corresponds to the principle of subgame perfection. In fact, a strategy of uncooperative behavior on every single day is also subgame perfect. With a sufficiently high discount factor, any pattern of cooperation and no cooperation can be supported as equilibrium behavior if the parties threaten to retaliate immediately with permanently uncooperative actions. This result can be generalized for each infinitely repeated situation of conflict: each payoff combination that guarantees each party at least the same payoff that she would also get in equilibrium in the basic situation, and which can be reached on the basis of the payoff structure, can be reached by a subgame perfect equilibrium in the infinitely repeated situation of conflict, provided the discount factor is sufficiently high. This result is known as the *folk theorem*. The condition that the payoff combination can be reached on the basis of the payoff structure means that the payoff combination can be described as a convex combination of payoffs of pure strategies in the basic situation.[6] The set of possible payoff combinations is therefore also referred to as a cooperative payoff region. Figure 5.3 depicts the complete set of possible payoff combina-

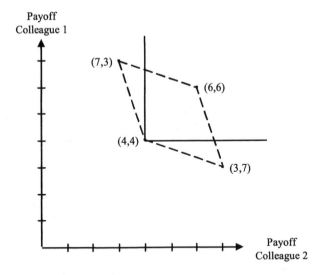

Figure 5.3. Payoff combinations that can be reached with subgame perfect equilibria of collaborating colleagues

tions as well as the specific set of those payoff combinations that can be reached with subgame perfect equilibria. The folk theorem states that there exists a multitude of strategically stable patterns of behavior when basic situations of conflict are repeated infinitely. A long-term relation between two organizational units does allow cooperative actions, although this behavior is not imperative. Which behavior the parties implicitly or explicitly agree upon depends on a number of other factors, which we did not yet consider in our model. In the following sections we will study two of the instruments that are necessary for successful self management: communication and bargaining.

2. The trigger strategy is not *renegotiation proof*. The threat of a colleague to retaliate is not credible, because with this behavior she would also punish herself. Not to cooperate reduces the payoff to four units, for both parties. This stands in contrast to a return to a mutually cooperative situation, where a payoff of six units would be possible. The parties therefore have an incentive not to punish their counterpart permanently. And thus there exists an incentive to renegotiate the previously agreed sanctions in order to collaborate again. Obviously, the possibility of renegotiation endangered the credibility of the trigger strategy. If both colleagues anticipate that a deviation of the cooperative behavior stays without consequences, both of them would have an incentive not to cooperative right at the beginning. In fact, in our example, the only renegotiation proof strategy would be not to cooperate from day 1 onwards. Renegotiations significantly constrain any room for cooperation.

3. Our argumentation for the strategic stability of the trigger strategy required that the basic situation of conflict has no definite end. Let us assume that the situation has a predetermined end, that is will only be played for certain number of periods (see Figure 5.4). Then there will be no incentive to cooperate, as we can show with the principle of backward induction. On the last day of their work relationship, both colleagues will always behave uncooperatively, irrespective of the previous course of conflict. But then any uncooperative behavior on the next to last day can not be punished on the last day anymore. Thus, the threat of sanctions lost its credibility and the parties will also not cooperate on the next to last day. We can continue this argumentation up to the first day of the relationship, effectively leading to a completely uncooperative behavior.

Out of our previous analysis we can deduct two conditions under which the cooperation is possible in a finitely repeated conflict. First, one of the two colleagues can credibly commit herself to the following trigger strategy: 'On day 1, choose to cooperate and repeat this until the other party deviates. Then, for the rest of the interaction, sabotage the work of the other.' As Figure 5.5 shows, sabotaging represents a third action in the basic situation of conflict, generating the following payoffs.

In this modified basic conflict there exist two strategically stable strategies. Both parties choose an uncooperative behavior and decide to sabotage

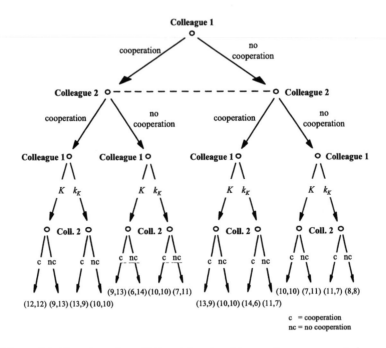

Figure 5.4. Situation of conflicting interests of two colleagues, repeated once, without discounting

	Employee 2		
	cooper- ation	no cooperation	sabo- tage
cooperation	6,6	3,7	0,2
Employee 1 no cooperation	7,3	4,4	1,2
sabotage	2,0	2,1	2,2

Figure 5.5. Modified basic conflict for the collaboration of two colleagues

the other's work. The trigger strategy specified above then has the following effect on the behavior of the parties. If the conflict is repeated once, then deviating from the cooperative behavior on day 1 leads to a payoff of two units for each party on day 2. A cooperation on day 1 leads to a payoff of four units on day 2, because both parties will decide not to cooperate. Adding the payoffs of both days generates the payoffs in Figure 5.6.

Employee 2

		cooper- ation	non- cooperation	sabo- tage
	cooperation	10,10	5,9	2,4
Employee 1	non- cooperation	9,5	6,6	3,4
	sabotage	4,2	4,3	4,4

Figure 5.6. Situation of conflict on the first day, if one of the colleagues can commit herself to sabotage on the second day

As one of the colleagues was able to commit herself to the trigger strategy, she will cooperate on the first day. The best response of the other party is to cooperate as well.

A second possibility to reach cooperative behavior in a finitely repeated conflict is to build up reputation. Assume that one party is uncertain whether her colleague really acts strategically. Specifically, she is wondering whether her colleague decided not to cooperate permanently, or whether she is following a different response pattern. In the later she can, for instance, assume that the colleague follows a Tit-for-Tat strategy: 'Cooperate on day 1 and then, on day T-1, choose the other party's alternative of the day before.' With a Tit-for-Tat strategy the colleague always imitates the other party with a lag of one day.

To what extent can this uncertainty about the strategy of the colleague lead to cooperative behavior? When a strategically acting colleague ever deviates from the Tit-for-tat strategy, the other party recognizes immediately that she does not adhere to a specific pattern of behavior. As explained above, the parties will then behave uncooperatively until the end of their relationship. Knowing this, the colleague has an incentive to imitate a player, who does in fact follow a fixed pattern of behavior. The best response of the uninformed party on the Tit-for-Tat strategy of the colleague can be to cooperate up to the last day of the work relationship. This depends on the payoff structure of the basic conflict and the probability with which the colleague follows the displayed strategy.

Considering all these limitations it seems to be quite a challenge to design a general framework of longer-term interactions between organizational units that induces cooperative behavior. However, we have to keep in mind that only the long duration of the relationship enables a cooperative behavior at all, either by building up trust, or reputation.

5.1.2 Communication

In the first part of this book we explained that a conflict of interest can exist despite cooperative interests of the parties involved. A typical example for this is the one-shot Prisoners' Dilemma, where the parties follow their own interest although this leads to a worse outcome than a joint pursuit of their cooperative interests. In such situations, in which a build-up of trust is not possible, the question arises how cooperative interests can nevertheless be supported. More specifically, as this is a coordination problem, one can ask to what extent communication between the parties before the actual conflict, commonly referred to as *pre-play communication*, changes the course of conflict.

In the cooperation dilemma the answer to this question is straightforward: communication between the parties has no effect on the course of conflict. Before the conflict both parties can assert they will cooperate, but as long as these promises are not binding, they will be insignificant when it actually comes to choosing the best response. The promises will be ignored, because uncooperative behavior always generates for both parties, irrespective of the other party's choice, a higher payoff than cooperation.

Considering the concept of equilibrium, this breakdown of communication in the cooperation dilemma is not surprising. The announcement of one party to choose a strategy that is not stable in equilibrium is simply not credible without commitment. As the announced behavior never represents a best response to the behavior of the other, there will always be an incentive to deviate from the announcement and to choose a more beneficial action.

We argued that communication without commitment can not influence the outcome of a conflict. But non-binding communication can nevertheless have a coordinating effect. In a situation of conflict, in which several equilibria exist in parallel, non-binding communication can be used by the parties as a *selection device*. This is obvious in a pure situation of cooperation. Pre-play the parties agree on that equilibrium which is payoff efficient, that is, which guarantees the highest payoff for each party. No party has an incentive to deviate from this non-binding agreement as there is no other action that could improve her situation.

What effect does non-binding communication have in situations where conflicting interest exists next to cooperative interests? Can the parties nevertheless self-manage on one equilibrium? Using two examples we will show to what extent coordination through communication is possible. In

Figure 5.7 there exist two equilibria in pure strategies. Both parties either decide on alternative A_1 or on alternative A_2. Party 1 prefers the former while Party 2 prefers the latter.

Party 2

		Alternative A_1	Alternative A_2
Party 1	Alternative A_1	3,1	0,0
	Alternative A_2	0,0	1,3

Figure 5.7. Situation of conflict with two leaders

Now, assume that party 1 says to Party 2 before the conflict: "Let's both choose alternative A_1." Which effect would this have on the actual behavior of the two parties? For simplicity let us assume that only Party 1 has the possibly to communicate pre-play. She can send Message M_1 'Let's both choose alternative A_1', or Message M_2 'Let's both choose alternative A_2'.

Figure 5.8 depicts this modified version, where Party 1 has four strategies: M_1A_1, M_1A_2, M_2A_1 and M_2A_2, where M denotes the message sent in pre-play communication, and A the action actually taken in the conflict. Party 2 also has four strategies A_1A_1, A_1A_2, A_2A_1 and A_2A_2, where, for instance, A_1A_2 denotes that she chooses Action 1 if Party 1 sent Message M_1 and Action 2 if Party 1 sent Message M_1. The following graph depicts this modified situation of conflict in its extensive form.

For each equilibrium in the original situation of conflict, there also exists an equilibrium in the modified version that leads to the same payoffs for both parties. Let us, for example, look at the equilibrium (M_2A_1, A_2A_1): Party 1 proposes Action A_2, but then chooses A_1. Party 2 decides in favor of A_1, but would have taken A_2, if Party 1 would have proposed Action A_1. This equilibrium guarantees Party 1 a payoff of three units and Party 2 receives one unit.

We call this equilibrium a *babbling equilibrium*. The announcement of a party has no impact on the real behavior of the parties. Thus, both parties treat pre-play communication as insignificant babbling. Despite the possibility of sending messages, none of the equilibria can be eliminated and there is no coordination by means of communication.

But this modified situation of conflict also has a prominent outcome (M_1A_1, A_1A_2): Party 1 proposes Action 1 and acts accordingly, and Party 2 adheres to Party 1's proposal. Again, Party 1 gains three units and Party

189

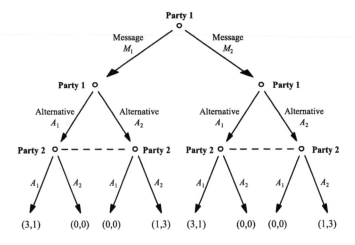

Figure 5.8. Situation of conflict with two leaders when pre-play communication is possible

2 only one unit. However, this is the only equilibrium where the announcement of Party 1 is actually implemented. Communication only supports coordination if both parties have a common understanding. Therefore, to effectively exclude Babbling Equilibria we have to make additional assumptions about such a common understanding, for example, about a common cultural background.

Up to now we only gave Party 1 the chance to announce an action. Now we assume a symmetric situation, where Party 2 can communicate as well. As the announcement of Party 1 leads to her most favored outcome, she will have an interest in breaking off any further communication so that Party 2 can not respond.

But in general this could lead to a very complex communication process with alternating announcements about their own actions or proposals for joint actions. To study the strategic behavior in such a situation, we have to expand our model to take account of this communication process. In the previous example we have seen that one-sided communication creates more equilibria than no communication. With two-sided communication we can expect an even greater multitude of equilibria. In the following we therefore choose a different path of analysis. First, we show which outcomes are possible with two-sided communication, and then we describe a simple communication mechanism, with which these outcomes can be realized.

Without the possibility of commitment, the parties will only communicate about strategically stable actions, as they know that the announcement of unstable behavior will be ignored in favor of better alternatives. We can therefore assume that, in the pre-play phase, the parties will only agree on payoffs that correspond to equilibrium behavior. Figure 5.9 exemplifies this with the conflict of two cowards.

Party 2

	Alternative A_1	Alternative A_2
Party 1 Alternative A_1	3,3	1,4
Alternative A_2	4,1	0,0

Figure 5.9. Situation of conflict with two cowards

In this situation of conflict there exist two pure equilibria (A_1,A_2) and (A_2,A_1) with the payoffs (1,4) and (4,1), respectively, as well as a mixed equilibrium – each party chooses one of her alternatives with a probability of $\frac{1}{2}$ – with the payoff (2,2). In Figure 5.10 the possible payoffs with communication lie within the convex hull of the three equilibrium payoffs.[7]

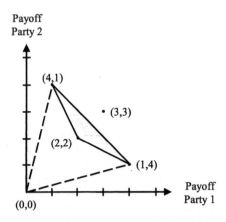

Figure 5.10. Payoff region in a situation of conflict with two cowards when pre-play communication is possible

Every point in this payoff region can be reached by randomization. Let us look at point $\left(2\frac{1}{2}, 2\frac{1}{2}\right)$. In pre-play communication both parties agree that a flip of the coin will determine the outcome of the situation of conflict and thus their behavior in the conflict. If heads comes up they agree on the strategy combination (A_1, A_2) and with tails on the strategy combination A_2, A_1. In a similar way they can also reach the payoff combination $\left(2\frac{3}{4}, 2\right)$:

$$\left(2\frac{3}{4}, 2\right) = \frac{1}{2}(4,1) + \frac{1}{4}(1,4) + \frac{1}{4}(2,2)$$

The two parties agree to determine the outcome of the conflict by flipping a coin twice. Two times heads result in (1,4), two times tails in (2,2), for all other cases they agree on (4,1). Each agreement represents a prominent outcome of the conflict, irrespective of the point that the parties choose in the above payoff region. For instance, if heads come up twice, (A_1, A_2) represent a prominent outcome. Although this is disappointing for Party 1 (she would rather have seen tails at least once), she will nevertheless anticipate that Party 2 will choose Action 2. This makes it optimal for Party 1 to adhere to the agreed behavior and choose A_1.

Which outcome the parties agree upon in the communication phase will be the result of a bargaining process. Based on the criterion of payoff efficiency we can conjecture that the parties will agree on a payoff combination that lies between the points (4,1) and (1,4).

Manipulation is of no interest, because any deviation from the announced behavior would lead to a more unfavorable outcome than the prominent outcome that the parties agreed upon in pre-play communication. Hence, in such a situation of conflict, where communication has a coordinating effect, the goal of every communicating party is to truthfully inform the other about her actions in order to align their actions.

Obviously, there are situations where parties want to manipulate through communication. To analyze this, we have to additionally assume that the communicating party has private information, which the other party can not directly verify. Depending on the type of private information, this party has an interest to appear in a better light than her information would actually allow her to. What role does communication play in such a situation? Will worse informed parties believe better informed parties at all?

In the first part of this book we already discussed these questions in connection with signaling games. A better informed party can communicate her private information convincingly, if she succeeds in revealing this information with supportive actions. In our example of further training for a motivated employee, the employee was able to prove her motivation and qualify herself for further training by showing a high effort in her job. To make this communication possible, three conditions had to be satisfied. The effort-related costs of the motivated employee had to be lower than the costs of an unmotivated employee. These were sunk costs that represented a non-recoupable prior investment. The quality of the work or chosen effort was verifiable by the supervisor.

But what happens in situations of conflict where these three prerequisites are not satisfied, that is, where the communication via supportive actions does not incur costs, may be reversed, or is not verifiable? Can the better informed party still communicate her private information credibly, despite the fact that the better informed party can only communicate with cheap talk?

If the better informed party does not succeed in signaling her superior information credibly, then cheap talk will not be informative in signaling games. In our example every employee is interested in further training, irrespective of her work motivation. If the supervisor had made her decision on the basis of an interview instead of the observed effort on the job, then she would not have been able to reliably reveal the motivation of the employee. Irrespective of the real motivation, the employee would have always communicated a positive work attitude in order to receive further training.

Therefore, if the better informed party has an interest that the worse informed party always reacts in the same way, irrespective of the former's type, then cheap talk can not be informative. Each party can imitate the type with the more beneficial information without any costs incurred and irrespective of her real information. Only if different types prefer different reactions from the informed party can the former credibly convey information to the latter with cheap talk.

5.1.3 Bargaining

Next to communication, bargaining represents an important instrument for the self management of parties in conflict. Particularly in allocation conflicts bargaining plays an important role between organizational units. Bargaining can be seen as a process where parties try to align their positions with offers, counteroffers, and concessions.

Allocation of financial resources in the marketing department

---

Two colleagues in a marketing department are responsible for the advertising campaigns of a brand new product. One colleague manages radio advertising, the other print advertising. The head of the department provides them with a single budget for print and radio advertising, which they are expected to allocate to the two advertising channels. As the two colleagues have no information about the relative impact of the two channels with regard to this new product, they both simply strive to get the biggest possible share for their own campaign. For the case where they do not come to terms, the head of marketing reserved the right to split the budget herself.

We assume that both parties bargain over the split of a budget of one unit. Figure 5.11 depicts the bargaining process:

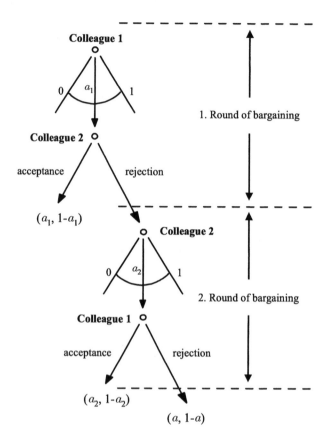

Figure 5.11. Bargaining process in the allocation of financial resources

- Colleague 1, who is responsible for radio advertising, opens the negotiation and proposes an offer $(a_1, 1 - a_1)$ where she receives a share a_1 and her Colleague 2 a share $1 - a_1$.
- Colleague 2, who is responsible for print advertising, decides to accept or decline the offer. In the first case, the bargaining process stops and she receives the share $1 - a_1$ of the total budget and Colleague 1 gets a_1. If Colleague 2 declines the offer, the process continues to a second round.
- In this second round, Colleague 2 makes a counteroffer $(a_2, 1 - a_2)$ where she receives the share $1 - a_2$ and Colleague 1 the share a_2.

- Subsequently Colleague 1 can accept or decline this counteroffer. If she declines, the head of marketing will split the budget.
- If the head of marketing has to split the budget, she will assign a share a of the budget to radio advertising and a share $1 - a$ to print, with $a \in (0,1)$. Both colleagues know this split at the start of the process.

Each unsuccessful bargaining round delays the advertising campaigns by a few days. This leads to opportunity costs for the company. We assume that the present value of the total budget decreases with each bargaining round by a discount factor $\delta \in (0,1)$ The present value of the budget after one unsuccessful round is δ and after an unsuccessful second round only δ^2 units.

How are the two colleagues going to behave in this situation of conflict? Are they going to agree on a split, and if yes, at which point in the process are they going to do this? Or will the head of marketing solve this conflict in the end? To answer these questions we will analyze the behavior of the two colleagues with backward induction.

Let us first look at the optimal offer of Colleague 2 in the second bargaining round. If her offer is declined, then Colleague 1 will definitely receive the share a in the third round of the process. In the second round of the process, this share has a value of δa. Colleague 1 will thus accept an offer from Colleague 2 that guarantees her a share $a_2 \geq \delta a$. Let us assume Colleague 2 wants to make an offer that her colleague will accept. Then she maximizes her payoff if she offers $a_2 = \delta a$ to Colleague 1. Her own payoff then is $1 - \delta a$. Then the present value of her share of the marketing head's allocation is $\delta(1 - a)$. This is less than $1 - \delta a$. Hence, if the second bargaining is reached, then the optimal offer from Colleague 2 is $a_2^* = \delta a$.

Let us now look at the optimal split of the total budget as offered by Colleague 1 in the first bargaining round. Anticipating the second round, she knows that Colleague 2 will receive $1 - a_2^*$ in the second round, if Colleague 2 declines her offer in the first round. The present value of this payoff in the first round is $\delta(1 - a_2^*)$. Therefore, in the first round, Colleague 2 will accept all offers from Colleague 1 where $1 - a_1 \geq \delta(1 - a_2^*)$ or, seen from the perspective of Colleague 1, where $a_1 \leq 1 - \delta(1 - a_2^*)$. If Colleague 1 wants her offer to be accepted she can receive a maximum payoff of $1 - \delta(1 - a_2^*)$. If she offers $a_1 > 1 - \delta(1 - a_2^*)^*$ and her offer is declined by Colleague 2, she will receive δa_2^*. As $\delta a_2^* < 1 - \delta(1 - a_2^*)^*$, it is optimal for Colleague 1 to offer a split $(a_1^*, 1 - a_1^*)$ with $a_1^* = 1 - \delta(1 - \delta a)$ in the first round.

The principle of backward induction enables a predictable outcome of the situation of conflict. Both colleagues will agree on an allocation of the budget in the first round. Colleague 1 will offer an optimal sharing rule, which Colleague 2 will accept. The optimal allocation will be a share $1 - \delta(1 - \delta a)$ for Colleague 1 and $\delta(1 - \delta a)$ for Colleague 2.

This bargaining solution is strongly influenced by the allocation of the head of marketing if she is forced to intervene in round 3. She does not fully delegate the splitting of the budget by reserving the right of arbitration. This poses the question, what would happen if the head of marketing pulled herself out of the bargaining process altogether, that is if she would fully delegate the authority of budget allocation to the two colleagues.

The bargaining process would change as follows. Instead of an exogenous budget split in round 3 the bargaining process would proceed with an infinite sequence of alternating offers (3a), (3b), (4a), (4b), and so on. Their structure would be analogous to the first two rounds. In every uneven round Colleague 1 would make an offer that Colleague 2 could accept or reject, and vice versa in every even round. This goes on until one of the two accepts the offer by the other party.

As in the previously discussed infinite situation of conflict we can not use the principle of backward induction to analyze the behavior of the parties, because there is no last bargaining round anymore. But we can deduce a solution by dividing the bargaining process in such a way that it fits into the analysis of the finite example. The structure of the bargaining process from the third round onwards, provided that this round is reached at all, is identical with the structure at the beginning of the bargaining situation: Colleague 1 is making an offer, after that the colleagues alternate in making offers until one of these is accepted by the other side.

Let us assume that the bargaining process over three rounds results in a sharing rule $(a, 1 - a)$. Using our above argumentation, we can then substitute the infinite bargaining process that starts in round three with the payoff of the finite process. We then find that the structure of the infinite bargaining process is similar to the finite process discussed above. In particular, this allows us to come back to the principle of backward induction and to infer the behavior in the first bargaining round from the third round. As discussed above, Colleague 1 will successfully offer a share of $1 - \delta(1 - \delta a)$ units for herself and a share of $\delta(1 - \delta a)$ units for Colleague 2 in the first round.

Let a_H and a_L denote the highest and lowest share, respectively, that Colleague 1 can ever reach as a result of a subgame perfect equilibrium. Because of backward induction the highest and lowest payoff of Colleague 1 in the first bargaining round then are $1 - \delta(1 - \delta a_H)$ and $1 - \delta(1 - \delta a_L)$, respectively. As a_H and a_L are also the highest and lowest share in the bargaining situation, it follows:

$$1 - \delta(1 - \delta a_H) = a_H, \text{ that is } a_H = \frac{1}{1 + \delta} \text{ and}$$

$$1 - \delta(1 - \delta a_L) = a_L, \text{ that is } a_L = \frac{1}{1 + \delta}$$

Therefore, the bargaining process has a unique subgame perfect outcome. In the first round Colleague 1 makes the offer to allocate the budget such that she receives $\frac{1}{1+\delta}$, while Colleague 2 gets the share $\frac{\delta}{1+\delta}$. The latter accepts the offer. If the discount factor is 1, there will be no discounting at all and each colleague receives one half of the budget.

This outcome implies that the two parties can cooperatively solve their allocation conflict in the very first round. Note that the party that starts the process by making the first offer has a strategic advantage: she has the opportunity to make a strategic move with which she can maneuver the second party into a position where she just accepts the offer. The second party is in a strategically unfavorable position as her rejection of the first offer (in order to make a more favorable counteroffer) leads to a delay and thus to a discounted, that is lower, total budget.

5.2 EXTERNAL MANAGEMENT BY LEADERSHIP

In previous sections we assumed that the conflict manager has no direct responsibilities as a superior authority with regard to the (self) manage- ment of the organizational units, with the exception of a possible mediating function. However, we have seen that self management does not always lead to goal-oriented collaboration. In contrast to vertical conflicts, the manager of lateral conflicts does not act as a superior authority that manages con- flicts of interest with the help of orders and guidelines. But the lateral conflict manager can use other measures to create a favorable environment for cooperation: mediation or organizational design.

As mediator the conflict manager only acts when the parties in conflict request her to. They themselves want her to change the outcome of the conflict to their joint benefit. Mediation, as a form of conflict management, has to satisfy two requirements. First, mediation has to be in line with the goals of the organization and must effectively increase the organization's ability to achieve these goals. Second, due to the general framework of the situation, an alternative vertical conflict management must be impossible or at least less effective.

In its simplest form, mediation just secures the equilibrium. The parties are in a pure cooperative situation in which several forms of coordination are possible. If the parties, despite payoff efficiency, can not agree on one of several strategically stable behaviors, a mediator can positively influence the coordination result by proposing an equilibrium. With this proposal the mediator introduces a focal point that coordinates the parties' expectations about their behavior.

Mediation becomes more difficult in situations of both competing and cooperative interests. If several equilibria exist then the proposal of a focal point mostly entails a disadvantage to one of the two parties. In such situations the mediator not only has to evaluate whether the outcome is efficient, but also has to appraise the competing interests of the parties with regard to the overall organizational goal. In particular, the mediator has to take great care that the proposal is acceptable to both parties.

An organizational designer creates institutional frameworks that support or enable the joint execution of tasks by the parties in conflict. At the same time the organizational designer makes sure that the parties' coordinated actions correspond to the goals of the organization as a whole.

This form of conflict management represents a general solution to the organizational problem. By considering interdependences and competing interests between the organizational units, the organizational designer solves both incentive and coordination problems. Next to the design of organizational structures and processes, this can also include the organization of information and communication systems or of incentive systems.

5.2.1 Designing Commitment Devices

In the last section we explained that communication alone does not always have a positive influence on the outcome of a conflict. For instance, in the cooperation dilemma, communication without commitment to the joint agreement does not solve the dilemma at all. The situation would be different if the parties could first write and sign a contract on the agreement. We illustrate this with the following example.

Minimal attendance in a work group

In a medium-sized company a secretary pool is responsible for much of the paperwork. They work with flextime such that each secretary can pick her favorite working time within a certain range. However, there is a minimal attendance requirement during core hours. To ensure minimal attendance in these core hours, the secretaries jointly coordinate who works when and how often: every Friday the secretaries meet and fix the attendance plan for the following week. Due to sickness or other unforeseen reasons it sometimes happens that one of the secretaries can not come as planned. The plan then provides for a colleague to jump in on short notice. Understandably, these emergency shifts are not very popular. The manager of the secretary pool fears that some of the secretaries may exploit such a stand-in procedure to the detriment of more considerate colleagues. This could create a bad working climate or even lead to the termination of the flextime model altogether. To prevent this, the manager makes the following arrangement with the secretary pool: if a secretary calls in sick for several times in a certain period without compensating her colleagues accordingly, she will receive up to three formal warnings and finally be dismissed.

Without the arrangement the secretary pool is confronted with a cooperation dilemma (see Figure 5.12). For simplicity, let us look at two secretaries only.

Secretary 2

		cooper-ation	non-cooper-ation
Secretary 1	cooperation	2,2	0,5
	non-cooperation	5,0	1,1

Figure 5.12. The cooperation dilemma of the secretaries

Each of the secretaries can choose between a cooperative and an uncooperative strategy. Cooperation means that a secretary jumps in when a colleague calls in sick. When choosing the alternative, that is not to cooperate, the secretary will try to make excuses why it is not possible for her to jump in this time. A mutually cooperative strategy would be beneficial for both secretaries; however, self interest leads to the worse, non-cooperative outcome of the conflict.

The arrangement with the manager can solve this cooperation dilemma, because it binds the secretaries to a cooperatives behavior. For this it is irrelevant whether the commitment is explicit in the form of a legal contract or implicit in the form of an informal agreement. In both cases it is necessary that the manager oversees the secretaries' compliance with the contract. This poses two conditions to the general framework of the situation of conflict. First, the compliance with the contract must be observable; second, the manager must be able to sanction non-compliance, that is, she must be able and willing to dismiss shirking secretaries after three formal warnings.

How does the possibility of binding the secretaries to a cooperative behavior affect their working hours? We assume again that the pool consists of two secretaries and model the contract with the manager as follows: if both secretaries sign the new contract with the manager then they commit themselves to behave cooperatively; however, if one secretary does not sign the contract then both will behave uncooperatively. As Figure 5.13 shows, this extends the strategic form of the situation of conflict with the signing of a binding contract as an additional action for both secretaries.

This modified version of the conflict has one equilibrium only: both secretaries will sign the contract and act cooperatively. But there exists an even better payoff for both secretaries. In principle, they can contractually

Secretary 2

		cooper- ation	non- cooper- ation	sign contract
Secretary 1	cooperation	2,2	0,5	0,5
	non- cooperation	5,0	1,1	1,1
	sign contract	5,0	1,1	2,2

Figure 5.13. The cooperation dilemma of the secretaries with an additional option to sign a binding contract

agree on anything more beneficial, provided that it guarantees the min-imal attendance in core hours. The secretaries could, for instance, agree on the following lottery. After signing the contract they flip a coin. Heads allows Secretary 1 to behave uncooperatively and Secretary 2 to behave cooperatively; and vice versa with tails. The secretaries can then expect the following payoff:

$$\frac{1}{2}(0,5) + \frac{1}{2}(5,0) = \left(2\frac{1}{2}, 2\frac{1}{2}\right).$$

Hence, the two secretaries could get a higher payoff than in the purely cooperative equilibrium. In general, this approach allows any payoff in the cooperative payoff region. Each payoff in the cooperative payoff region can be reached with a convex payoff combination of pure strategy combinations. In our example, all payoff combinations in the bi-matrix of the cooperation dilemma (Figure 5.12) define the cooperative payoff region in Figure 5.14. If the secretaries have the opportunity to agree by contract which pure strategy they are going to pursue, then they can reach any point in this cooperative payoff region. We can thus interpret each of these points as a probability distribution $(\alpha_{11}, \alpha_{12}, \alpha_{21}, \alpha_{22})$ over the set of all pure strategy combinations. Such a probability distribution is referred to as *correlated strategy*.

The possibility of writing a binding contract allows the parties to agree on a random mechanism that conditions their hitherto independent decisions on each other. Without a superior authority that enforces this contract, a correlated strategy would not be followed: if this strategy is not an equilib-rium strategy, at least one of the parties would have an incentive to deviate from the non-enforceable agreement after the random draw is done.

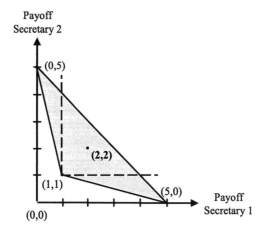

Figure 5.14. The cooperative payoff region of the cooperation dilemma

On which correlated strategy will the parties agree? Figure 5.15 shows a general correlated strategy for our example.

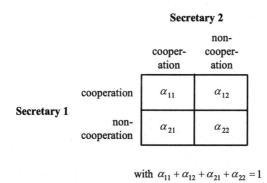

with $\alpha_{11} + \alpha_{12} + \alpha_{21} + \alpha_{22} = 1$

Figure 5.15. A general correlated strategy for the cooperation dilemma

First, we can exclude all payoff combinations where a party would receive less than in the non-cooperative equilibrium. An agreement that is permitted for a correlated strategy therefore has to satisfy the incentive compatibility constraint of each party. For example, a secretary would never agree to a contract, where she will commit herself always to cooperate while her colleague can choose never to cooperate. With such a contract the secretary would receive a payoff of no units. However, if she does not agree to

201

the contract she can at least get a payoff of one unit. In the above figure, the set of permitted correlated strategies is defined by a triangle with the corners $(1,1)$, $(4,1)$, and $(1,4)$.[8]

Which of the permitted correlated strategies the parties will actually implement is normally determined in more or less complex contract negotiations. The bargaining process we described in one of the previous sections on self management would, for instance, result in a correlated strategy with $\alpha_{12} = \alpha_{21} = \frac{1}{2}$. The expected payoff would then be $2\frac{1}{2}$ units for each party.

5.2.2 Providing Information

In the previous section we assumed that the organizational units could commit themselves contractually to their agreements. Some superior authority guaranteed the compliance with these contractual commitments. It was therefore possible for the organizational units to agree on a solution of the conflict situation that was advantageous for them and for the organization. Leadership in this sense helps significantly to establish cooperation and coordination.

In many conflicts the enforcement of a contract poses problems to the supervisor. Two distinct problems can arise: either the compliance with the contract can not be observed, and thus also not be controlled by the supervisor, or the supervisor does not possess adequate possibilities to sanction in order to discourage deviations from agreements. If, due to the framework of the situation of conflict, one of those two problems is present, the contractual agreement has no binding effect anymore.

The advantage of joint research

Two employees in the research and development department of a firm are supposed to collaborate on a research project. Both know that the success of the research project depends on the effort they invest. In principle, they are striving to contribute high effort to the project. But both also know that a high effort of the other would also contribute significantly to the success from the project, even if oneself is just working on a routine level. Both would in fact prefer to rely on the effort of the other. But in that case, the success of the project would be jeopardized. Prior to the start of the project both employees consider how they could eventually capture any benefits from joint research in such a situation. A binding contract would be the best solution, because both parties would commit themselves to contribute a high effort level. However, both also know that such a contract would not have any effect on their behavior, because their supervisor would not be able to assess their respective research input and would therefore also not be able to enforce the contract. Another solution seems to make sense here: the supervisor should tell both, whether their specific contribution is important or less important for the success of the project. She should emphasize the importance of at least one of the two employees' contribution. The supervisor may tell something different to the two employees. Here it is important that she does not reveal what she told the other employee. Both employees will use the information of the supervisor as a recommendation for their behavior. If their contribution is important, this implies that they should provide a high effort, otherwise a routine effort is sufficient.

Why should this agreement between the two researchers help to find a solution to this problem of cooperation? Figure 5.16 specifies the situation of conflict.

Researcher 2

		high effort	low effort
Researcher 1	high effort	3,3	1,4
	low effort	4,1	0,0

Figure 5.16. Research cooperation as a situation of conflict with two leaders

In this strategic form of the situation of conflict there are three equilibria: Employee 1 chooses a low effort and Employee 2 chooses a high effort. Or reversed, Employee 1 chooses a high effort and Employee 2 chooses a low effort. Or both parties choose one of their alternatives with a probability of 50 percent. In the last case they would both get a payoff of two units. The mutually best payoff combination of (3,3) can not be achieved, since this is not a result of equilibrium behavior and contractual agreements are also not enforceable.

Suppose that the two employees inform their supervisor about their ideas of how to improve the research cooperation. Of course, it will be in the interest of the supervisor to support this proposal, as she is also interested in a high effort contribution from both researchers. What are the consequences of her mediation on the cooperation of the two employees? Suppose prior to her mediation the supervisor determined the value of the employees' effort contributions as follows: with a probability of $\frac{1}{3}$ she tells both employees that their effort is important; with a probability of $\frac{1}{3}$ she tells this to either one of the two employees.

Although the message of the supervisor has no binding consequences for the actions of the two employees, it nevertheless leads to a more advantageous equilibrium in the modified situation of conflict, in which both employees will follow the recommendation.

In order to see this let us first consider the case in which the supervisor tells Employee 1 that his effort is important for the project. The employee knows that the supervisor will tell the other employee with equal probability that the other's effort is important, or that it is not important. Therefore Employee 1 will be indifferent between her two actions and will expect a payoff of two units from both alternatives.

In case the supervisor informs Employee 1 that her effort is less important for the project, Employee 1 can conclude that her colleague will be informed about the high importance of her contribution to the project. Therefore a low effort is the best response to her colleague's high effort.

In both cases Employee 1 will adhere to the agreement and take the supervisor's recommendation as an indicator for her agreed-upon effort. Since this holds analogously also for Employee 2, we find that both employees can come to a self-supporting agreement about the future situation of conflict if the supervisor lives up to her attributed role of a mediator. Both employees can expect the following payoff:

$$\frac{1}{3}(1,4) + \frac{1}{3}(3,3) + \frac{1}{3}(4,1) = \left(2\frac{2}{3}, 2\frac{2}{3}\right)$$

The parties' agreement is thus more advantageous than the equilibrium in mixed strategies. It is also more advantageous than the agreement to coordinate behavior with the help of flipping a coin, because this would lead to an expected payoff of $2\frac{1}{2}$ units for each party.

But the suggested solution to the coordination problem requires the mediating participation of the supervisor. If the supervisor, for example, revealed to Employee 1 what she told her colleague about the importance of the latter's effort, then Employee 1 would choose low effort although the supervisor also told her that her effort is important for the project's success. Only the partial private information each party receives makes the solution advantageous.

The suggested self-enforcing solution is less advantageous than a contractual agreement. If the two employees could commit to their behavior prior to the start of the joint project, each party could earn a payoff of three units.

This leads to the question whether the suggested solution could be improved by any alternative self-enforcing agreement. According to our previously introduced terminology we are looking for a correlated strategy that maximizes the joint payoff of the parties and additionally is also self-enforcing. In this sense such a strategy can be denoted as the parties' correlated strategically stable strategy. No employee has an incentive to deviate from the supervisor's recommendation.

For this purpose consider the general correlated strategy $(\alpha_{11}, \alpha_{12}, \alpha_{21}, \alpha_{22})$ in Figure 5.17.

**Recommendation of the
supervisor for Employee 2**

		effort is important	effort is un-important
Recommendation of the supervisor for Employee 1	effort is important	α_{11}	α_{12}
	effort is unimportant	α_{21}	α_{22}

with $\alpha_{11} + \alpha_{12} + \alpha_{21} + \alpha_{22} = 1$

Figure 5.17. A correlated strategy as a recommendation for the research cooperation

The joint payoff of the two employees is given as $6\alpha_{11} + 5\alpha_{12} + 5\alpha_{21}$. The correlated strategy would be self-enforcing if none of the two parties had an incentive to deviate from the recommendation. This can be specified by the following incentive compatibility conditions:

$$3\alpha_{11} + \alpha_{12} \geq 4\alpha_{11}$$

$$4\alpha_{21} \geq 3\alpha_{21} + 4\alpha_{22}$$

$$3\alpha_{11} + \alpha_{21} \geq 4\alpha_{11}$$

$$4\alpha_{12} \geq 3\alpha_{12} + \alpha_{22}$$

The first two conditions concern the behavior of Employee 1, the last two the behavior of Employee 2. For example, the first inequality establishes that a high effort from Player 1 will lead to a higher payoff for her than a low effort, when the supervisor tells her that her effort is important to the project's success. If she conforms to the agreement and invests a high effort, she receives a payoff of three units with probability α_{11} and a payoff of one unit with probability α_{12}. If she deviates from the agreement and chooses a low effort, she earns four units with probability α_{11}. The conditions for Employee 2 can be interpreted analogously. The last inequality for example establishes the incentives for Employee 2 when the supervisor tells her that her effort is not important for the project's success. When conforming to the agreement and choosing a low effort, she can expect a payoff of four units with probability α_{12}. If she chooses a high effort instead she would get an expected payoff of $3\alpha_{21} + \alpha_{22}$.

Due to the symmetry of the relation between the two employees it must be that $\alpha_{12} = \alpha_{21}$ holds in the optimum. The two incentive constraints for each employee are therefore identical and can be reduced to $\alpha_{12} \geq \alpha_{22}$ and $\alpha_{12} \geq \alpha_{11}$. Since a low effort from both employees would lead to a payoff of no units, we find $\alpha_{22} = 0$. Taking into account that the sum of all probabilities adds up to one, the joint payoff is given as $-6 - 2\alpha_{12}$. As it is optimal to reduce α_{12} as much as possible, that is, $\alpha_{12} = \alpha_{11}$, the above suggested correlated strategy with $\alpha_{11} = \alpha_{12} = \alpha_{21} = \frac{1}{3}$ constitutes an optimum. The maximum possible payoff of three units for each player with a contractual agreement is thus not achievable.

So far we have assumed that the supervisor mediates at the beginning of the situation of conflict. She gives the two parties a recommendation for their behavior that, if it is incentive compatible, will be followed by both parties, and will thus lead to better cooperation and coordination. In this case she can not determine the timing of her intervention. In general it is important at which point in time the supervisor intervenes. The example in Figure 5.18 illustrates this.

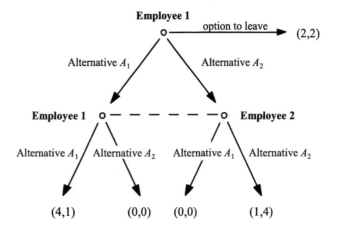

Figure 5.18. A situation of conflict with two leaders and the option to leave

In this dynamic situation of conflict Employee 1 has the possibility to either risk confrontation with Employee 2 or to avoid it. In the second case she chooses to leave and receives a payoff of two units. In the first case she has to decide between alternatives A_1 and A_2. Since she can expect a payoff of one unit at maximum when choosing A_2, she will never choose this alternative. The option to leave strictly dominates alternative A_2. Therefore, when making her decision, Employee 2 can assume that her colleague has chosen alternative A_1. In this case she would also choose A_1. This results in a payoff of four units as opposed to two units when taking the option to leave. Employee 2 then expects to receive one unit.

In this situation the supervisor could improve the joint payoff of the two employees by the mediation plan in Figure 5.19. First, the supervisor

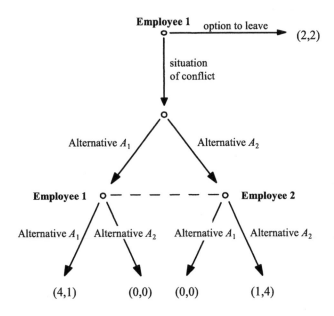

Figure 5.19. Modified situation of conflict with two leaders and the option to leave

instructs Employee 1 not to take the option to leave. Only if the employee follows this suggestion does she proceed to recommend the following. With a probability of $\frac{1}{2}$ she recommends both employees to choose alternative A_1, with a probability of $\frac{1}{2}$ she recommends both to choose alternative A_2. With this mediation both parties would earn an expected payoff of $\frac{1}{2} \cdot 1 + \frac{1}{2} \cdot 4 = 2\frac{1}{2}$, which is more than they could earn if Employee 1 opted to leave. Since no party has an incentive to deviate from the supervisor's recommendation, the mediation plan is strategically stable.

The timing of the supervisor's recommendations is essential for the success of the mediation. If the supervisor told the employees right at the beginning of the situation of conflict whether she will suggest alternative A_1 or A_2 at a later stage, we would be back in the original situation of conflict. Only the fact that Employee 1 receives the recommendation for A_1 or A_2 after she has already decided not to leave, makes the supervisor's recommendation incentive compatible.

5.2.3 Mechanism Design

In the previous sections we focused on one-sided communication between the parties in conflict and the superior authority. The supervisor as a mediator informs the parties partially, which improves coordination and cooperation. In this situation, one-sided communication represented an appropriate and sufficient conflict management instrument. As the organizational units did not possess any private information, the supervisor was able to determine the optimal communication system and then inform the parties in conflict accordingly.

In the following we will now analyze the role of conflict management in situations where the parties do possess private information that is relevant for the set-up of their work relation. Certainly, the supervisor will try to consider an individual party's private information in her communication to all parties. The communication process between the parties in conflict and the supervisor are therefore bilateral: the parties inform the supervisor about their private information and she in turn incorporates this information and informs the parties about the general framework of their collaboration.

In this sense we can interpret the task of the supervisor as designing a situation of conflict under incomplete information. The game-theoretical literature refers to this task as *mechanism design*: the supervisor as principal designs a mechanism and communicates it to the agents as subordinate parties. This mechanism specifies the general framework of a situation of conflict, in which the agents are called upon to provide their private information. This information then determines the actual form of collaboration between the agents.

Awarding a customer's order

Two production plants in the same company are directly competing for customer orders. They both produce the same products and then deliver them to the company's central division for sales and distribution. The plants' success depends on their internal prices that they get from the central sales and distribution division. Most prices are negotiated up-front, particularly for larger orders. The success of the sales and distribution division depends on the spread between the price quoted to the customer and the production units' prices. As the sales and distribution unit does not know the production costs of any of the plants, it tenders the customer order to both plants and decides on the basis of their internal offers.

How should the customer order be awarded on the basis of the production plants' offer? The search for the optimal method to allocate the customer order is the search for an optimal mechanism. We will determine the optimal design of this mechanism based on the following specifications.

The customer order has a production volume of 100 units. The capacity of each of the plant would be big enough for such an order. Their cost structure is linear with constant marginal costs k and without any fixed costs. The marginal costs of Plant 1 and Plant 2 are private information, which we denote k_1 and k_2 respectively. The marginal costs can be either one or two units and both are equally likely; thus have a probability of 0.5 each. This is common knowledge.

If the sales and distribution division knew about the marginal costs, the assignment of the customer order would be simple: at equal costs it would split the order between the two plants and at different marginal costs it would award the contract to the cheaper plant. With a chance of 0.25 the costs would be 200 units $(0.5 * 0.5)$, and with a chance of 0.75 the costs would be 100 units $(1 - 0.5 * 0.5)$. On average, the expected costs of the customer order would be 125 units.

However, if the sales and distribution division is uncertain about the real production costs of the plants, it can not use this simple allocation rule anymore. Let us assume that the central division would ask both plants up-front about their costs and then award the order. Then both plants would always communicate high costs, irrespective of their real costs. Assume Plant 1 has costs of two units. Then it would report this, because there is no incentive to report lower costs: otherwise it could happen that the other plant also reports lower costs and then Plant 1 would make a loss of 50 units on a split order. This loss would even increase to 100 units if the other plant should report high costs.

Now assume that Plant 1 really has low production costs. If it reports this truthfully the plant would have to produce at marginal costs and make no profit. If it reported high costs instead, the plant could expect a profit: with a probability of more than 0.5 the other plant will also report high costs. The order is then split and Plant 1 will make a profit of 50 units. As the situation is symmetric, both plants will always report high costs and the central division always faces total costs of 200 units.

The central division can only improve this situation if it can motivate both plants to report their real production costs. The revelation principle guarantees that the central division can resort to a mechanism that induces honest and direct information.[nine]

- If both plants report high costs, the order is split and the central division pays a price of two units/piece.
- If both plants report low costs, the order is also split and the central division pays a price of p_1/piece, $p_1 \geq 1$.
- If one plant reports high costs and the other low costs, the more efficient plant gets the order for a price of p_2/unit, with $p_2 \geq 1$.

Figure 5.20 shows the revenues of the two plants when this mechanism is implemented. The amounts in the matrix represent the payments or revenues that the plant receives from the central division. These revenues do not incorporate production costs. The net payoff or profit of the plant would additionally depend on the fact as to whether the reported costs correspond with the real costs or not.

		Production unit 2	
		reports low costs	reports high costs
Production unit 1	reports low costs	$50p_1, 50p_1$	$100p_2, 0$
	reports high costs	$0, 100p_2$	$100, 100$

Figure 5.20. Revenues of the production plants

We will now examine under which conditions the above mentioned mechanism induces an honest reporting of the two plants.[10] For simplicity we assume that Plant 2 always reports truthfully. Figure 5.21 shows the expected (net) payoffs of Plant 1.

		Real production cost	
		low	high
Reported production cost	low	$25(p_1 - 1)$ $+50(p_2 - 1)$	$25(p_1 - 2)$ $+50(p_2 - 2)$
	high	25	0

Figure 5.21. Net payoffs (profits) of Plant 1 if Plant 2 always reports truthfully

Assume that Plant 1 has high costs. Truthful reporting generates no profit: either the other plant reports low costs and gets the order, or the order is split and Plant 1 produces at marginal costs. If the plant pretends to have low costs then the expected payoff will be: with a probability of 0.5 the other plant has low production costs, the order will be split, and the (net) payoff will be $50 (p_1 - 2)$. In the alternative case the other plant reports high costs and the payoff will be $100 (p_2 - 2)$. A truthful reporting of the real costs therefore requires that the following incentive compatibility constraint is satisfied:

$$0 \geq \frac{1}{2} \cdot 50 (p_1 - 2) + \frac{1}{2} \cdot 100 (p_2 - 2)$$

Now assume that Plant 1 has low marginal costs. If the plant reports this truthfully it can reckon on the full order – with a chance of 0.5 that the other plant has high costs – and on a respective payoff of $100 (p_2 - 1)$ However, with a chance of 0.5 the other plant also has low marginal costs. In that case the order will be split and the payoff for Plant 1 is $50 (p_1 - 1)$ If Plant 1 pretends to have high production costs it would receive half the order with a probability of 0.5, and thus could expect a payoff of 25 units. The second incentive compatibility constraint guarantees that Plant 1 truthfully informs the central division about the real marginal costs also when these are low.

$$\frac{1}{2} \cdot 50 (p_1 - 1) + \frac{1}{2} \cdot 100 (p_2 - 1) \geq 25$$

If both incentive compatibility constraints are satisfied both parties will report their real production costs. The central division will try to specify the parameters of the mechanism such that the internal purchasing costs are minimized. The central division's expected costs are:

$$100 \left(\frac{1}{4} p_1 + \frac{1}{2} p_2 + \frac{1}{4} \cdot 2 \right).$$

With a probability of 0.25, both plants have low costs and receive a price p_1. p_1 per produced unit. With the same probably both plants have high costs of two units. And with a probability of 0.5 one of the two plants has low costs and receives the full order at a price p_2. The expected costs that the central division wants to minimize thus are $25p_1 + 50p_2$. Further, the second incentive compatibility constraint requires that $25p_1 + 50p_2 \geq 100$. In the optimum this constraint will be satisfied with equality, that is $p_1 + 2p_2 = 4$, and the expected costs of the central division will be 150 units. The first incentive compatibility constraint is automatically satisfied, because $p_1 + p_2 < 4$.

With this we have defined the basis for a number of mechanisms that induce a truthful reporting of the real production costs and minimize the costs of the central division: each pair of transfer prices (p_1, p_2), that satisfies the condition $p_1 + 2p_2 = 4$ characterizes such a mechanism.

Our argumentation does not yet take account of the fact that such a mechanism can also induce other strategically stable equilibria, next to the equilibrium where it is strategically stable to report truthfully. If the central division wants to make sure that there exists a unique equilibrium, the mechanism has to satisfy additional constraints.[11]

Assume Plant 2 always reported high costs. Then we would have to prevent Plant 1 from having an incentive to report high costs, too. Otherwise the unconditional reporting of high costs would be a strategically stable behavior. If Plant 1 has low costs and reports this truthfully, it can expect the complete order and will have a payoff of $100 (p_2 - 1)$. If the plant pretends to have high costs instead, the order will be split and Plant 1 can expect a payoff of 50 units. Therefore, the central division must ensure that

$$100 (p_2 - 1) \geq 50$$

to exclude that both plants always report high costs. This condition can be reduced to $p_2 \geq 1\frac{1}{2}$.

On the other hand, the central division also has to make sure that none of the two plants has an advantage in always reporting low costs. In fact, if $p_2 = 2$ and $p_1 = 0$, then this would also lead to a strategically stable behavior: Plant 2 always reports low costs, while Plant 1 always reports high costs. If Plant 1 reports low costs it would, according to the mechanism, receive no payment and incur a loss of 50 units. Consequently it would always quote high costs and make a profit, provided Plant 2 always reports low costs. Although Plant 2 receives no payment, it is not worse off than with the alternative of producing half an order at marginal costs, which also results in a profit of no units. To exclude this strategically stable behavior of both plants, p_2 must be smaller than two.

We can now specify a single mechanism that induces the quoting of real costs. If both plants report low costs, then the order is split and the central division pays a price that just covers marginal costs, that is $p_1 = 1$. If one plant reports low costs, while the other reports high costs, the one with the lower costs gets the complete order at a price that reflects the average production costs, that is $p_2 = 1\frac{1}{2}$. And if both plants report high costs, the central division awards the order to both plants at marginal production costs.[12]

5.3 LITERATURE NOTES

The literature on repeated game is substantial. Stigler (1964) was one of the first who studied retaliation as a possible explanation for collusion in oligopolistic markets. Green and Porter (1984) as well as Abreu, Pearce and Stacchetti (1986) formalized and extended these ideas in a game-theoretic context. Aumann (1986, 1989), Mertens (1987), as well as Mertens, Sorin and Zamir (1990) provide survey articles for repeated games.

Friedman (1971) developed the folk theorem, which was then generalized by Rubinstein (1979) and Fudenberg and Maskin (1986). A detailed discussion can be found in Fudenberg and Tirole (1991). The literature on renegotiation of contracts is based on works from Coase (1937) and Williamson (1985), who study this problem in connection with the question as to whether an economic transaction should be conducted via a market, via a contract, or via a change in ownership. For prominent models on renegotiation, see, for example, Grossman and Hart (1986), Hart and Moore (1988), Dewatripont (1988), or Fudenberg and Tirole (1991).

Our discussion about the impact of communication on players' behavior is based on Schelling (1960). A formal discussion of pre-play communication can be found in Farrell (1988) and Myerson (1989). Gibbons (1992) discusses the differences between cheap-talk and signaling games. For applications of cheap-talk models, see Matthews (1989), Stein (1989), Austen-Smith (1990), or Farrell and Gibbons (1991). Aumann (1974) introduced the idea of correlated equilibria. Also see Myerson (1991), who discusses games with communication in detail.

There also exists a large body of literature on bargaining. The approach presented in this chapter is based on Rubinstein (1982) and focuses on the dynamics of bargaining processes. An alternative approach is axiomatic. It first characterizes the conditions that have to be satisfied for a bargaining solution and then analyzes which solutions are possible at all. This approach was presented by Nash (1950b) and is also referred to as cooperative bargaining. Osborne and Rubinstein (1990) offer a general introduction in bargaining theory.

As with repeated games and bargaining, the literature on mechanism design is extensive, too. Green and Laffont (1977) offer a good way to enter this topic. Laffont and Tirole (1987) study optimal mechanisms in a situation of adverse selection and moral hazard. A detailed discussion of the topic can be found in Myerson (1991), and in Fudenberg and Tirole (1991).

5.4 EXERCISES

5.4.1 Product Innovation

A firm has to decide about implementing a product innovation. The marketing department as well as the production department have elaborated a
concept for a product innovation. The marketing department always prefers
a customer-oriented product innovation, while the production department
prefers a lot-size-oriented innovation. In a joint meeting the departments
have to agree upon a subsequent action plan (by voting). If both departments agree to construct a compromising plan of product innovation, both
departments gain status, because both contributed to the implementation
of the product change. However, if the departments do not want to compromise and decide to strive for implementing their own plan of product
innovation, the winning department reaches an even higher gain in status,
while the other department loses some of its status. Before the meeting both
departments commit to their voting strategies with respect to both types
of product innovation. Figure 5.22 depicts the resulting conflict situation.

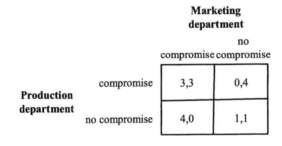

Figure 5.22. Product innovation

1. Model the conflict situation of the voting process during the common
   meeting, in case the plans of product innovation are taken to vote subsequently. (Hint: when voting about the second plan of product innovation,
   the behavior of both parties in voting about the first plan is known to
   both departments.) Determine the subgames in this conflict situation
   and define the concept of information set.
2. Determine the equilibrium outcome of this conflict situation and elucidate the adequate equilibrium concept.
3. The manager of the marketing department proposes that her department
   will be compromising in the first voting if the other department does the
   same in she next voting. How do you judge this proposal? How does the
   outcome change when the game is subsequently repeated three (or four)

times in which the departments have to decide about three (or four) different plans of product innovation?

5.4.2 Delta

The normal form game in Figure 5.23 is played repeatedly according to the following rule: the game will end after each round with a probability of δ and will be repeated with a probability of $(1 - \delta)$. The payoffs per period will be added up for each player. The total utility of each player equals the sum of all her payoffs.

Player 2

		L	R
	O	3,3	0,6
Player 1			
	U	6,0	1,1

Figure 5.23. Normal form game

1. What should be the level of δ to make sure that the strategy below will lead to a subgame perfect Nash equilibrium of (O,L) in all periods?
   Player 1: Play O in Period 1. If the game is repeated and the outcome in the previous period was (O,L), play U in all subsequent periods.
   Player 2: Play L in Period 1. If the game is repeated and the outcome in the previous period was (O,L), play R in all subsequent periods.
2. Prove that the resulting equilibrium is subgame perfect.

5.4.3 Joint Venture

Two firms, 1 and 2, are planning a joint project (called 'joint venture'). When the project is completed, each partner receives a payoff of $V = 100$. The costs needed to complete the project amount to $R = 8$. The contribution of each firm can not be enforced by the other partner. Therefore, both firms agree upon the following course of action. In Period 1, Firm 1 will pay a contribution of c_1. If this contribution is large enough to complete the project, the game comes to an end and both firms receive V. However, if the contribution of Firm 1 is insufficient ($c_1 < R$), Firm 2 will pay a contribution of c_2 in the second period. If the (undiscounted) sum of both contributions is large enough to complete the project, each firm receives V. However, if the sum appears insufficient both firms receive nothing.

Both firms have to finance their contributions by means of alternative profitable activities. These opportunity costs cause an increase in the total costs of contributing to the project for each firm, from $c\{i\}$ to $c\{i\}^2$. Assume that firm 1 discounts a return that occurs in the second period by a factor δ.

1. Calculate the outcome of this two-stage game (that is calculate the level of the contribution for each firm in terms of the discount factor δ).
2. How does the outcome change when $R = 12$?

5.4.4 Foreign Project

A firm has to perform a project abroad, which will be supervised by a local engineer. Only two engineers are found suitable candidates for performing the task; Mr Hughes and Mrs Radon. Because a civil war is going on in the foreign country, the engineer who has to manage the project abroad faces costs of the magnitude c. The engineer operating in the home country does not face such costs (for her $c = 0$). Their manager has to decide who of the two engineers will be sent abroad. However, the manager is not very decisive and does not want to force any of the engineers to go abroad. She therefore explains to Mr Hughes that she will stick to the following procedure to come to a decision about who will be sent abroad: If Mr Hughes agrees voluntarily to be sent abroad to manage the project, he receives a bonus of b. If Mr Hughes refuses, the bonus will be offered to Mrs Radon, who may subsequently decide whether to accept the foreign project or not. In case Mrs Radon also refuses the task, no one will get a bonus and the decision will be taken by throwing a coin (that is each engineer faces a probability of $p = \frac{1}{2}$ of being sent out).

1. Depict the conflict situation of both engineers in a sequential manner.
2. At what level will the manager have to fix the bonus in order to make sure that at least one of the engineers applies for the project voluntarily? At what level will the manager have to fix the bonus in order to make sure that Mr Hughes will apply for the project voluntarily?
3. Elucidate the correct equilibrium concept. Do you think this is a democratic procedure? How do you assess the initial position in the conflict of both Mr Hughes and Mrs Radon?

5.4.5 Home Production or Outsourcing?

Booz Corp. specializes in the production of high-grade spirits. The firm has to decide whether it will print the labels for the liquor bottles itself, or outsource the printing to a middleman. If Booz Corp. decides to produce the labels itself, the production costs amount to $c\{I\}$. If, however, the firm decides to outsource the printing, the production costs come up to $c\{V\}$, where $c\{I\} < c\{V\}$. Assume that Booz Corp. knows the costs of producing the labels itself, but that it does not know the costs for the middleman when the printing is outsourced.

1. Formulate the mechanism design problem of Booz Corp.. Assume that the firm strives for cost minimization.
2. Determine the optimal direct-revelation mechanism. Can this optimal mechanism be implemented in a simple pricing scheme? Explain.
3. Suppose that an adjustment of the prefabricated standard labels may result in a third possible level of production costs; $c\{S\} > c\{V\}$. Now, solve again the previous two questions in case this additional third production method belongs to the possibilities of Booz Corp..

5.5 NOTES

1. The following discussion on the building of trust does not only apply to lateral relationships, but also to vertical collaborations between supervisors and employees.
2. The payoffs in this situation of conflict should be interpreted as expected payoffs of the two colleagues and are determined as follows. With a probability of 50 percent, neither Colleague 1 nor Colleague 2 has clients waiting when the bank closes. The colleague that has to work longer receives a payoff of no units if her colleague does not cooperate and a payoff of six units if she receives help from her colleague. The colleague that does not have to work longer receives a payoff of eight units if she goes home in time and does not cooperate and a payoff of six units if she stays and cooperates.
3. The relationship between the discount factor δ and the discount rate i is as follows:

$$\delta = \tfrac{1}{1+i}$$

At a discount rate of $i = 0$, no discounting takes place with $\delta = 1$. At an extremely high discount rate, future payments become irrelevant, as the discount factor δ is extremely small.

4. For simplicity, we assume in the following that both colleagues can observe the behavior of the other at the end of the day. It could be argued that only one of the two colleagues can observe the behavior of the other, but even if this aspect is considered in the modeling of the repeated version of the game, the results below do not change qualitatively.
5. $6 + 6\delta + 6\delta^2 + ... = \tfrac{6}{1-\delta}$.
6. A convex combination of a set of payoffs is a weighted sum of these payoffs, where each weight is non-negative and the sum of all weights adds up to 1.
7. The convex hull of a set of payoffs includes all convex combinations of these payoffs.
8. In a general situation of conflict only those points in the cooperative payoff space, which guarantee each party at least her security level, are considered for a contractual agreement. The security level denotes the highest expected payoff that a party can get, if all other parties choose their worst correlated strategy. If this incentive compatibility constraint is satisfied for each party, all parties find a contractual agreement prior to the actual conflict. See Myerson (1991).
9. A general mechanism would specify an allocation $(a_{ij}^1, a_{ij}^2, p_{ij}^1, p_{ij}^2)$ for each possible pair of reports ij of the two plants: if the first plant reports $i \in \{1,2\}$ and the second plant reports $j \in \{1,2\}$ then the customer order will be allocated with the

217

ratio $a_{ij}^1 : a_{ij}^2$. p_{ij}^1 and p_{ij}^2 are then the prices, which the central division pays to the plants.

10. Four conditions have to be satisfied for a general mechanism: two incentive compatibility constraints, which ensure that a party truthfully reports low (high) production costs, provided the other party reports real costs, too; and two participation constraints, which ensure that the party with low (high) production costs at least receives a reservation payoff.

11. The incentive compatibility constraint discussed above excludes the case that, for instance, the second plant always reports wrong production costs.

12. This mechanism requires that the parties always decide in favor of the organization as a whole when they are indifferent. This additional assumption would not be necessary if we specify $p_1 = 1.01$ and $p_2 = 1.51$. However, the central division would then have costs of 150.5 units.

References

Abreu, D., D. Pearce and E. Stacchetti. 1986. Optimal Cartel Equilibrium with Imperfect Monitoring. *Journal of Economic Theory* 39:251-269.

Arrow, K. 1986. Agency and the Market. In K. Arrow and M. Intriligator (eds), *Handbook of Mathematical Economics*. Amsterdam: Elsevier Science Publishers B.V.

Aumann, R. 1974. Subjectivity and Correlation in Randomized Strategies. *Journal of Mathematical Economics* 1:67-96.

Aumann, R. 1986. Repeated Games. In G. Feiwel (ed.), *Issues in Contemporary Microeconomics and Welfare*. London: Macmillan.

Aumann, R. 1989. Survey of Repeated Games. In *Essays in Game Theory and Mathematical Economics in Honor of Oskar Morgenstern*. Mannheim: Bibliographisches Institut.

Aumann, R., S. Hart and M. Perry. 1996. The Absent-Minded Driver. Center for Rationality and Interactive Decision Theory. *The Hebrew University of Jerusalem*. Discussion Paper No. 94.

Austen-Smith, D. 1990. Information Transmission in Debate. *American Journal of Political Science* 34:124-152.

Banks, J. and J. Sobel. 1987. Equilibrium Selection in Signaling Games. *Econometrica* 55:647-662.

Bernheim, B. 1984. Rationalizable Strategic Behavior. *Econometrica* 52:1007-1028.

Binmore, K. 1990. *Essays in the Foundations of Game Theory.* Oxford: Basil Blackwell.

Binmore, K. 1992. *Fun and Games: A Text on Game Theory.* Lexington, MA: D. C. Heath and Co.

Brandenburger, A. 1992. Knowledge and Equilibrium in Games. *Journal of Economic Perspectives* 6:83-101.

Brandenburger, A. and E. Dekel. 1990. The Role of Common Knowledge Assumptions in Game Theory. In F. Hahn (ed.), *The Economics of Missing Markets Information and Games*. Oxford: Oxford University Press.

Cho, I.-K. and D. Kreps. 1987. Signaling Games and Stable Equilibria. *Quarterly Journal of Economics* 102:179-221.

Coase, R. 1937. The Nature of the Firm. *Economica* 4:386-405.

Dasgupta, P., P. Hammond and E. Maskin. 1979. The Implementation of Social Choice Rules. *Review of Economic Studies* 46:185-216.

Demski, J. and D. Sappington. 1984. Optimal Incentive Contracts with Multiple Agents. *Journal of Economic Theory* 33:152-171.

Dewatripont, M. 1988. Commitment through Renegotiation-Proof Contracts with Third Parties. *Review of Economic Studies* 55:377-390.

Doyle, A. Conan.1990. *A Complete Facsimile Edition of Sherlock Holmes.*

Mallard Press.

Dye, R. 1986. Optimal Monitoring Policies in Agencies. *The Rand Journal of Economics* 17:339-350.

Farrell, J. 1988. Meaning and Credibility in Cheap-Talk Games. In M. Dempster (ed.), *Mathematical Models in Economics*. Oxford: Oxford University Press.

Farrell, J. and R. Gibbons. 1991. *Union Voice*. Cornell University. Mimeo.

Friedman, J. 1971. A Non-Cooperative Equilibrium for Supergames. *Review of Economic Studies* 38:1-12.

Fudenberg, D. and E. Maskin. 1986. The Folk Theorem in Repeated Games with Discounting and Incomplete Information. *Econometrica* 54:533-554.

Fudenberg D. and J. Tirole. 1991. *Game Theory*. Cambridge, MA: MIT Press.

Geanakopolos, J. 1992. Common Knowledge. *Journal of Economic Perspectives* 6:53-82.

Gibbard, A. 1973. Manipulation for Voting Schemes. *Econometrica* 41: 587-601.

Gibbons, R. 1992. *A Primer in Game Theory*. Hemel Hempstead: Harvester Wheatsheaf.

Green, J. and J.-J. Laffont. 1977. Characterization of Satisfactory Mechanisms for the Revelation of Preferences for Public Goods. *Econometrica* 45:427-438.

Green, E. and R. Porter. 1984. Non-cooperative Collusion under Imperfect Price Information. *Econometrica* 52:975-994.

Grossman, S. 1981. The Informational Role of Warranties and Private Disclosure about Product Quality. *Journal of Law and Economics* 24:461-484.

Grossman, S. and O. Hart. 1982. Corporate Financial Structure and Managerial Incentives. In J. McCall (ed.), *The Economics of Information and Uncertainty*. Chicago: University of Chicago Press.

Grossman, S. and O. Hart. 1983. An Analysis of the Principal-Agent Problem. *Econometrica* 51:7-46.

Grossman, S. and O. Hart. 1986. The Costs and Benefits of Ownership: A Theory of Vertical and Lateral Integration. *Journal of Political Economy* 94:691-719.

Guasch, L. and A. Weiss. 1981. Self-Selection in the Labor Market. *American Economic Review* 73:275-284.

Güth, W. and H. Kliemt. 1996. One Person – Many Players? On Björn Frank's 'The Use of Internal Games: The Case of Addiction'. *Journal of Economic Psychology* 17:661-668.

Harris, M. and A. Raviv. 1979. Optimal Incentive Contracts with Imperfect Information. *Journal of Economic Theory* 20:231-259.

Harsanyi, J. 1967. Games with Incomplete Information Played by 'Bayesian' Players, I: The Basic Model. *Management Science* 14:159-182.

Harsanyi, J. 1968a. Games with Incomplete Information Played by 'Bayesian' Players, II: Bayesian Equilibrium Points. *Management Science* 14:320-334.

Harsanyi, J. 1968b. Games with Incomplete Information Played by 'Bayesian' Players, III: The Basic Probability Distribution of the Game. *Management Science* 14:486-502.

Harsanyi, J. 1973. Games with Randomly Disturbed Payoffs: A New Rationale for Mixed Strategy Equilibrium Points. *International Journal of Game Theory* 2:1-23.

Harsanyi, J. and R. Selten. 1988. *A General Theory of Equilibrium Selection in Games.* Cambridge, MA: MIT Press.

Hart, O. and J. Moore. 1988. Incomplete Contracts and Renegotiation. *Econometrica* 56:755-785.

Holloway, C. 1979. *Decision Making Under Uncertainty: Models and Choices.* Englewood Cliffs, NJ: Prentice-Hall.

Holmstrom, B. 1979. Moral Hazard and Observability. *Bell Journal of Economics* 10:74-91.

Holmstrom, B. 1982. Moral Hazard in Teams. *Bell Journal of Economics* 13:324-340.

Holmstrom, B. and R. i Costa. 1986. Managerial Incentives and Capital Management. *Quarterly Journal of Economics* 101:835-860.

Hume, D. 1888. *Treatise on Human Nature* (ed.), L. Selby-Bigg. Oxford: University Press.

Jost, P.-J. 1988. *On Control in Principal-Agent Relationships.* Bonn: Rheinische Friedrich-Wilhelms-Universität.

Jost, P.-J. 1996. On the Role of Commitment in a Principal-Agent Relationship with an Informed Principal. *Journal of Economic Theory* 68:510-530.

Jovanovic, B. 1982. Truthful Disclosure of Information. *Bell Journal of Economics* 13:36-44.

Kofmann, F. and J. Lawarree. 1993. Collusion in Hierarchical Agency. *Econometrica* 61:629-656.

Kreps, D. 1990a. Out-of-Equilibrium and Out-of-Equilibrium Behaviour. In F. Hahn, ed., *The Economics of Missing Markets Information and Games.* Oxford: Oxford University Press.

Kreps, D. 1990b. *A Course in Microeconomic Theory.* Princeton, NJ: Princeton University Press.

Kreps, D., P. Milgrom, J. Roberts and R. Wilson. 1982. Rational Cooperation in the Finitely Repeated Prisoners' Dilemma. *Journal of Economic Theory* 27:245-252.

Kreps, D. and R. Wilson. 1982a. Sequential Equilibrium. *Econometrica* 50:863-894.

Kreps, D. and R. Wilson. 1982b. Reputation and Imperfect Information. *Journal of Economic Theory* 27:253-279.

Laffont, J.-J. and J. Tirole. 1987. Auctioning Incentive Contracts. *Journal of Political Economy* 95:921-937.

Lambert, R. 1986. Executive Effort and the Selection of Risky Projects. *Rand Journal of Economics* 16:77-88.

Luce, R. and H. Raiffa. 1957. *Games and Decisions: Introduction and Critical Survey.* New York: Wiley.

Machiavelli, N. [1532] 1950. *The Prince and the Discourse.* New York: Modern Library.

Maskin, E. and J. Tirole. 1990. The Principal-Agent Relationship with an Informed Principal: The Case of Private Values. *Econometrica* 58:379-409.

Maskin, E. and J. Tirole. 1992. The Principal-Agent Relationship with an Informed Principal II: Common Values. *Econometrica* 60:1-42.

Mathewson, G. and R. Winter. 1985. The Economics of Franchise Contracts. *Journal of Law and Economics* 28:503-526.

Matthews, S. 1989. Veto Threats: Rethoric in a Bargaining Game. *Quarterly Journal of Economics* 104:347-369.

McLennan, A. 1985. Justifiable Beliefs in Sequential Equilibrium. *Econometrica* 53:889-904.

Melumad, N. and D. Mookherjee. 1989. Delegation as Commitment: The Case of Income Tax Audits. *The Rand Journal of Economics* 20:139-163.

Mertens, J.-F. 1987. Repeated Games. In *Proceedings of the International Congress of Mathematicians* 1986.

Mertens, J.-F. and S. Zamir. 1985. Formulation of Bayesian Analysis for Games with Incomplete Information. *International Journal of Game Theory* 14:1-29.

Mertens, J.-F., S. Sorin and S. Zamir. 1990. *Repeated Games.* Manuscript. Berkley, CA.

Milgrom, P. 1981. Good News and Bad News: Representation Theorems and Applications. *Bell Journal of Economics* 12:380-391.

Milgrom, P. and J. Roberts. 1982. Predation, Reputation, and Entry Deterrence. *Journal of Economic Theory* 27:280-312.

Milgrom, P. and J. Roberts. 1986. Price and Advertising Signals of Product Quality. *Journal of Political Economy* 94:796-821.

Myerson, R. 1979. Incentive Compatibility and the Bargaining Problem. *Econometrica* 47:61-73.

Myerson, R. 1985. Bayesian Equilibrium and Incentive Compatibility. In L. Hurwicz , D. Schmeidler and H. Sonnenschein, (eds), *Social Goals and Social Organization.* Cambridge: Cambridge University Press.

Myerson, R. 1983. Mechanism Design by an Informed Principal. *Econometrica* 51:1767-1797.

Myerson, R. 1989. Credible Negotiation Statements and Coherent Plans. *Journal of Economic Theory* 48:264-303.

Myerson, R. 1991. *Game Theory: Analysis of Conflict.* Cambridge, MA: Harvard University Press.

Nash, J. 1950a. Equilibrium Points in N-Person Games. *Proceedings of the National Academy of Sciences* 36:48-49.

Nash, J. 1950b. The Bargaining Problem. *Econometrica* 18:155-162.

Okuno-Fujiwara, M., A. Postlewaite and K. Suzumura. 1990. Strategic Information Revelation. *Review of Economic Studies* 57:25-47.

Ordeshook, P. 1986. *Game Theory and Political Theory: An Introduction.* Cambridge, MA: Cambridge University Press.

Osborne, M. and A. Rubinstein.1990. *Bargaining and Markets.* San Diego: Academic Press.

Osborne, M. and A. Rubinstein. 1994. *A Course in Game Theory.* Cambridge, MA: MIT Press.

Pearce, D. 1984. Rationalizable Strategic Behavior and the Problem of Perfection. *Econometrica* 52:1029-1050.

Poundstone, W. 1992. *Prisoners' Dilemma.* New York: Doubleday.

Pratt, J. and R. Zeckhauser. 1985. Principals and Agents: An Overview. In J. Pratt and R. Zeckhauser, (eds), *Principals and Agents: The Structure of Business.* Boston, MA: Harvard Business School Press.

Radner, R. 1985. Repeated Partnership Games with Imperfect Monitoring and No Discounting. *Review of Economic Studies* 53:43-58.

Rapoport, A. 1964. Tacit Communication in Experiments in Conflict and Cooperation. *International Psychatric Clinic* 1:225-244.

Rapoport, A. and M. Guyer. 1966. A Taxonomy of 2x2 Games. *General Systems* 11:203-214.

Ross, S. 1973. The Economic Theory of Agency: The Principal's Problem. *American Economic Review, Papers and Proceedings* 63:134-139.

Rothschild, M. and J. Stiglitz. 1976. Equilibrium in Competitive Insurance Markets: An Essay On the Economics of Imperfect Information. *Quarterly Journal of Economics* 90:629-666.

Rubinstein, A. 1979. Equilibrium in Supergames with the Overtaking Criterion. *Journal of Economic Theory* 21:1-nine.

Rubinstein, A. 1982. Perfect Equilibrium in a Bargaining Model. *Econometrica* 50:97-109.

Salop, J. and S. Salop. 1976. Self-Selection and Turnover in the Labor Market. *Quarterly Journal of Economics* 90:619-628.

Sappington, D. 1991. Incentives in Principal-Agent Relationships. *Journal of Economic Perspectives* 5:45-66.

Schelling, T. 1960. *The Strategy of Conflict. Cambridge*, MA: Harvard University Press.

Selten, R. 1965. Spieltheoretische Behandlung eines Oligopolmodells mit Nachfrageträgheit. *Zeitschrift für die gesamte Staatswissenschaft* 12:301-

324.

Selten, R. 1975. Reexamination of the Perfectness Concept for Equilibrium Points in Extensive Games. *International Journal of Game Theory* 4:25-55.

Selten, R. 1978. The Chain-Store Paradox. *Theory and Decision* 9:127-159.

Sen, A. 1987. *On Ethics and Economics.* Oxford: Basil Blackwell.

Shavell, S. 1979. Risk Sharing and Incentives in the Principal and Agent Relationship. *Bell Journal of Economics* 10:55-73.

Spence, M. 1973. Job Market Signaling. *Quarterly Journal of Economics* 87:355-374.

Stein, J. 1989. Cheap Talk and the Fed: A Theory of Imprecise Policy Announcements. *American Economic Review* 79:32-42.

Stigler, G. 1964. A Theory of Oligopoly. *Journal of Political Economy* 72:44-61.

Stiglitz, J. and A. Weiss. 1983. *Sorting out the Differences between Screening and Signaling Models.* Princeton University. Mimeo.

Thomas, K. 1976. Conflict and Conflict Management. In M. Dunette (ed.) *Handbook of Industrial and Organizational Psychology.* Chicago: Rand McNally.

Twain, M. 1876. *The Adventures of Tom Sawyer.* New York: New American Library.

Tirole, J. 1986. Hierarchies and Bureaucracies: On the Role of Collusion in Organizations. *Journal of Law, Economics and Organization* 2, 181-214.

Van Damme, E. 1987. *Stability and Perfection of Nash Equilibrium.* Berlin: Springer.

Williamson, O. 1985. *The Economic Institutions of Capitalism.* New York: The Free Press.

Index